Rethinking Peace and C

Series Editor
Oliver P. Richmond
University of Manchester
Manchester
United Kingdom

This agenda-setting series of research monographs, now more than a decade old, provides an interdisciplinary forum aimed at advancing innovative new agendas for approaches to, and understandings of, peace and conflict studies and International Relations. Many of the critical volumes the series has so far hosted have contributed to new avenues of analysis directly or indirectly related to the search for positive, emancipatory, and hybrid forms of peace. New perspectives on peacemaking in practice and in theory, their implications for the international peace architecture, and different conflict-affected regions around the world, remain crucial. This series' contributions offers both theoretical and empirical insights into many of the world's most intractable conflicts and any subsequent attempts to build a new and more sustainable peace, responsive to the needs and norms of those who are its subjects.

More information about this series at
http://www.springer.com/series/14500

Who needs Trump? As David Chandler shows in this book, critical peacebuilders began to lose faith in a liberal international order long before Donald Trump won the White House. Read this book if you want to understand better the rise and fall of the liberal peace over the last twenty years, if you want to uncover the roots of our current impasse, and if you want glimpses of what our post-liberal international order may look like.

– **Philip Cunliffe**, *Editor-in-Chief, International Peacekeeping, University of Kent*

An impressive synthesis of the trajectory of peacebuilding over the past two decades. Chandler's sustained critique of peacebuilding philosophies and practices highlights the perils of good intentions in the absence of critical politics and analysis.

– **Keith Krause**, *Director, Centre on Conflict, Development and Peacebuilding, Graduate Institute of International and Development Studies, Geneva*

For more than two decades, peacebuilder policymakers and scholars in the international community have considered at length the question "How do we build peace after war?" The simple answer, as David Chandler's masterful review of the evolution of peacebuilding ontology penetratingly demonstrates, is, "We can't." In this incisive volume, Chandler shows exactly why this is the case and how peacebuilding – if it is to occur – is at the end of the day a primarily internal or endogenous process. Policymakers and scholars will to well to shelve their off-the-shelf solutionist toolkits, logframes, and task matrices after reading this important book.

– **Timothy D. Sisk**, *Professor of International and Comparative Politics, University of Denver*

David Chandler

Peacebuilding

The Twenty Years' Crisis, 1997–2017

palgrave
macmillan

David Chandler
Department of Politics & International
  Relations
University of Westminster
London, United Kingdom

Rethinking Peace and Conflict Studies
ISBN 978-3-319-50321-9   ISBN 978-3-319-50322-6 (eBook)
DOI 10.1007/978-3-319-50322-6

Library of Congress Control Number: 2017931582

Cover illustration: epa european pressphoto agency b.v. / Alamy Stock Photo

Printed on acid-free paper

This Palgrave Macmillan imprint is published by Springer Nature
The registered company is Springer International Publishing AG
The registered company address is: Gewerbestrasse 11, 6330 Cham, Switzerland

ACKNOWLEDGEMENTS

I would like to thank the series editor Oliver Richmond for inviting me to survey the rise and fall of peacebuilding as an international project and, of course, the publishers at Palgrave-Macmillan for allowing me to borrow from the title of EH Carr's classic work on International Relations.

The intention of this book is to work through and reappraise the 'Twenty Years' Crisis' of international peacebuilding. This neither involves a chronological story of peacebuilding, as a set of distinct international missions or specialist policy areas, nor does it seek to establish a normative set of 'lessons learned'. It is a study of the discourses and understandings of the meaning of peacebuilding for both its advocates and its critics. The individual chapters reassemble and rework material from a wide range of my research in this field over the time period. Much of the material focuses upon the Balkans, particularly the Bosnian example, in order to illustrate the changing discourses of peacebuilding as a set of techniques and practices in a scenario where international peacebuilders were free to experiment from a position of control and influence rather than fighting a rearguard action against an armed insurgency.

The organisational thematic of the material presented here would not have been possible without the opportunity of preparing and reworking material for a large number of keynotes, lectures, papers and presentations over the last couple of years, enabling me to work through my own process of reassessing the rise and fall of peacebuilding approaches. I would therefore like to extend some important thanks to the organisers and participants of recent workshops, conferences and panels at: the Danish Institute for International Studies, Copenhagen; Georgia State University; Leeds

University; the University of Copenhagen; University College, Dublin; the University of Manchester; the Virginia Tech Steger Center for International Scholarship, Riva San Vitale, Switzerland; the University of Ghent; the École Normale Supérieure; the School of Oriental and African Studies, University of London; University College London; the University of Tübingen; the University of California, Berkeley; the University of Osnabrueck; Oxford Brookes University; the Centre for Poverty Analysis, Colombo; the Centre for Global Cooperation Research, Duisburg; and recent annual conferences of the International Studies Association and the European International Studies Association and the European Consortium for Political Research Joint Sessions of Workshops,

Beyond this, so many debts have accrued over the twenty years that I have worked on this thematic that the list of individuals would be ridiculously long, suffice to say that I would not be writing these acknowledgements had I not had the privilege of working within such a dynamic, generous and collegial academic and practitioner community.

CONTENTS

PART I

Introduction

CHAPTER 1

The Twenty Years' Crisis

INTRODUCTION

This book, on the twenty years' crisis of peacebuilding, seeks to trace the rise and fall of international peacebuilding, understood as a field of external policy intervention with the intention of assisting post-conflict or conflict-prone states to build a sustainable peace on the basis of liberal institutional frameworks of constitutionalism, market freedoms, democracy and the rule of law. The book is not a survey of peacebuilding missions themselves but rather is concerned with the changes in the understanding of the peacebuilding project itself. The chapters are organised broadly chronologically in five sections. The second part essentially concerns the emergence of discourses of international intervention, the shift from peacekeeping to peacebuilding and the critiques of sovereignty in the 1990s, closing with the peacebuilding protectorates of Bosnia and Kosovo. The third part considers the impasse of peacebuilding approaches at the levels of policy interventions to build state institutions and to encourage civil society engagement. The fourth part of the book considers policy discourses and academic work in the 2010s, focusing on analysing the rise of the local and the shift to resilience and the concluding part focuses on the broader critique of peacebuilding as flawed on the basis of its liberal, universal, linear and reductive assumptions.

This book is the product of my own twenty-year academic engagement in the field of international intervention and peacebuilding (I was in the

© The Author(s) 2017
D. Chandler, *Peacebuilding*, Rethinking Peace and Conflict Studies,
DOI 10.1007/978-3-319-50322-6_1

middle of my PhD research when the international protectorate powers were formalised in Bosnia in 1997) and reworks some of the material from my publications over this period. I consider myself lucky to have been engaged in the study of international peacebuilding during the 1990s, 2000s and 2010s and to have witnessed major changes in both policy-making and academic attitudes, approaches and conceptual frameworks in the field. I have had first-hand opportunities to engage in policy and academic discussions attempting to understand, legitimate and to negotiate first the expansion of liberal internationalist framings, policies and practices and then the retreat from these approaches towards more pragmatic, 'local', 'organic' and indirect approaches, which have increasingly rejected the international peacebuilding paradigm.

This book derives its subtitle from E. H. Carr's classic work on International Relations theory and interwar history, *The Twenty Years' Crisis 1919–1939: An Introduction to the Study of International Relations*, first published by this publisher (under the former ownership of Macmillan Press in 1939). Carr's book was originally intended to be titled 'Utopia and Reality' (Cox, 2001, p. xi) (which the publishers found to be too abstract) indicating that the twenty years' crisis of the title was not merely about a series of problems or an on-going set of issues, but rather concerned a secular trend, a contestation between two approaches and a shift from one way of thinking to another: from an idealist, utopian, abstract, morality-based view of liberal universalism to a more strategic, pragmatic and interest-based 'science' of realism; starting from the world as it exists rather than how we would like it to be. The suggestion of this book is that peacebuilding is now understood as having taken a similar trajectory, starting off as a liberal (today most commentators would also say idealist or utopian) project and ending up in a 'realist' or pragmatist mode of resignation and disillusionment.

Carr himself had little at stake in this shift, apart from to highlight that it indicated the ideological nature of International Relations itself as a discrete body of thought, which he saw as merely a pseudo-discipline, aping other social sciences and designed to rationalise the exercise of power of dominant nations over weaker ones (Cox, 2001, p. xiii). Likewise, I take no pleasure in the end of peacebuilding as an international framework of problem-solving; the shift from a 'utopia' of managed liberal transformation to a 'reality' of pragmatism and monitoring from afar brings little improvement to the lives of those benighted by war and conflict and is merely the rationalisation of the 'reality' of the implosion of the liberal frameworks of meaning which drove the initial 'utopian' aspirations of the mid- and late-1990s.

The shift in fortunes of international peacebuilding – from the exaggerated, even hubristic, demands for universalist transformation to an idealised liberal model to today's craven retreat to aerial drones and crowdsourced monitoring from afar (Lynch, 2016; Pugliese, 2016) – are not just a blow to the aspirations of international intellectuals and policymakers, they also herald a much broader shift in international political thinking about the problems of governance and our relationship to the external world today. Carr's study started with the triumphalism of the United States' entry into international politics at the Versailles peace conference following the First World War and he clearly had little sympathy for the moral crusading liberal idealism in the cause of US interests, personified by US President Woodrow Wilson. The interwar period of the *Twenty Years' Crisis* was the story of the collapse of liberal international idealism, which was dealt a major blow by the world economic collapse of 1929 that rekindled open inter-imperialist rivalries, leading rapidly to the resumption of World War.

The 'twenty years' crisis' of international peacekeeping from 1997 to 2017 does not have the drama on the world scale of the interwar period but holds some similarities to Carr's story of disappointment and disillusionment in liberal internationalism driven by a 'voluntarist' moral idealism in the service of power politics. The repeat of a new internationalist moral moment with the end of the Cold War was also short-lived and contested and the new 'realism', that is the upshot of failures of the grand schemes of international intervention, can equally be seen as a sterile deterministic 'codification of the status quo'. However, there are, of course, major differences. Carr's 'twenty years' crisis' was driven by the breakdown of the fragile international order established with the League of Nations, damaged by US isolationism and the exclusion of major powers Germany and the Soviet Union. The auspices for success for international peacebuilding, under a US-guided international order in the 1990s, seemed much more promising.

Ironically, it was not international rivalries that undermined liberal dreams of international peacebuilding as much as the lack of contestation of the international sphere. Rather than a new period of international intervention and the carving up of the territories of the world after the end of the Cold War it appears that there has been a grand retreat from the international sphere itself. This retreat can be articulated in the words of

Carr as 'consistent realism'; a realism that 'fails to provide any ground for purpose or meaningful action' (Carr, 2001, p. 86). The idealism of the 1990s may have evaporated but no positive vision has taken its place. Whereas Carr assumed that it was straightforward for moral claims to enable and legitimise the interests of the powerful this seems to be no longer the case. Both idealism and strategic realism seem in short supply today, as long as this remains the case we are unlikely to see the revival of international peacebuilding in any recognisable form.

THE END OF PEACEBUILDING

In 2000, at the height of the United Nation's confidence in the transformation of the international agenda, in the *Report of the Panel on United Nations Peace Operations*, presented by the United Nation's Secretary-General, Section A, 'Defining the elements of peace operations', defined the new concept of peacebuilding in these terms:

> Peace-building is a term of...recent origin that, as used in the present report, defines activities undertaken on the far side of conflict to reassemble the foundations of peace and provide the tools for building on those foundations something that is more than just the absence of war. Thus, peace-building includes but is not limited to reintegrating former combatants into civilian society, strengthening the rule of law (for example, through training and restructuring of local police, and judicial and penal reform); improving respect for human rights through the monitoring, education and investigation of past and existing abuses; providing technical assistance for democratic development (including electoral assistance and support for free media); and promoting conflict resolution and reconciliation techniques. (UN, 2000b, p. 3)

The definition was kept open with a non-inclusive list of examples of international peacebuilding responsibilities listed, covering a wide range of institutional capacity-building measures including everything from the legal and political system to education and health and welfare.

In 2017, peacebuilding is no longer a term on the international agenda. Even the United Nations has shifted away from the use of this terminology. The UN's shift away from peacebuilding, to enabling countries to manage their own 'sustainable' solutions, stems from a rejection of the interventionist approaches developed and popularised in the 1990s and now seen to be based on 'supply-driven templates and an overly techno-cratic focus on capitals and elites' and counterproductively increasing 'the risk of unintentionally exacerbating divisions' (UN, 2015a, p. 12). In fact, the UN report of the advisory group of experts for the 2015 review of the United Nations Peacebuilding Architecture, went as far as to state that mistakes had resulted from no less than 'a generalized misunderstanding of the nature of peacebuilding' itself (UN, 2015b, p. 7). Instead, prag-matism has increasingly become the order of the day with the call for 'more realistic and contextualized political strategies' (UN, 2015a, p. 13).

Peacebuilding has been eased off the policy agenda on the grounds that there is no longer the assumption of clarity in terms of problems or solutions, as the UN's High-level Independent Panel on Peace Operations review stated 'there is no linear path to peace' (UN, 2015a, p. 18): 'complex linkages' and interconnections between actors and inter-vening agencies mean that the UN needs less focus on 'template mandates and missions' and instead more emphasis upon fluid and flexible 'situation-specific' strategies (ibid, p. 23). The idea that external actors can either develop solutions or implement them on the ground has been undermined by the reality that 'conflicts have become more complex, increasingly frag-mented and intractable' (UN, 2015b, p.7).

The UN no longer wants to set itself up as the external expert and manager of processes of transitional 'peacebuilding' but rather seeks to increasingly situate itself as part of domestic processes of support and facilitation. This pragmatic approach, working with and through local processes:

> demands that United Nations personnel in the field engage with and relate to the people and communities they are asked to support. The legacy of the 'white-SUV culture' must give way to a more human face that prioritizes closer interaction with local people to better understand their concerns, needs and aspirations. (UN, 2015a, p. 30)

The UN has thus moved to distance itself from 'peacebuilding' and towards stressing peace as sustainability and local legitimacy rather than as an externally led transformation conforming to preconceived goals and attained through externally managed social and political engineering:

> Peacebuilding is not State-building . . . Countries emerging from conflict are not blank pages and their people are not 'projects'. They are the main agents

of peace. However, the international approach is often based on generic models that ignore national realities...Efforts to sustain peace must build upon [local] institutions and the resilience and reconciliation processes of local communities, and not undermine them...When countries set out their priorities and they enjoy strong national support, they must be respected. Too often they are not. (UN, 2015a, p. 48)

Peacebuilding has been rejected by the UN because it has been understood to be too linear and too reductionist. Today it may be alleged that 'peacebuilding' is not 'statebuilding' but this has not always been the case and the two concepts seem to be intimately connected and are often used interchangeably, largely because the UN itself conceptualised peacebuilding as the building or rebuilding of states, as considered in the following section of this Introduction. Peacebuilding made a lot of easy assumptions that something that was broken could be easily fixed, returning societies to the status quo or establishing a new one on the basis of the liberal institutions of democracy, the rule of law and market efficiency. The focus upon liberal institutional frameworks was the cornerstone of peacebuilding conceived as a liberal internationalist project. This project is now over, as the UN states: '[T]he term "post-conflict peacebuilding" should be abandoned as misleading, the same can be said for the term "peacebuilding architecture"' (UN, 2015b, p. 47).

Today, the UN argues that peacebuilding needs to be replaced by a more general and amorphous conception of 'sustaining peace' and that the focus on building liberal institutions was mistaken for two key reasons (UN, 2015b, p.17). Firstly, that rather than peacebuilding occurring after conflict, problems have to be engaged with along an 'arc' or continuum, from prevention to reconstruction: sustaining peace is a complex process not a set of discrete linear stages, calling for different institutional operations and sets of expertise. Second, and relatedly, peacebuilding had implied that peace could be built according to some universal set of policies to be implemented, rather than through engaging in complex, interrelated and cross-cutting policy concerns which are always going to be case specific, involving going beyond policy and expertise 'silos' in order to 'unite the peace and security, human rights and development "pillars" of the UN' (UN, 2015b, p. 8). In short, the policy space of what was called 'peacebuilding' no longer exists as a distinct set of goals, techniques, practices and expertise, separate to UN activities put in a more holistic policy context of the UN's Sustainable Development Goals (UN, 2015b, p. 57). The aim of this book is to examine how the crisis of peacebuilding developed in the late 1990s and how it seems to have been resolved through the development of a new pragmatist consensus.

THE 'HUBRIS' OF LIBERAL PEACEBUILDING

From the position of looking back from 2017, the twenty years' crisis seems the product of accident, of hubris and of a fundamental misunderstanding of the nature of peace, of politics and of the unintended consequences of external policy interventions. This did not seem to be the case in the 1990s when the policy discourse of peacebuilding was central to what was seen to be a new liberal international order, with the end of the Cold War division. In the closing years of the Cold War and into the early 1990s the UN began to extend post-conflict missions and peacekeeping mandates of ceasefire monitoring in ways which began to be openly political, interfering directly in civilian matters including constitutional, judicial and electoral reforms, for example, in the UN-led missions deployed in Namibia, Angola, El Salvador, Cambodia and Mozambique (see Doyle and Sambanis, 2006).

With the end of the Cold War, there was a new sense of optimism regarding the international liberal order and the idea of peacebuilding began to formalise with the UN Secretary-General's *Agenda for Peace* report of 1992. Paragraph 17 of the report argued that while the state was the central institution: 'The time of absolute and exclusive sovereignty, however, has passed; its theory was never matched by reality.' (UN, 1992) Paragraph 59 claimed, under the rubric of the new concept of 'peacebuilding', that the UN could have the authority to directly intervene in the political process providing 'support for the transformation of deficient national structures and capabilities, and for the strengthening of new democratic institutions'.

The rise and fall of peacebuilding was premised on the blurring of the key binary boundaries of international society: the boundaries between peace and war and between sovereignty and intervention. Peace was no longer primarily a matter of the international, an issue concerning interstate relations, but migrated to being a problem of domestic politics. At the same time, the domestic matter of peace became internationalised as the boundaries between sovereignty and intervention blurred. This double blurring of the boundaries of international politics constituted the twenty years' crisis of peacebuilding.

The extension of international authority to intervene in the management of post-conflict peacebuilding was reinforced in the Secretary-General's follow up position paper, the *Supplement to the Agenda for Peace*, in 1995. Here it was argued that international intervention must extend 'beyond military and humanitarian tasks and must include the promotion of national reconciliation and the re-establishment of effective government' (UN, 1995a, Para 13). In the position paper, under the section headed 'Post-Conflict Peace-Building', for the first time, the UN Secretary-General envisaged the possibility of new forms of UN temporary protectorates with the goal of peacebuilding:

> In a country ruined by war, resumption of such activities may initially have to be entrusted to, or at least coordinated by, a multifunctional peace-keeping operation, but as that operation succeeds in restoring normal conditions, the programmes, funds, offices and agencies can re-establish themselves and gradually take over responsibility from the peace-keepers, with the resident coordinator in due course assuming the coordination functions temporarily entrusted to the special representative of the Secretary-General. (UN, 1995a, Para 53)

The stage was set for the twenty years' crisis the moment the Secretary-General's conception of peacebuilding with the goal of liberal institution-building was fully implemented for the first time, following the post-war elections in Bosnia-Herzegovina, when the temporary international mandates were extended and civilian control over the peacebuilding process taken over by international appointees in February 1997. The hubris of the late 1990s was highlighted in the UN blessing for an international protectorate in Kosovo in 1999, marking these years as the highpoint of the peacebuilding moment. The Balkans were the crucible through which peacebuilding was developed, tested and renegotiated and the confidence of the late 1990s quickly waned with the over extension of the belief in external responsibility for overseeing post-conflict political processes of reconstruction and the debacles of Afghanistan and Iraq.

Today, there is an emergent consensus over what has gone wrong with peacebuilding over the last 20 years. In both policymaking and in academia there has been a reappraisal of the peacebuilding paradigm; one which has sought to rationalise and to a certain extent excuse and legitimate the policy errors which led to a situation where, by 2017, a key area of US concern – the Middle East – now seemed to be beyond US control and influence as a direct product of US-led interventionist practice in Afghanistan, Iraq, Libya and Syria. It appears that the lesson being learned is the lesson of pragmatism, that peace cannot be exported as a set of policies, institutions and practices. That to do so, in the words of leading US scholar David Lake, is 'criminally stupid' (2016, p. ix) or 'astounding in its audacity' (2016, p. 197). Lake's monograph *The Statebuilder's Dilemma: On the Limits of Foreign Intervention* (published in late 2016) is a clear and representative example of the current acceptance of pragmatist approaches and serves here as a basis for discussing their implications.

Pragmatism could be understood as a 'realist' response to the liberal idealism of international peacebuilding. According to Lake, who uses statebuilding and peacebuiding as interchangeable concepts, the problematic is simple – peacebuilding only came into existence as a liberal project with the end of the Cold War in 1990. Prior to then, the US and the Soviets were keen to support loyal regimes and there was no conception of peacebuilding as the external promotion of liberal institutional frameworks. 'Liberal statebuilding, beginning with the end of the Cold War, elevated the goal of building legitimate states and premised strategy on the belief that democracy and free markets would be sufficient to legitimate a government in the eyes of its people.' (Lake, 2016, p. 6) It is worth quoting Lake's formulation of the problem:

> The liberal model of statebuilding so widely applied in the post–Cold War period was not selected because it was a tried and true method. Rather, it was an ideology that fit an emerging academic paradigm on the positive role of limited political institutions that, in turn, reflected the euphoria of the 'end of history' moment. Contrary to the prevailing wisdom, however, legitimacy is not inherent in institutions in general nor only in institutions with representative qualities. Institutions are not 'strong' or accepted by society simply because they are institutions. This puts the proverbial cart before the horse...This is the mistake of nearly all statebuilders in recent decades, and of all institutionalist scholars, who have placed inordinate faith in the legitimating power of democratic institutions...
>
> The arrogance behind this particular theory of politics, however, grew out of our own time. Given the world in 1991, as history was just ending, how could democracy, free markets, and limited but effective states not be 'good things' – and why should all good things not go together? In the end, the model said more about the statebuilders than about statebuilding. (2016, p. 198)

We can see a simple inversion of liberal peacebuilding understandings: exporting institutions and legal frameworks makes no sense and ignores the social basis of governing legitimacy – establishing hybrid orders where the state has no de facto purchase on society or further destabilising society by offering enrichment opportunities to elites etc.

Here, Lake sets up the liberal peacebuilding framework as an accident of the historical moment and liberal overconfidence in the 1990s. A policy blip that was always destined to fail – based as it was more on our naïve idealism than any understanding of the world. In the terminology of popular French sociologist Bruno Latour, it now appears that really 'We Were Never Liberal Peacebuilders' (see Latour, 1993). Peacebuilding it seems was just an unfortunate and accidental mistake. This is both a problematic and apologetic or self-serving interpretation of the end of the peacebuilding paradigm as will be considered below.

THE PRAGMATIC APOLOGIA

Pragmatism, as a critique of peacebuilding, problematised the idea of institution-building both from the 'top-down' and from the 'bottom-up'. Pragmatic positions were critical both of the idea that international experts could develop institutional solutions that could just be exported or imposed by external actors (prevalent in the late 1990s) and also of the idea that deeper social, economic or political external 'engineering' might enable liberal institutional frameworks to work without frictions (the 'peacebuilding-as-statebuilding' approach of the 2000s). Both these 'liberal' framings assumed that external actors could shape social and political processes and outcomes on the basis that power worked in a linear or cause-and-effect manner (i.e. that certain policy interventions would lead to certain desirable results or outcomes). Pragmatist positions tended to resist the idea that there were pre-set or pre-packaged 'off-the-peg' solutions to universal or generalisable 'problems', instead problems should be grasped in their concrete and relational context (as will be considered further in the closing chapters). From a pragmatic perspective, Western interests in creating liberal democracies or ideological desires to spread liberal values therefore needed to be tempered by a much greater appreciation of 'realism'.

This 'realist turn' inverted the international peacebuilding paradigm, starting from the problem rather than from the Western or international provision of 'solutions' or external goals. This inversion was powerfully expressed through the view that there was a paradox or contradiction at the heart of the peacebuilding programme. The more there was an attempt to shape outcomes based on external interests or values the less likely it was to succeed: '...the greater the interests of the statebuilder in the target country, the less likely statebuilding is to succeed in building a legitimate state that can survive on its own into the indefinite future' (Lake, 2016, p. 2). The pragmatic paradox is interesting in that it is not just a critique of the limits and difficulties of exporting liberal institutions, it also suggests that to do so is inherently problematic, making the situation worse. Lake argued that: 'current practice reveals great faith in externally led social engineering' (2016, p. 1):

> The existing literature emphasizes getting national political institutions 'right.' This emphasis recurs both at the deep level of politics, where observers and practitioners identify predatory institutions as the root evil, and at the surface, where analysts debate the proper strategy and tactics of statebuilding. This concentration on institutions implicitly accepts and is premised on a particular theory of state legitimation, one grounded in liberalism. Institutions are, no doubt, important. But in this focus the underlying social cleavages that undermine institutions and ultimately bring down states are ignored. (2016, p. 11)

In this, now consensual, critique, Lake echoed the current perspective of the UN, cited at the opening of this chapter, against the idea that external preferences or blueprints could be exported or imposed. The UN described this externally led or 'top-down' approach as a 'template' culture or the 'the so-called "Christmas tree mandate" dilemma, where template language for many tasks routinely appeared in mission mandates' (UN, 2015a, p. 60). The pragmatic paradox appeared to be that the more 'enthusiastic' reformers were to transform other societies the more they risked unintentional consequences, which could be counterproductive. The pragmatic lesson was that 'less can sometimes be more': that peace could not in fact be built by good intentions of external dogooders but needed to be understood in more 'local' and 'organic' ways. This shift towards the 'pragmatic' or the 'organic' was also prefigured in more critical policy and academic work which suggested that peacebuilding was a complex organic process of self-organising adaptation and resilience. For example, Cedric de Coning, a leading policy analyst, concluded that:

> when international peace interventions try to engineer specific outcomes, they produce the opposite effect of that which sustaining peace aims to achieve; they generate on-going instability, dependence and fragility, because such interventions undermine self-organisation and thus resilience. A complexity-informed approach to self-sustainable peace suggests that peacebuilders limit their efforts to safeguarding, stimulating, facilitating and creating the space for societies to develop resilient capacities for self-organisation. (de Coning, 2016, p. 14)

Thus, the pragmatic alternative sought to move away from external or universal goals and looked for more 'organic' metrics that could serve as a guide instead, such as local 'legitimacy', starting with the existing social and political order rather than 'universal' views of desirable liberal institutional frameworks. It was important to focus on how the actually existing society worked, rather than Western ideals. Pragmatism worked with what there was rather than imposing liberal goals and aspirations. As Lake stated:

> My approach differs from the prevailing institutionalist view ... institutionalists are fundamentally liberals, in the classic sense of this term, who believe the legitimacy of the state follows from democracy and free markets.... [T]his liberal model of statebuilding is itself deeply flawed and has repeatedly failed to provide the legitimacy necessary for successful statebuilding ... legitimacy follows from social order, not the other way around as in the prevailing model. (2016, p. 17)

For this doyen of US policymaking academia, the pragmatist framing thus neatly inverted the 'top-down' and 'liberal' paradigm of international peacebuilding. In what is now the established consensus on the death of the peacebuilding moment, it was suggested that intervention guided by liberal universalist understandings could only make conflict situations worse. Amitai Etzione, a leading communitarian theorist, for example, picking up on US Presidential candidate Hillary Clinton's call for a more 'active' foreign policy, argued that any return to liberal universalist assumptions would be disastrous:

Take Afghanistan. If the US would extend its involvement there as it did during the years between 2003 and 2014, we would suffer many more thousands of casualties (which are now down to single digits); kill or cause to be killed many more Afghans; and sink many more hundreds of billions into a government that is ranked by Transparency International as one of the most corrupt in the world. We would continue to stand in the way of the Afghan government working out its differences with the Taliban and Pakistan, because we believe we know that the Afghan people prefer a liberal secular democracy (or would, if they would just listen to us). In short, things could get much worse (Etzione, 2016)

Despite the fact that existing conditions are far from ideal, the new consensus seems to be that, no matter how bad things are, international peacebuilding interventions will fail to make a positive difference. Both policymakers and radical critics increasingly agree that accepting the status quo can often be better than attempts at any positive transformation. Thus disillusionment with international intervention has been given coherence and even a positive spin by pragmatic and 'organic' approaches, which have strongly reinforced the potentially dangerous and self-satisfying understanding that 'they' are not ready for liberalism. Thus even radical critiques of Western hubris and liberal certitude have been played out against the backdrop of 'their' unsuitability for modern liberal frameworks of governance.

The error of Western policymakers then becomes merely that of naivety and over confidence in 'their' capacities and abilities to be like 'us'. This definitely softened the 'critical' blow and enabled pragmatic approaches to salve Western policy consciences. Today it appears that the real 'crime' of international peacebuilders was that of caring too much. As Lake put it: 'The limits of external statebuilding are reached precisely when the statebuilder cares the most about the future policies of the failed state.' (2016, p. 16) 'Caring too much' implied that peacebuilders wanted to go too far and too quickly, in essence, attempting to short cut the 'organic' process of building sustainable peace.

THE RETURN OF REALISM

The pragmatist critique of international peacebuilding goals left three general policy options. Lake set up the first option as that advocated by Stephen Krasner, of 'good enough governance', where the international community enforced a minimal set of rights standards and key international security threats were dealt with and stability was seen as more important than democracy (2016, p. 201). This perspective could be seen as pragmatism in its everyday usage and as a return to Cold War clientelist regimes:

> This is the direction in which US policy, at least since Iraq, has been trending under President Obama: target individual terrorists and organizations but avoid large-scale interventions, even into such clearly failed states as Libya, and tolerate authoritarian leaders who promise stability, as with the military in Egypt after the coup against President Mohamed Morsi. (Lake, 2016, p. 202)

The second option was that of a 'neutral' peacebuilding intervention (2016, p. 203) where the concern was focused on building up organic processes of social formation. Interestingly, Lake spent little time considering how this 'neutral' approach to peacebuilding intervention might work, suggesting that it was a highly unlikely possibility as a multi-lateral framework would still rely on 'interested' states, which would pervert the process to their own ends or would attract little international support (2016, p. 204). This 'organic' option, of working with the resources and capacities available rather than seeking to direct and shape policy processes, similarly took peacebuilding off the policy agenda, making peacebuilding a marginal preoccupation of non-governmental agencies, concerned with community development and social welfare.

Lake's preference was the third option, which involved no direct international intervention, instead focusing on providing indirect institutional incentives:

> ...focus instead on creating an international environment conducive to indigenous state formation. Through the use of carrots and sticks, states might shape incentives for fragile states by making access to the security and economic benefits of the Pax Americana, in general, or the European Union, in particular, contingent on domestic groups settling their differences, agreeing on a social order, and governing themselves effectively. (2016, p. 21)

It is noticeable that the only option of the three with the goal of supporting liberal peacebuilding goals, formally the sine qua non of the peacebuilding project, was one that did not involve any policy intervention in the states and societies concerned. The two options that could be seen to be involved in domestic political processes only operated at the margins, either with a concern with compliant state elites or with building community capacities and neither of these approaches aimed at supporting liberal institutional frameworks of markets, democracy, rights and the rule of law. In the turn to realist and pragmatist understandings, peacebuilding as a major paradigm of international policymaking is doubly erased: firstly, in being reinterpreted as a momentary accident or misunderstanding; and, secondly, in discussions of alternatives that betray no legacy of previous doctrines.

THE CONTENTS OF THE BOOK

This book is organised in five parts, the Introductory section continues with the next chapter, introducing the 'political' and 'pragmatic' critiques of peacebuilding, construed as a specifically 'liberal' project. Firstly, the 'political' critics who focused on the ideological use of liberal discourses to selectively promote Western interests and perpetuate new international hierarchies, and secondly the emergence of 'pragmatic' approaches highlighting the problems of the liberal episteme itself. These critiques serve to put the following chapters in context, with analysis of the political impasse of international peacebuilding, as the difficulty of evading the reproduction of the hierarchical binaries of the counter-position of Western authority and local incapacity, and the emergence of pragmatic approaches seeking to move beyond 'liberal' conceptions of peacebuilding.

Part II contains two chapters. Chapter 3 looks at the development of the *Agenda for Peace*, initiated by the UN Secretary-General Boutros Boutros-Ghali in 1992, intended to reform international peacekeeping operations with the proposal for 'post-conflict peacebuilding'. Boutros-Ghali defined peacebuilding as 'action to identify and support structures which will tend to strengthen and solidify peace in order to avoid a relapse into conflict'." These reforms were confirmed at the 2000 UN Millennium Assembly and were shaped by the need for a new 'people-centred' approach to conflict situations, no longer strictly bound by traditional 'state-centred' principles, such as non-intervention and state sovereignty. This chapter considers the impact of the proposals for UN peace negotiations, peacekeeping, peacebuilding and long-term conflict prevention. It concludes with a discussion of the implications of these reforms as confirmation of the new policy sphere of peacebuilding as the external management of post-conflict and conflict-prone states.

Chapter 4 focuses on the development of international mechanisms for international peacebuilding in the 2000s. This chapter analyses the development, content and consequences of the 'peacebuilding-as-statebuilding' discourse. In this period, peacebuilding was reformed through a shift away from an emphasis upon the direct protectorate powers of the 1990s. The chapter engages with the changing theoretical approaches to state sovereignty, which redefined sovereignty as state capacity rather than as political independence, recasting peacebuilding as strengthening sovereignty rather than undermining it. In the 2000s, peacebuilding often no longer appeared as external coercion but as an internal matter of administrative assistance for 'good governance' or 'institutional capacity-building'. The consequences of this move are also considered and it is suggested that 'peacebuilding-as-statebuilding' left states with only formal self-government, resulting in the institutionalisation of weak states which had little relationship with their societies and lacked legitimate authority.

Part III contains two chapters considering the limits of attempts to socially and politically engineer liberal institutions at the informal and formal level. Chapter 5 concerns 'Civil Society Building', for many commentators, considered a precondition for the development of consolidated peaceful societies. Nowhere was this more the case than where ethnic and nationalist identification indicated a deeply politically segmented society. To challenge this segmentation, international institutions provided financial and technical support to a growing civil society sector based on non-governmental organisations. Civil society promotion was key to 'democratization' strategies and 'a key component of peacebuilding' addressing the 'economic, social, cultural, humanitarian and political roots of conflict' according to the UN. Democratisation was broadly defined by the UN to constitute a 'comprehensive approach' covering the broad range of new peacebuilding priorities: 'top-down' international regulation of elections, institutional development and economic management, accompanied by 'bottom-up' assistance to develop a democratic political culture through civil society-building. While top-down economic and political interventions were often seen to perpetuate social segmentation and ethnic nationalism, bottom-up support for the sphere of civil society was held to have an empowering and transformative content. This chapter considers how civil society promotion worked in relation to institutionalist understandings and opened up the sphere of society for international intervention and analyses its limits in practice.

Chapter 6 considers the limits of work at the level of building formal institutions: the belief that external experts could provide the institutional scaffolding which would form the preconditions for successful peacebuilding (Paris, 2004 is the classic academic reflection of this). This approach reached its highpoint with the discussions over governance reform in Iraq in 2003 and many policymakers turned to the Bosnia-Herzegovina experience for lessons in peacebuilding. The key lesson advocated at this point by international officials was the prioritisation of the 'rule of law' rather than the focus on political processes and elections. It was held that while regular elections had merely reinforced the dominance of political elites hostile to reform, internationally imposed legal changes could galvanise the peacebuilding process. This chapter analyses the limits of this perspective through focusing on three areas of legal activism in Bosnia: constitutional change, property return and employment laws. It suggests that the 'rule of law' approach saw legal or administrative solutions as a short cut to addressing political problems, fetishising the legal framework at the same time as marginalising the political sphere.

Part IV contains two chapters. Chapter 7 reflects upon the shift away from institution-building approaches and the critique of linear understandings of peacebuilding, which assumed that Western 'blueprints' could be imposed upon non-compliant elites. In the late 2000s and early 2010s it was increasingly suggested, in both policy and academic literatures, that there should be a shift towards non-linear approaches. Rather than focusing upon Western policy prescriptions intra-elite bargaining and formal institutional structures, these understandings stressed non-linearity, hybridity, local societal processes and practices and the importance of 'hidden' agency and resistance. This chapter highlights that, while these approaches set up a critique of liberal linear approaches, they tended to reify hybrid, non-liberal or non-linear outcomes as the product of local inter-subjective attachments. In this way, they reproduced the voluntarist and idealist understandings of liberal peace, locating the problems or barriers to peace and development at the cognitive or ideational level rather than considering the barriers of economic and social context.

Chapter 8 considers how, in the late 2000s and early 2010s there was a shift towards critical understandings of 'liberal peace' approaches to international intervention, which argued that local culture held the key to the effectiveness of peace interventions. In this 'bottom-up' approach, peace, reconciliation, and a 'culture of law' then became secondary effects of sociocultural norms and values. However, these liberal peace critiques remained trapped in the impasse of peacebuilding: the inability to go beyond the binaries of liberal universalism and cultural relativism. This understanding is then contrasted with the rise of 'resilience' approaches to intervention – which built on this attention to the particular context of application but moved beyond the impasse through philosophical pragmatism and the focus on concrete social practices. This chapter clarifies the nature of this shift through the focus on the shifting understanding of international peacebuilding in addressing the failings of the 'war on drugs' in the Americas.

The concluding Chapter 9 examines the transformation in the conceptual understanding of international peacebuilding over the twenty years' crisis. It suggests that this conceptual shift can be usefully interrogated through its imbrication within broader epistemological shifts highlighting the limits of causal knowledge claims: heuristically framed in this article in terms of the shift from policy interventions within the problematic of causation to those concerned with the pragmatic management of effects. In this shift, the means and mechanisms of international intervention have been transformed, no longer focused on the universal application of Western causal knowledge through policy interventions but rather on the effects of specific and unique local and organic processes at work in societies themselves. The focus on effects took the conceptualisation of intervention out of the traditional terminological lexicon of International Relations theory and instead recast problems in increasingly organic ways, suggesting that artificial or hubristic attempts at sociopolitical intervention should be excluded or minimised.

CHAPTER 2

The Pragmatic Critique

INTRODUCTION

As highlighted in the introductory chapter, for many commentators, the lack of success of international peacebuilding efforts has been explained through the pragmatic discourse of 'liberal peace', where it is assumed that 'liberal' Western understandings and assumptions have influenced policymaking leading to counterproductive results. At the core of the critique is the assumption that the international peacebuilding approach sought to reproduce and impose liberal models: focused on the formal liberal institutional framework of state sovereignty, markets, human rights and democracy. This chapter challenges this view of Western policymaking and suggests that post-Cold War post-conflict intervention and peacebuilding can be better understood as reflecting disillusionment with classical liberal assumptions about the autonomous subject – framed in terms of sovereignty, law, democracy and the market. The loss of credibility of liberal modernist frameworks of understanding the world (dealt with further in the concluding chapter) enabled pragmatic critiques of liberal peacebuilding to rewrite post-Cold War intervention in ways that have exaggerated the 'liberal' nature of the policy frameworks and acted as apologia, excusing policy failure on the basis of the self-flattering view of Western policy elites: that non-Western subjects were not ready for 'Western' freedoms.

From the late 1990s, commentators developed critical frameworks of the 'liberal peace' to understand the new, more interventionist,

© The Author(s) 2017
D. Chandler, *Peacebuilding*, Rethinking Peace and Conflict Studies,
DOI 10.1007/978-3-319-50322-6_2

approaches to the problems of post-conflict peacebuilding (see, for example, Duffield, 2001; Paris, 2002; Pugh, 2005; Richmond, 2005; Richmond and MacGinty, 2007). In essence, liberal peacebuilding was held to go beyond traditional approaches of conflict prevention, or 'negative peace'; towards the external engineering of post-conflict societies through the export of liberal frameworks of 'good governance', democratic elections, human rights, the rule of law and market relations (for an overview, see Richmond, 2008a). As Alex Bellamy summarised: 'The principle aim of peace operations thus becomes not so much about creating spaces for negotiated conflict resolution between states but about actively contributing to the construction of liberal polities, economies and societies.' (2008a, pp. 4–5). The critical discourse of peacebuilding flagged up the problem that – under the guise of universalising Western liberal frameworks of democracy and the market – the needs and interests of those subject to intervention were often ignored, resulting in the maintenance of inequalities and conflicts and undermining the asserted goals of external interveners. The critique of international intervention and peacebuilding, framed by the construction of the liberal peace, was highly effective in challenging assumptions of easy fixes to post-conflict situations (see, for example, Chesterman et al., 2005; Dobbins et al., 2007; Paris and Sisk, 2009a).

This chapter seeks to introduce and examine the use of the 'liberal peace' rubric to describe and analyse international peacebuilding interventions in the post-Cold War period. It will be argued that the critique of liberal peace bore little relation to policy practice while importantly preparing the ground for today's realist or pragmatist consensus. The desire to critique the peacebuilding project as a 'liberal' project led to a set of assumptions and one-sided representations that eventually succeeded in portraying peacebuilding policy interventions as 'too liberal': as too fixated on Western models and too keen to allow democratic freedoms and market autonomy. It will be explained here that this view of 'liberal' interventions transforming post-conflict societies through 'immediate' liberalisation and 'rapid democratization and marketization' (Paris, 2004, p. 235) was a self-serving and fictional policy narrative.

This narrative fiction was used, in the frameworks of pragmatic policy-orientated critiques, as the framework upon which to reflect upon Western policy and to limit policy expectations on the basis that the aspirations of external interveners were too ambitious, too interventionist, and too 'liberal' for the states and societies which were the subject of intervention.

This policy narrative, which succeeded in becoming the dominant appraisal of international peacebuilding was given legitimacy by ostensibly radical critiques of post-Cold War intervention, similarly framed through the critique of 'liberal' peacebuilding. For example, Oliver Richmond re-read the catastrophe of the invasion and occupation of Iraq in terms of an 'attempt to mimic the liberal state', which had 'done much to discredit the universal claims of the transferability of the liberal peace in political terms' (Richmond, 2008b, p. 458). Michael Barnett argued that 'liberal values' clearly guided peacebuilding activities and that their 'explicit goal' was 'to create a state defined by the rule of law, markets and democracy' (Barnett, 2006, p. 88). Beate Jahn held that 'the tragedy of liberal diplomacy' lies in the ideological drive of liberalism, in which intervention is intensified despite the counterproductive results (Jahn, 2007a, b). Foucauldian-inspired theorists, Michael Dillon and Julian Reid, similarly reinforced the claims that the key problematic of peacebuilding intervention was its liberal nature, asserting that there was a liberal drive to control and to regulate the post-colonial world on the behalf of neoliberal or biopolitical power, seeking 'to globalize the domesticating power of civil society mechanisms in a war against all other modes of cultural forms' (Dillon and Reid, 2009, p. 20).

This radical view of a transformative drive to regulate and control through peacebuilding based upon liberal framings of power and knowledge, stood in stark contrast to the views articulated in much of the policy world. By the end of the Cold War, leading policy institutions were highly pessimistic of the capacities of non-liberal subjects to cope with liberal political, economic and social forms and suspicious of even East and Central European states coping with democracy and the market, let alone those of sub-Saharan Africa. Bringing the radical critique back in relation with the policy practices seems to suggest that the policy critics of liberal peacebuilding have offered succour and consolation to the policy-makers along with their desire to provide critique. This second introductory chapter thus maps the critical positions which converged in the pragmatic consensus that peacebuilding was problematic because of its inherently 'liberal' nature.

There have been many different approaches taken to the critique of peacebuilding approaches and often authors have not clearly staked out their methodological frameworks or instead developed a 'scattergun approach' using a range of different critiques (see, for a survey, Richmond, 2005). Nevertheless, for heuristic purposes, it is useful to frame these diverse critiques within two broad, distinctive, but often interconnected, approaches; which are here categorised as the 'political', and the more policy-orientated, 'pragmatic' critique. The former approach tended to see the discourse of peacebuilding as ideological and instrumental, arguing that the rhetoric of freedom, markets and democracy was merely a representation of Western self-interest, which had little genuine concern for the security and freedoms of those societies intervened in. The latter approach suggested that rather than the concepts being misused by Western powers, the problem lay less with power relations than with the universal conceptualising of the liberal peace itself.

The 'Political' Critique

In this framework, international peacebuilding was critiqued on the basis that it reflected the hegemonic values and the political, economic and geo-strategic needs of Western states. This 'political' critique focused on the role played by the interests of Western powers in shaping policy and the impact of the economic and structural inequalities of the world economy. It also paid attention to the naturalising of policy assumptions based upon this perspective. There were two main versions of this critical political perspective.

Firstly, there was a Left or neo-Marxist structural critique of international peacebuilding approaches. This framing suggested that Western intervention inevitably reproduced hierarchies of power due to the structural constraints of neoliberal market relations – opening up societies and economies through the demands for democratisation and the free market. This approach focused on the problems of neoliberal economic policies for the reconstruction of post-conflict societies and suggested that, in serving the interests of dominant Western powers and the international financial institutions, liberal peacebuilding policies inevitably reproduced the conditions and possibilities for conflict (see also, Abrahamsen, 2000; Barbara, 2008; Cramer, 2006; Jacoby, 2007).

This approach often drew upon Robert Cox's critical theory to suggest that the narrow problem-solving approach taken by Western policymakers was problematic as it took for granted the interests of these actors and treated market-based economic solutions as merely technical 'problem-solving' approaches to address problems of post-conflict development (Cox, 1981). These critical approaches to international peacebuilding suggested that it was necessary to reflect on these assumptions to reveal the power interests that lay behind them and to question the presentation of these policies in policy neutral technical terms (see, for example, Bellamy, 2008). Michael Pugh, for example, highlighted how neoliberal economic practices were naturalised as technical solutions to development and reconstruction, marginalising or preventing political discussions of economic alternatives better suited to post-conflict societies (see, for example, Pugh, 2005; Pugh et al., 2008).

Secondly, there was a more Foucauldian approach, which critiqued international peacebuilding not so much on the basis of its interventionary policies per se as on the regulatory and controlling interests behind these policies: understood as perpetuating the needs and interests of liberal, neoliberal or biopolitical capitalism in the West. Mark Duffield pioneered this approach in his book, *Global Governance and the New Wars* (2001). The focus was less on the opening up of non-Western economies to the world market and more on the reshaping and transformation of these societies in order to prevent instability. Duffield argued that the project of 'liberal peace reflected a radical development agenda of social transformation' with the aim 'to transform the dysfunctional and war-affected societies that it encounters on its borders into cooperative, representative and, especially, stable entities' (2001, p. 11).

This transformative liberal intervention necessitated the radicalisation of both development and security discourses, giving the external institutions of global governance new mandates to: 'shift the balance of power between groups and even to change attitudes and beliefs' (2001, p. 15). In his later work, Duffield expanded on this framework of the projection of liberal interests in stabilising 'zones of conflict' through the use of the Foucauldian conception of biopolitics, where intervention was understood as saving, developing, or securing the Other, at the same time legitimising and extending external regulatory control (Duffield, 2007; see also, Dillon and Reid, 2009, p. 20). Duffield argued that in the interests of stabilising the neoliberal economic order, the divisions between the 'developed' and the 'undeveloped' world were reproduced through policies of containment such as 'sustainable' or 'community-based' development (see also Jabri, 2007, p. 124).

THE EMERGENCE OF 'PRAGMATIST' CRITIQUE

The 'pragmatist' critique of peacebuilding as being a specifically 'liberal' project presented itself as a critique of the grounding universalising assumptions of the liberal policy discourse itself, rather than merely as a critique of the ideological or interest-based forms of its implementation. These critics of international peacebuilding initially advocated the continuation of international intervention but only if it could be done in less 'liberal' ways; for example, with less attention to the reconstruction of sovereign states, democracy and the free market. While upholding the values of democracy and the free market aspirationally, these critics argued against the liberal peacebuilding approach on the basis that it was unsuitable in the context of post-conflict states and situations of state failure.

This approach tended to focus on the problem of Western interventionist 'ideas' or 'values' rather than on hegemonic interests or power relations. While their critique of the liberal peacebuilding thesis therefore appeared to be more radical, their intentions could be understood as more conservative or policy-orientated. Rather than problematising relations of power or the interests behind policymaking, there was a tendency to view the liberal peacebuilding approach as a projection of Western ideals in a context where they can be counterproductive. Like the 'political' critique, there was two variants, the more radical version, which had close connections with the 'political' critique above (and which will be considered first) and a more conservative version, particularly influential in US policy and academic discourse (which will be considered second).

The first, radical, variant engaged from the approach of critical theory and human security. Like the 'political' critiques, it highlighted that international peacebuilding policies should be seen as power-based, rather than as purely technical solutions (see, for example, Bellamy, 2008). However, the focus was less on the assumptions about market relations or securing the needs of global neoliberal or biopolitical regulatory power and more on the assumptions made about the political and institutional framework and positivist and rationalist forms of Western knowledge. For writers, such as Alex Bellamy (2008), a central concern was the problematic focus on the rebuilding of Westphalian state forms, for Oliver Richmond (2008a), the focus was on the liberal assumptions of political community assumed in the approach of 'liberal peace', which tended to ignore vital local concerns of identity and culture.

Radical pragmatist approaches clearly took on board the concerns over universalising Western liberal assumptions, central to pragmatist critiques, which are prevalent today. However, they differed in their normative conclusions, often suggesting that peacebuilding could be successfully reformed through including other, 'non-liberal', approaches which were more reflective, pluralist, or 'bottom-up'. The intimation was that if international peacebuilding could adapt away from its universal liberal starting assumptions it could be more successful and be more easily accepted by those being intervened upon (Richmond, 2008b, p. 462). Some commentators from within this perspective argued that becoming less 'liberal' was in Western politicians own interests, in a globalised and interconnected world, or alternatively suggested that non-state actors could intervene in ways which engaged more equally and empathetically with those on the ground (see, for example, Tadjbakhsh and Chenoy, 2007; Maclean et al., 2006).

This second, more conservative, pragmatist approach sought to problematise universalist understandings of the 'export' or 'transplanting' of liberal institutions, suggesting that societal differences had to be taken much more seriously. Commentators who problematised the 'black-boxing' of societies being intervened in included Jack Snyder, Fareed Zakharia, Stephen Krasner, Robert Keohane and Roland Paris, amongst others, who argued that liberal universalist assumptions had undermined the effectiveness of international peacebuilding (see, for example, Snyder, 2000; Zakharia, 2003, pp. 98–9; Krasner, 2004, 2005; Keohane, 2002; Paris 2004).

One of the core universal liberal assumptions questioned in this pragmatist approach was that of sovereign statehood. These critics argued that focusing on (re)constructing sovereign states was unlikely to solve the problems of post-conflict societies, merely to reproduce them. Krasner argued that sovereignty was problematic for many states because they lacked the capacity for good governance and required an external regulatory framework in order to guarantee human rights and the rule of law (Krasner, 2004, p. 89; see also; Fearon and Laitin, 2004). Robert Keohane forwarded a similar perspective with differing levels of statehood applicable to different levels of governance capacity: 'We somehow have to reconceptualise the state as a political unit that can maintain internal order while being able to engage in international cooperation, without claiming exclusive rights . . . traditionally associated with sovereignty' (Keohane, 2003, p. 277; see also Keohane, 2002).

It was not just the autonomy of states that was seen to be problematic and potentially counterproductive but also the institutional frameworks of autonomy. For example, Roland Paris argued that the assumptions of liberal peacebuilding – that democracy and the free market would ensure social progress and stability – neglected to consider the problematic nature of post-conflict transition. Questioning the assumption that 'liberalization fosters peace', Paris advocated less emphasis on interventionist policies that promoted democracy and the market, both of which were seen to encourage competition and conflict without adequate institutional safe-guards (Paris, 2004, pp. 40–51). Instead, Paris advocated a policy of 'Institutionalization before Liberalization' in order to establish the regu-latory frameworks necessary to ensure that post-conflict societies could gradually (and safely) move towards liberal models of market democracy (ibid., pp. 179–211). This critique of the export of liberal models to non-liberal societies echoed that made in the 1960s by Samuel Huntington (1968; see also Chandler, 2006b).

Both the radical and conservative 'pragmatic' critics of 'liberal' peace-building did not argue that they themselves were anti-liberal; merely that liberalism, as projected in international peacebuilding frameworks, had to take into account the non-liberal context in which intervention took place. Fareed Zakharia, for example, argued that, while in the West, modernity was historically associated with both liberalism and democracy, much of the non-Western world had to make a choice between liberalism and democracy as, without the institutional framework of limited government, 'elections provide a cover for authoritarianism' and are 'merely legitimized power grabs'; in this context, therefore, 'what Africa needs more than urgently than democracy is good governance' (Zakharia, 2003, pp. 98–9; see also Snyder, 2000).

The pragmatist critique of liberal peacebuilding was that, rather than being based on the needs and interests of Western hegemonic powers and international financial institutions, the problem was one of projecting an idealised understanding of the West's own historical development; one which tended to naturalise the smooth working of the market and under-stand liberal political frameworks as an organic product of democratic processes such as free elections. For these critics, the founding assump-tions of international peacebuilding were the problem: attempts to uni-versalise Western models in non-liberal contexts, would merely reproduce, and maybe even exacerbate, the problems of conflict and instability.

A 'CRITICAL' CONSENSUS?

This chapter suggests that the radical intent of the 'political' critics of interventionist Western policies was blunted by their articulation within the pragmatist problematic of 'liberal' peacebuilding, enabling their cri-tique to be assimilated into the policy discourse of how policy might be reformed and made 'less liberal' in the wake of the discrediting of the claims of Western peacebuilding after the debacles of Iraq and Afghanistan. The two fairly distinct critical framings of 'liberal' peacebuilding stemmed from very different methodological perspectives and political and policy intents. While the 'pragmatist' critics tended to seek to defend and legitimate regulatory external intervention, the 'political' critics tended to challenge and oppose these frameworks as the projection of Western power and interests. Nevertheless, in critiquing Western policy interventions within the problematic of 'liberal' peacebuilding it seemed that there was often much less distance between the approaches than might be assumed on the basis of political intent and occasionally there was a surprisingly large area of confluence.

Both 'political' and 'pragmatist' approaches regarded the limits of international peacebuilding as determined by its 'liberal' essence. Yet, little attention was paid to the meaning and practice of 'liberalism'. This was perhaps understandable as the 1990s witnessed a new confidence in Western power with assumptions that the collapse of non-market alternatives (with the end of the Cold War) meant the 'End of History' and the end of any political or ideological challenge to the ascendency of liberal perspectives and discursive judgements on the economic, political and social frameworks of states and societies. However, while understandable, these assumptions were mistaken or at least one-sided, ignoring the internal crisis of liberalism, especially apparent once the competition of the Cold War was over. The rest of this chapter seeks to highlight that the rapid rise of critiques of 'liberal' peacebuilding was, in fact, indicative of a lack of confidence in classical liberal assumptions about human behaviour and the political and socio-economic institutions needed for human flourishing.

In the critiques of international peacebuilding, the growing consensus on the problematic nature of liberalism began to cross the political and policy spectrum. The fundamental and shared claim of the critics was that the lack of success of external interventions, designed not only to halt conflict but to help reconstruct the peace, was down to the 'liberalism' of the interveners. If only they were not, in various ways, so liberal, then it was alleged external intervention or assistance would potentially be much less problematic. It thus appeared that the main academic and political matter of dispute was whether the liberal peace discourse was amenable to policy change. Here the divide seemed to roughly approximate to the division highlighted above, in terms of the heuristic categories of 'political' and 'pragmatic' critics of peacebuilding.

The more ostensibly radical, 'political', critics, with a more economically deterministic approach to the structural dynamics of international hierarchies and the needs of 'neo-liberalism' were less likely to be optimistic of policy reform. On the 'pragmatist' side, critics of 'liberal' peace frameworks tended to be more engaged in policy-related work and were more optimistic with regard to a shift away from a 'liberal' policy-emphasis. Radical and more conservative pragmatist approaches both advocated for a more pluralist emphasis on the different needs and processes of societies, with some advocates arguing that liberal goals should be tempered through a greater engagement with plural 'local' voices and other advocates suggesting that more extended forms of societal intervention could enable liberal institutions to be successful after an extended period of managed transition. Pragmatist positions emerged in opposition to 'liberal' frameworks of peacebuilding but there was a range of potential alternatives, pragmatism was a critical approach rather than a fixed set of policy prescriptions.

In an influential article, Endre Begby and Peter Burgess argued that the majority of the critics of 'liberal' peacebuilding seemed to share two key assumptions about external intervention: firstly, that external Western intervention (of some kind) was necessary, and secondly, that the goal of this intervention should be the liberal one of human freedom and flourishing (Begby and Burgess, 2009). They stated that, in this case, the problem was not so much with the aspirations or goals of 'liberal peace' but with the practices of intervention itself. They had a valid point regarding the limited nature of much of the 'critical' discourse, but did not reflect adequately on the diminished content of the 'liberalism' of the policy interventions themselves nor the 'liberal' aspirations of those who advocated for the reform of practices of external intervention. Today it is clear that the common ground in the broad and disparate critiques of 'liberal' peacebuilding was not the critique of external intervention per se as much as the classical assumptions of liberalism itself.

The critique of liberalism as a set of assumptions and practices drove the approach to the study of post-Cold War peacebuilding in ways which tended to produce a fairly one-sided framework of analysis in which the concept of liberalism was ill-equipped to bear the analytical weight placed upon it and appeared increasingly emptied of theoretical or empirical content. Liberalism was used promiscuously to explain a broad range of, often contradictory, policy perspectives and practices across very differing circumstances and with very differing outcomes. In this sense, liberalism operated as a 'field of adversity' (Foucault, 2008, p. 106) through which a coherent narrative of peacebuilding was articulated both by critical and policy-orientated theorists. The promiscuous use of liberalism to explain very different policy approaches was, of course, facilitated by the ambiguous nature of the concept itself.

It is this ambiguity that enabled liberalism to be critiqued from opposing directions, sometimes by the same author at the same time. Good examples of this were Roland Paris and Timothy Sisk who criticised 'liberal' peacebuilding for being both too laissez-faire and too interventionist in its approach to the regulation and management of conflict. In the peacebuilding literature, the experience of the early and mid-1990s and the 'quick exit' policies of the extended peacekeeping operations in Nambia, Nicaragua, Angola, Cambodia, El Salvador, Mozambique, Liberia, Rwanda, Bosnia, Croatia and Guatemala was repackaged as evidence that Western interveners had too much faith in the liberal subject (Paris and Sisk, 2009b). Similarly, the ad hoc responses to the problems of the early 1990s in the development of formal peacebuilding missions with protectorate powers, in Bosnia, Kosovo and East Timor, was criticised as liberal hubris, on the assumption that international overlords could bring democracy, development and security to others. It seemed that, rather than adding clarity, the critique of the 'liberalism' of interventions shed very little light on their content.

Rather than a critique of liberalism for its inability to overcome social, economic and cultural inequalities, both the policy, 'pragmatist', critique of peacebuilding and the more radical, 'political', critiques argued that social, economic and cultural inequalities and differences had to be central to policy practices and invalidated universalising liberal attempts to reconstruct and rebuild post-conflict societies. In this context – in which the dichotomy between a liberal policymaking sphere and a non-liberal sphere of policy intervention came to the fore – there was an inevitable tendency towards a consensual framing of the problematic of liberal peacebuilding intervention as a problem of the relationship between the liberal West and the non-liberal Other.

The rock on which the peacebuilding expectations were held to crash was that of the non-liberal Other. The non-liberal Other increasingly became portrayed as the barrier to Western liberal aspirations of social peace and progress; either as it lacked the institutional, social, economic and cultural capacities that were alleged to be necessary to overcome the problems of peacebuilding or as a subaltern or resisting subject, for whom liberal peacebuilding frameworks threatened their economic or social existence or fundamental values or identities. The 'critique' became an apologia in that this discursive focus upon the non-Western or non-liberal Other was often held to explain the lack of policy success and, through this, suggest that democracy or development were somehow not 'appropriate' aspirations or that expectations needed to be substantially lowered or changed to account for difference.

International Peacebuilding and the Critique of Liberalism

The 'liberal' assumptions held to be driving international peacebuilding approaches were very much in the eye of their critical beholders. The most obvious empirical difficulty was that international policy regarding intervention and peacebuilding seemed to have little transformative aspiration: far from assumptions of liberal universalism, with the failure of post-colonial development, especially from the 1970s onwards, international policymakers had developed historically low expectations about what could be achieved through external intervention and assistance. The lack of transformative belief was highlighted by one of the key concerns of the pragmatist critics of international peacebuilding – the focus on capacity-building state institutions and intervening to construct 'civil' societies. The focus on institutional solutions (at both the formal and informal levels) to the problems of conflict and transition was indicative of the narrowing down of aspirations from transforming society to merely regulating or managing it – often understood critically as the 'securitising' of policymaking. This was a long way from the promise of liberal transformation and the discourse of 'liberating' societies economically and politically.

In fact, it was the consensus of opinion on the dangers of democracy, which informed the focus on human rights and good governance. For the pragmatist and the political critics of international peacebuilding, liberal rights frameworks were often considered problematic in terms of the dangers of exclusion and extremism. The shift to institutionalism of 'illiberal' peace approaches was not based on arguing for the export of democracy – the freeing up of the political sphere on the basis of support for popular autonomy. The language of institutionalist approaches was that of democratisation: the problematisation of the liberal subject, held to be incapable of moral, rational choices at the ballot box, unless tutored by international experts concerned to promote civil society and pluralist values. In these frameworks, the holding of elections served as an examination of the population and the behaviour of electoral candidates, rather than as a process for the judgement or construction of policy (which it was assumed needed external or international frameworks for its production).

The focus on societal processes underpinning liberal institutions did not stem from a critique of peacebuilding programmes; institutionalist approaches developed from the 1970s onwards in the field of international development and sought to explain why market-orientated policies did not lead to the equalisation of development possibilities but the perpetuation of structural inequalities. For institutionalist approaches, the problem was never the market itself but rather the formal and informal institutions of the societies concerned, which were held to prevent or block the market from working optimally (see the theoretical framing developed in North and Thomas, 1973; North, 1981, 1990). From 1989 onwards, Western governments and donors stressed that policy interventions could not just rely on promoting the freedoms of the market and democracy, but needed to put institutional reform and 'good governance' at the core (see, for example, World Bank, 1989, 1992, 1997, 1998).

Even in relation to Central and Eastern Europe it was regularly stressed that the people and elected representatives were not ready for freedom and that it would take a number of generations before it could be said that democracy was 'consolidated' (see, for example, Dahrendorf, 1990). The transitology literature was based on the critique of liberal assumptions – this was why a transitional period was necessary. Transition implied that markets and democracy could not work without external institutional intervention to prevent instability. While markets needed to be carefully managed through government policymaking it was held that civil society was necessary to ensure that the population learnt civic values to make democracy viable (see, for example, Fukuyama, 1995; Schmitter and Karl, 1991; O'Donnell, 1996; Gunther et al., 1996).

It was through the engagement with 'transition' and the problematic negotiation of EU enlargement that the discursive framework of liberal institutionalism – where human rights, the 'rule of law', civil society and anti-corruption were privileged over democracy – was programmatically cohered. It was also through the discussion of 'transition' that the concept of sovereign autonomy was increasingly problematised, initially in relation to the protections for minority rights and then increasingly expanded to cover other areas of domestic policymaking (see, for example, Cordell, 1998). The key concepts and values of 'liberal' peacebuilding held to have been promoted with vigour with the 'victory of liberalism' at the end of the Cold War were never as dominant a framing as the pragmatist policy critics have claimed (see also Hehir, 2008).

Rather than attempting to transform non-Western societies into the liberal self-image of the West, external interveners had much more status quo aspirations, concerned with regulatory stability and regional and domestic security, rather than transformation. Rather than imposing or 'exporting' alleged liberal Western models, international policy making revolved around the promotion of regulatory and administrative measures that increasingly suggested the problem was not the lack of markets or democracy but rather the culture of society or the mechanisms of governance. Rather than promoting democracy and liberal freedoms, the discussion was how to keep the lid on or to manage the 'complexity' of non-Western societies, usually perceived in terms of fixed ethnic and regional divisions. The solution to the complexity of the non-liberal state and society was the internationalisation of the mechanisms of governance, removing substantive autonomy rather than promoting it.

While it is true that the reconstruction or rebuilding of states was at the centre of external projects of peacebuilding, these processes did not construct a liberal international order. External peacebuilding was a problematic conception for classic liberal thought because the states being constructed in these projects of post-conflict and failed state interventions were not liberal states in the sense of having self-determination and political autonomy. The state at the centre of the peacebuilding projects of the 1990s and 2000s was not the 'Westphalian state' of traditional International Relations theorising. Under the internationalised regulatory mechanisms of intervention and peacebuilding the state was increasingly reduced to an administrative level, in which sovereignty no longer marked a clear boundary line between the 'inside' and the 'outside' (Walker, 1992). Whether we consider European Union statebuilding, explicitly based on a sharing of sovereignty, or consider other peacebuilding interventions, such as those by the international financial institutions in sub-Saharan Africa, it was clear that the state was central as a mechanism for external coordination and regulation rather than as a self-standing actor in so-called 'Westphalian' terms (see Ghani and Lockhart, 2008; Chandler, 2006a; Harrison, 2004).

Too Liberal?

There was little evidence then of the assertions of the critics of 'liberal' peacebuilding, that external interveners imagined that they had the power to reshape state institutions and societies in accordance with Western norms. The limited results would appear to demonstrate that the process of internationalising the governance of non-Western states, through the process of liberal institution-building, increasingly resulted in states which had little connection with their societies, and where the formal political process was increasingly marginalised. Empirically, the 'political' critics of peacebuilding were correct to argue that external policies of intervention – which operated at the formal level of exporting human rights frameworks, the rule of law and mechanisms of 'good governance' – marginalised the people of these societies. This, however, was not the same as arguing that this was because the frameworks of intervention were too liberal.

It would have been possible to argue that external mechanisms of international engagement ignored the political, economic and social context of these societies, and were satisfied with non-Western states paying lip-service to external donor and institutional requirements, rather than asserting that these external actors were attempting to transform these states into Westphalian liberal democracies. At the empirical level it was unproblematic to argue that the result of these external programmes could be seen as 'façade democracy' or as 'reproducing state failure' (Bickerton, 2007; Chopra, 2003) or highlight that Western policy aspirations had little purchase on very different realities and often therefore resulted in 'hybrid polities' where the state formally accorded to Western norms but informally still operated on the basis of traditional hierarchies and exclusions (see, for example, Roberts, 2008, 2009).

Where the critical 'political' and 'pragmatic' discourse was problematic was in the confidence with which its proponents asserted that the reasons for these policy failings could be located in the liberalism of the interveners or the non-liberalism of the subjects of intervention. Roland Paris, for example, argued that 'there is no logical requirement for international agencies to resurrect failed states as states, rather than [as] some other type of polity', and insisted that this was the 'latest chapter in the globalisation of the Westphalian state', where this state form was being propped up despite its failings (2002, p. 654). Paris argued that just as the non-liberal Other could not deal with the liberal state form, they were similarly ill-suited to handle electoral democracy, warning particularly against the holding of elections in post-conflict situations. It was asserted that holding elections when societies were still divided or segmented would be counter-productive, often giving enhanced legitimacy to warring parties and bol-stering the legitimacy of the forces successful in conflict. Often the solutions advocated by the pragmatist critics were along similar lines with regard to both sovereignty and democracy: the need for greater international engagement in the state institutions, under the guise of guaranteeing that no voices were 'excluded' and the need to constrict the autonomy of elected authorities. Under the rubric of the critique of 'liberal' peacebuilding, these critics often advocated the reform of policy interventions away from the focus on liberal rights frameworks and elec-toral democracy.

Dominik Zaum, for example, through a series of case studies, argued that the aspirations of the technocratic approach of international peace-building failed to appreciate that the liberal discourse of self-government undermined the authority of external interveners and enabled local elites to assert pressure and influence (Zaum, 2007). These liberal normative commitments meant that international interventions were limited both in time and scope and therefore found it difficult to resist compromising their initial goals through giving greater authority to local actors (see also Ignatieff, 2003). Other authors had a similar perspective, explaining the failures of international intervention as a product of external actors assum-ing that liberal models could merely be exported, rather than understand-ing the contradictions involved in bringing liberalism to non-liberal societies. Michael Barnett and Christopher Zürcher, for example, sought to analyse why liberal interventions tended to be no more than surface, on the basis that elites at both national and subnational levels could 'capture' and 'compromise' peacebuilding, leading to the reproduction of state-society relations and patrimonial politics (Barnett and ZüRcher, 2009; see also Kahler, 2009, p. 296).

Some of the policy critics argued not merely that these Western models were perverted by the power of the non-liberal Other but that the attempt to export Western models to non-liberal societies would inevitably fail to bridge the gulf between liberal and non-liberal state-society forms. Noah Feldman, for example, suggested that these non-Western states and socie-ties were so alien to Western liberal interveners that 'the high failure rate strongly supports the basic intuition that we do not know what we are doing' (2004, p. 69). Feldman suggested that external assistance should continue but the idea that 'our comparative advantages of wealth and power

[give] us any special ability to identify the institutional structures that will succeed in promoting democracy' should be rejected (ibid, p. 71). Michael Ignatieff similarly argued that 'we do not actually know how to make states work in non-liberal societies that are poor, divided on religious or ethnic lines or lacked a substantial state tradition in the first place' (Ignatieff, 2005, p. 73). The work of Roland Paris and Timothy Sisk supported this view, suggesting that, in dealing with the non-liberal Other, the issues were so complex and dilemma-laden that pragmatic 'muddling through' was the only solution (2009c).

Discursively, the alleged 'voice' of the non-liberal Other was also central to the shifting discourse of international development. While some commentators suggested that little substantive had changed in the shift from the modernising frameworks of the liberal 'Washington Consensus' to the post-liberal, post-conditionality, 'New York Consensus' focus on pro-poor policy making, sustainable development and poverty reduction strategy papers (for example, Pugh, 2005; Cammack, 2006, 2004; Harrison, 2001), there was little doubt that the aspirations for social and economic transformation had been scaled back (Crawford, 2006; see also Easterly, 2006). It was quite clear that broad frameworks of development intervention had much lower horizons than during the Cold War period (Leys, 1996; Pender, 2001); for example, with the replacement of Cold War desires for modernisation with the Millennium Development Goals (MDGs). The MDGs focused not on social and economic transformation but on the situation of the poorest in society with the aspiration that, by 2015, people will be able to live on $1 a day (Sachs, 2005).

With regard to the critique of universal liberal aspirations for progress, it was often difficult to tell the anti-universalist and hierarchical pragmatist perspectives apart from the viewpoints of some of the more radical 'political' critics of 'liberal' peacebuilding. Liberalism was criticised not for its inability to universalise economic growth and overcome the problems of combined and uneven development, but for the aspirations of development itself. For example, Michael Pugh asserted that rather than the 'economic rationalism of (capitalistic) entrepreneurship', other, 'non-liberal', values needed to be taken into account. Following the work of those critical of liberal development models, such as Amartya Sen (1999), he argued that in non-liberal societies:

> Inequalities and non-physiological needs are considered more significant than either absolute poverty or, beyond a survival point, physiological

needs. This means that provided people are not destitute [...] they may choose to live humbly in order to be fulfilled. Such an approach recognises that the paths to modernisation may not be convergent at all, and the marginalised peoples of the world are entitled to choose the extent to which, and how, they integrate in the global economy. (Pugh, 2005, p. 34)

At the core of the 'pragmatist' and 'political' critiques of 'liberal' peacebuilding was a critique of liberal universalist aspirations rather than a critique of the new international hierarchies and divisions based on the institutionalisation of the divide between 'liberal' peacebuilders and 'non-liberal' Others. The critique reflected the ease with which 'liberalism' had become a 'field of adversity', through which both policy reformers and radical critics could both stake out their positions. The construction of a liberal 'field of adversity' had little relation to policy realities. This was reflected in the fact that, while there was a consensus on the view that Western policies were problematic in that they were too 'liberal', there was much less attention to how the problems of the post-colonial world might have been alternatively addressed. Here, as discussed below, the discursive critique of liberal peacebuilding unfortunately had very little to offer and merely established the conceptual basis for today's pragmatic consensus.

BEYOND THE CRITIQUE OF THE LIBERAL PEACEBUILDING?

It would appear that the ostensibly more radical or 'political' critics, those who drew out the problematic nature of power relations, in fact, had very little to offer as a critical alternative to the policies of intervention and peacebuilding, other than a scaling back of the possibilities of social change. The leading 'political' critics of liberal peacebuilding, like Mark Duffield and Michael Pugh – working through critical theoretical frameworks which problematised power relations and highlighted the importance of difference – suggested that the difference between the liberal West and the non-liberal Other could not be bridged through Western policy-making. For Pugh, as we have seen above, taking critical theory to its logical conclusion, capitalist rationality was itself to be condemned for its universalising and destabilising impulses. Similarly, for Duffield, it seemed that the problem of hegemonic relations of power and knowledge could not be overcome, making any projection of the ideals of development or democracy potentially oppressive (2007, pp. 215–34). Oliver Richmond systematised these critiques, bringing them within the radical pragmatist perspective, highlighting the problems of the disciplinary forms of knowledge of liberal peacebuilding approaches and suggesting that while it may be possible to go beyond them through the use of post-positivist and ethnographic approaches – enabling external interveners to have a greater access to the knowledge of 'everyday life' in non-liberal societies being intervened in – any attempt to know, rather than merely to express 'empathy', was open to hegemonic abuse (see 2008a, p. 157).

Without a political agent of emancipatory social change, the radical 'political' critiques of liberal peacebuilding, which drew upon the modernist perspectives of critical Marxist or Foucauldian theory, could not go beyond the bind which they had set themselves, of overcoming hegemonic frameworks of knowledge and power. In fact, it could be argued that these critical approaches, lacking the basis of a political subject to give content to critical theorising, ultimately took an uncritical approach to power. Power was assumed rather than theorised, making the limits to power appear merely as external to it. It was assumed that there was an attempt to transform the world in liberal terms and that the failure to do so could therefore be used to argue that liberal forms of knowledge were inadequate ones. The critique was amenable to being 'co-opted' into pragmatist frameworks and became one not essentially of power or of intervention per se but of the limited knowledge of liberal interveners. The alternative was not that of emancipatory social transformation but of the speculative and passive search for different, non-liberal, forms of knowledge or of knowing. This came across clearly in the conclusions reached by Duffield, Richmond and others, and highlighted the lack of a critical alternative embedded in these approaches.

The more ostensibly conservative pragmatic critics of peacebuilding, drawn largely to the policymaking sphere, had much clearer political aims in their critique of liberal universalism. This was manifest in their focus on institutional reform, understood as a way of reconciling non-liberal states and societies both to the market and to democratic forms. This, like the transitology discourse before it, was a radical critique of classical liberal assumptions. In their advocacy of these frameworks, discursively framed as critiques of liberal peacebuilding, they had a clear point of reference. Although, as highlighted above, this point of reference was largely a fictional one: a constructed narrative of post-Cold War intervention, which enabled them to ground the scaling back of policy expectations against a framework of allegedly unrealistic or 'hubristic' liberal aspirations.

This critique of 'liberalism' became more an apologia for interventionist policymaking, rather than a critique, the more policymakers were condemned for being 'liberal'. Institutionalist approaches, which informed the interventionist frameworks of international institutions and donors in the 1990s and 2000s, were explicit in their denunciation of the universalist assumptions of classical liberalism. This critique of liberalism was however an indirect one, inevitably so, as the institutionalist critique developed at the height of the Cold War (see, for example, Leys, 1996). This is why, while the classical concepts of the liberal rights framework remained – 'sovereignty', 'democracy', 'rule of law', 'civil society' – they were given a new content, transforming the universal discourse of the autonomous liberal rights-holder from that of the subject of rights to the object of regulation (see Chandler, 2010). This new content was unfortunately of little interest to the more radical 'political' critics of liberal peacebuilding. But, in understanding the content of institutionalist approaches, it is possible to tie together the superficial nature of external engagement with the fact that it had a non-liberal content rather than one that was too liberal.

The institutionalist discourse of intervention and regulation was not one of liberal universalism and transformation but one of restricted possibilities, where democracy and development were hollowed out and, rather than embodying the possibilities of the autonomous human subject, become mechanisms of control and ordering. Institutionalisation reduced law to an administrative code, politics to technocratic decision-making, democratic and civil rights to those of the supplicant rather than the citizen, replacing the citizenry with civil society, and the promise of capitalist modernity with pro-poor poverty reduction (see further Chandler, 2006a, 2010; Foucault, 2008; Hay, 2007; Williams, 2000; Krastev, 2004). Critical conceptualising of this inversion of basic liberal assumptions and ontologies as 'liberalism' made the word meaningless at the same time as claiming to stake everything on the assumed meaning and stakes involved in the critique of 'liberal' peacebuilding.

CONCLUSION

The end of the experiment of international peacebuilding has been rationalised and accepted on the pragmatist basis that Western peacebuilding interventions were too 'liberal'. The fact that 'liberalism' was to blame is allegedly revealed in the lack of success on the ground: in the failure to achieve liberal outcomes. For the pragmatist critics, the sources of this failure are held to be located in the non-liberal nature of the societies intervened upon. In the dominant policy framing of interventionist agendas, this failing is because of the lack of capacity of domestic societies and political elites; for more radical readings, the problematic impact of external policymaking is often re-read as the resistance of indigenous ways of life and knowledges, which should instead be understood and empathised with.

The critique of 1990s and 2000s policies of peacebuilding for their liberalism suggests that the self-image of the West was being projected where it could not take hold. As we have seen, this critique easily flattered the self-understanding of liberal interveners that if they were incapable of transforming the post-conflict societies and failing states, that they were engaged with, it was merely because they could not easily be anything other than liberal and that the societies being intervened in were not ready for liberal frameworks of governance. These critiques have thereby cohered and naturalised the reproduction of the ideological binary of the civilisational divide between 'the West and the Rest', which was seen to be confirmed the more interventionist approaches appeared to have little impact and to have to be scaled back.

There are obviously a number of problems with the critical pragmatic consensus of the failure of 'liberal peacebuilding'. These stem not merely from the fact that the interventionist policies being critiqued were far from 'liberal'. Of greater concern is the way that the term 'liberal' became an easy and unproblematic assertion of critical intent. The critique of liberal peacebuilding – and its ability to encompass both policy advocates and radical critics of intervention – revealed much more about the problematic state of radical and liberal thought than it did about the policies and practices of intervention and peacebuilding. The ostensible framework of liberal peacebuilding – of the transformative dynamic ontology of the universal rational subject – had already long since been critiqued and displaced by the framework of governance and regulatory power. It was peculiar, in these circumstances, that the dominant policy discussion and the radical discursive framing of post-Cold War peacebuilding should therefore have taken this form.

While apologetic intent could perhaps be reasonably applied to some critics working within policymaking circles and attempting to justify the drawing back from the optimistic claims of transformation in current pragmatic policy framings, this charge cannot so easily be placed at the feet of those articulating more 'political' critiques of international peacebuilding.

That the radical critique of liberal peacebuilding reproduced similar framings to those of the policy-orientated institutionalist critiques, highlighted the problematic use of the liberal paradigm as a 'field of adversity' to give coherence to radical frameworks of critique. However, in focusing on the target of liberalism rather than on the policy practices and discourses themselves, radical criticism became enlisted in support of the pragmatist project, which succeeded in rewriting the failures of peacebuilding intervention as a product of the universalising tendencies of the liberal approach and suggested that the liberal aspirations of the past should be rejected on the basis of an appreciation of the irreconcilable 'difference' of the non-liberal subject.

PART II

The Rise of Peacebuilding

CHAPTER 3

The Birth of a Mission

INTRODUCTION

The 'twenty years' crisis' of peacebuilding from 1997 onwards cannot be grasped without an understanding of the rise of peacebuilding in the decade of the 1990s. In this decade, the framework of international sovereignty and of non-intervention rapidly corroded, opening up a new international agenda based on the blurring of the domestic and international realms. Peacebuilding was not a matter of international relations based on sovereign equality but one premised on the selective opening up of the domestic realm to international regulation and external conditionalities. While the UN Secretary General's 1992 *Agenda for Peace* introduced the concept of 'post-conflict peacebuilding' as an ad hoc extension of international peacekeeping, it was not until after the interventions in the wars of the break-up of the former Yugoslavia and the establishment of formalised international peacebuilding regimes that the UN was able to clarify the meaning of peacebuilding and the transformed nature of its relationship to international peacekeeping.

The September 2000 UN Millennium Assembly confirmed the need for a fundamental reform of UN peacekeeping operations. This reform was shaped by the liberal internationalist discourse that had cohered throughout the 1990s, no longer strictly bound by traditional 'realist' 'state-centred' principles, such as non-intervention and state sovereignty. The UN Secretary General's Millennium Report, *'We the Peoples'*, started the formal process of revising the UN's approach to

© The Author(s) 2017   45
D. Chandler, *Peacebuilding*, Rethinking Peace and Conflict Studies,
DOI 10.1007/978-3-319-50322-6_3

peace operations after criticism of UN peacekeeping failures in Rwanda, Bosnia and Sierra Leone in the 1990s and NATO action over Kosovo which bypassed Security Council controls. As the Millennium Report noted in its introduction: 'No shift in the way we think or act can be more critical than this: we must put people at the centre of everything we do' (UN, 2000a, p. 7). The report noted that a 'new understanding of the concept of security is evolving' (2000a, p. 43). International security during the Cold War was 'synonymous with the defence of territory from external attack' and was bound up with the principle of state sovereignty and its corollary of non-intervention (UN, 2000a, p. 43).

However, the post-Cold War conception of international security was to be different: 'The requirements of security today have come to embrace the protection of communities and individuals from internal violence', far from upholding sovereignty and the principle of non-intervention the demands of international security were deemed to necessitate a fundamental rethinking of the UN's strategy (2000a, p. 43). The Secretary General described this new strategy as a 'more human-centred approach to security' as distinct from the previous 'state-centred' approach (ibid.). This Report was followed by the Brahimi UN Panel Report, detailing further proposals for reform, which was ratified at the UN Millennium Summit in New York in September 2000.

This chapter considers the contrast between the assumptions of the new international liberal 'people-centred' or 'human-centred' approach and the earlier state-centred one and seeks to establish the impact of this approach on the reform of UN peacekeeping operations and the ratification of peacebuilding as a separate and distinct sphere of policymaking. It further considers the implications of peacekeeping reform for the shift towards international peacebuilding and the erosion of the sovereign barriers that separated domestic and international concerns. The precondition for peacebuilding missions and projects of the 1990s and 2000s was the erosion of the traditional international legal framework of sovereign statehood, enabling peacebuilding projects focused on the internationalisation of liberal institutional frameworks. With the closure of the peacebuilding era, the dynamic of international intervention seems to have come to an end, not on the basis of a restored interest in sovereign autonomy but on the grounds that the project of peacebuilding intervention was itself flawed.

THE CRITIQUE OF THE REALIST PARADIGM

Prior to the outbreak of the Second World War, in a world shaped by imperial relationships and the ideology of race and empire, there was only partial international acceptance of the rights of state sovereignty and self-determination (Chandler, 2000). In the post-war settlement, the United States' dominance of the world economy enabled the construction of a new system of international regulation. As Justin Rosenberg wrote, the US planners realised that 'the British Empire...will never reappear and that the United States may have to take its place', but that in the face of growing nationalism and the discrediting of empire, new institutions of management of international relations would be necessary to 'avoid conventional forms of imperialism' (Rosenberg, 1994, p. 37). Central to this new mechanism of international regulation was the conception of sovereign equality. The Nazi experience and the rise of non-European powers had undermined the elitist ideologies of race and empire and led to the defensive acceptance of a law-bound international system. As Norman Lewis noted:

> The impact of the war and the sense of a loss of legitimacy ended what had, until then, been the inter-war consensus upon the non-applicability of the right to self-determination to colonial peoples... However, this consensus could no longer be sustained in the face of the new legal order, the ideological conflicts of the Cold War and the rise of nationalism within the colonial world. (Lewis, 1997)

The political pressure on the leading world powers meant that the 1945 settlement, preserved in the principles of the UN Charter, was a decisive moment in the transformation of the international system. The UN Charter system, the first attempt to construct a law-bound international society of states, recognised all nation-states as equal. Article 1(2) called for 'respect for the principle of equal rights and self-determination of peoples'; Article 2(1) emphasised 'the principle of sovereign equality' of member states; and Article 55 stressed respect for the principle of equal rights and self-determination of peoples (Ramsbotham and Woodhouse, 1996, p. 38). The UN system did not realise full sovereign equality in its own internal workings. The five permanent members of the powerful Security Council, the United States, Britain, France, Russia and China, were obliged to reach a consensus on policy, thereby giving the major powers the right of veto. Nevertheless, sovereign equality was formally recognised through equal representation in the General Assembly and through the principle of non-interventionism.

Sovereign states were clearly unequal in terms of power, wealth and resources. However, despite these limitations, the universal recognition of sovereign equality was a thoroughly radical conception of the authority of the non-Western state. Its authority was derived exclusively from its people and, as a consequence of this, the international order became one in which non-Western states had the same political legitimacy as the more developed Western states, despite the inequalities of economic and military power. This equality was confirmed on many occasions in UN resolutions, notably the Declaration on the Inadmissibility of Intervention in the Domestic Affairs of States and Protection of their Independence and Sovereignty of 21 December 1965 (Resolution 2131 (XX)) and the Declaration on Principles of International Law Concerning Friendly Relations and Cooperation among States in Accordance with the Charter of the United Nations of 24 October 1970 (Resolution 2625 (XXV)). The latter Declaration made it clear that: 'All States enjoy sovereign equality. They have equal rights and duties and are equal members of the international community, notwithstanding differences of an economic, social, political or other nature' (Mills, 1997, p. 269). The official commentary to the latter document stated:

> No State or group of States has the right to intervene, directly or indirectly, for any reason whatever, in the internal or external affairs of any other State. Consequently, armed intervention and all other forms of interference or attempted threats against the personality of the State or against its political, economic and cultural elements, are in violation of international law. (Littman, 1999, p. 33)

The liberal internationalist approach directly challenged this realist perspective of state sovereignty. Instead of the nation-state at the centre of policy priorities it was held to be the people of the state, particularly those most in need. This framework followed the approach of human rights advocates, who had argued for an explicitly people-centred approach, making the subject of international policy the universal citizen, not the political citizen defined by the nation-state. The discourse of putting people first was held to have inaugurated 'a new kind of citizenship, the citizenship of humanity' (Pieterse, 1997, p. 72). As leading international human rights theorist Nicholas Wheeler wrote: 'The notion of common humanity/human solidarity is diametrically opposed to the statist paradigm which is predicated on the contention that state leaders and citizens do not have moral responsibilities or obligations to aid those beyond their borders' (Wheeler, 1997, p. 10).

People's human rights were seen to be particularly vulnerable in conflict situations. As the Millennium Report observed, despite international resolutions, 'the brutalization of civilians, particularly women and children, continues in armed conflicts':

> Women have become especially vulnerable to violence and sexual exploitation, while children are easy prey for forced labour and are often coerced into becoming fighters... In the most extreme cases, the innocent become the principal targets of ethnic cleansers and genocidaires. (UN, 2000a, p. 46)

The emphasis on the rights of vulnerable people rather than the rights of states was explained as necessary because many non-Western states could no longer be assumed to be able, or willing, to safeguard the rights of their citizens. As the Millennium Report argued: 'States are sometimes the principal perpetrators of violence against the very citizens that humanitarian law requires them to protect' (UN, 2000a, p. 46). Given the changing perspective of the non-Western state, the advocates of human rights argued that the international community must have the power to step in to safeguard the rights of the vulnerable.

The concept of empowering vulnerable people extended to the post-conflict situation and the prioritisation of conflict prevention and peace-building: 'Strategies of prevention must address the root causes of conflicts, not simply their violent symptoms' (UN, 2000, pp. 44–5). The Secretary General suggested that the 'root causes' of international conflict were no longer to be located in the geo-political competition of major states but rather in the internal political and social arrangements of much less influential powers:

> The majority of wars today are wars among the poor. Why is this the case?... In many poor countries at war, the condition of poverty is coupled with sharp ethnic or religious cleavages. Almost invariably, the rights of subordinate groups are insufficiently respected, the institutions of government are insufficiently inclusive and the allocation of society's resources favours the dominant faction over others. (UN, 2000a, p. 45)

The new context of international security concerns considered smaller and economically less developed states to be the most likely to be prone to conflict due to problems of poverty, ethnic and cultural division and political exclusion. It was these states that would be increasingly subject to new peacekeeping approaches and were the focal point of ongoing policy discussions that attempted to establish a new balance between the rights of state sovereignty and the protection of human rights. This new people-centred approach, concerned with how small states treated their most vulnerable citizens, was a fundamentally different approach to that taken by the UN prior to the 1990s, when international peace was seen to be guaranteed through protecting the sovereign rights of smaller states from encroachment and intervention by the major powers.

The Implications for Sovereignty and Intervention

The problems of renegotiating the UN's previous framework of non-intervention and state sovereignty were highlighted in the Millennium Report's discussion of the 'dilemma of intervention' (UN, 2000a, p. 47). The Millennium Report set out clearly why the UN believed that its previous principle of non-intervention in the sovereign affairs of states should be overturned. The Secretary General acknowledged concerns 'that the concept of "humanitarian intervention" could become a cover for gratuitous interference in the internal affairs of sovereign states' (ibid.). He also recognised that 'there is little consistency in the practice of intervention ... except that weak states are far more likely to be subjected to it than strong ones' (UN, 2000a, p. 48). He recognised 'both the force and the importance of these arguments' and accepted 'that the principles of sovereignty and non-interference offer vital protection to small and weak states' (ibid.).

But in response to these objections General-Secretary Kofi Annan asked, if the current principles of sovereignty and non-intervention were allowed to stand, 'how should we respond to a Rwanda, to a Srebrenica – to gross and systematic violations of human rights that offend every precept of our common humanity?' (UN, 2000a, p. 48) Intervention may have been politically difficult, 'but surely no legal principle – not even sovereignty – can ever shield crimes against humanity' (ibid.). Where such crimes occurred, the Security Council now claimed a 'moral duty' to act on behalf of the international community (ibid.).

The problem was in defining where the balance between protecting human rights and sovereignty lay. During the Cold War, genocide was considered to be the only grounds for international intervention in internal affairs. By the late 1990s this was no longer the case. Security Council resolution 1296 (2000) established that the targeting of civilians in armed conflict and the denial of humanitarian access to civilian populations afflicted by war may themselves constitute threats to international peace and security and thereby trigger intervention (UN, 2000b, p. 9). The question of where to draw the line of sovereignty was the central question of international peace concern. The dynamic of the liberal internationalist approach was continually to renegotiate the boundaries of state sovereignty. As former UK Prime Minister Tony Blair stated in his keynote speech in Chicago on 22 April 1999: 'The most pressing foreign policy problem we face is to identify the circumstances in which we should get involved in other peoples' conflicts' (UKJCC, 2000, p. 5). The assumption was that it was an increasingly open question whether major Western powers decided to respect sovereignty or to intervene in the cause of protecting the vulnerable. This was an evolving process because the demands of human rights advocates for the protection of vulnerable people and groups would inevitably conflict with the rights of states to assert control over their internal affairs.

Once the idea of sovereignty and self-government was put to question in poorer, less developed regions, the liberal internationalist approach legitimised increasing levels of international involvement at every stage of the peace process. The Brahimi Panel criticised traditional peacekeeping, because it treated 'symptoms' rather than the sources of conflict, and therefore 'has no built-in exit strategy' and was 'slow to make progress', leaving traditional peacekeepers in place for 10, 20, 30 or even 50 years in Cyprus, the Middle East and India/Pakistan (UN, 2000b, p. 3). However, there was little evidence that increased levels of international interference in peace settlements or in post-conflict peacebuilding were any more effective in resolving the 'sources' of conflict or in offering a more effective 'exit strategy'.

The logical conclusion of the focus on extending peacebuilding regulation in post-conflict societies was the creation of new protectorate powers of transitional civil administration headed by the UN. The first fully developed peacebuilding mandate of this sort was established in 1995, when the UN took over the civil administration of Bosnia, followed in

1999 by civil administration mandates in Kosovo and then East Timor. The Brahimi Report offered a positive vision of the future:

> We see an SRSG [Special Representative of the Secretary-General] ending a mission well accomplished, having given the people of a country the opportunity to do for themselves what they could not do before: to build and hold onto peace, to find reconciliation, to strengthen democracy, to secure human rights. (UN, 2000b, pp. 46–7)

The UN's starting assumption was that the 'people' at the centre of their interventions could not build peace and reconciliation or secure democracy or human rights 'for themselves'. However, the experience of Bosnia, Kosovo and East Timor would suggest that this approach, which assumed that people lacked an adequate capacity for political problem-solving, was in danger of excluding people of the region from the political process of peacebuilding and reconstruction.

As the Brahimi Panel noted, UN administrators had been given responsibility for micro-managing these societies: making and enforcing the law, establishing customs services, collecting business and personal taxes, attracting foreign investment, adjudicating property disputes, reconstructing and operating public utilities, creating a banking system and running the schools (UN, 2000b, p. 13). This diminished view of the capacity of people in the region, and exaggerated view of the benign civilising powers of external administration, led to the increasing accumulation of powers in the hands of international regulators appointed by the UN, reducing the formal (political) and informal (social and economic) mechanisms available for people in these states to take responsibility for negotiating and maintaining a sustainable peace settlement (Chandler, 1999). There appeared to be little incentive to roll back international regulative mechanisms, leaving the internationalist approach of the UN unable to lay the basis of any long-term solution accountable to the people of the region.

These UN peacebuilding missions were to reveal that the peacebuilding project of protecting and empowering the vulnerable was highly likely to be just as long term as that of traditional peacekeeping, the major difference being that during the process of internationalising peace state sovereignty was effectively surrendered by the post-conflict state. This brought into question the claims to empowerment, democracy and rights, which figured prominently in the arguments of the advocates of this approach. In fact, there could be little doubt that far from empowering people in non-Western states, the extension of peacebuilding mandates heralded a public retreat from the principles of self-determination and democracy. The Brahimi Panel's suggestion that the UN Security Council should in fact establish a centre of responsibility for the tasks of transitional administration to manage future direct mandates indicated that it saw a long-term future for the new internationalist mandate system. This perspective of a return to colonial protectorates in the cause of peacebuilding was supported by the British government, which suggested that 'there is a strong case for reassessing the role of the Trusteeship Council', suspended since the last UN protectorate Palau was granted a form of independence in 1994 (UKJCC, 2000, p. 9).

For many commentators, the weakening of the concept of state sovereignty indicated a stronger UN. This was partly borne out in the extension of the UN role from light peacekeeping to extended and multi-functional peacebuilding. Nevertheless, the relationship between the sphere of state sovereignty, particularly of smaller and more marginal states, and the sphere of UN decision-making control was not necessarily a zero-sum one. While the internationalist approach enabled new powers of international regulation in post-conflict societies, the critique of sovereignty and the political sphere in post-conflict states raised more fundamental questions about the role of the UN in regulating questions of war and peace. The central contradiction at the heart of UN reform was how to develop an internationalist approach within the UN's structures, which were designed and legitimised in 1945 on the basis of an entirely different set of assumptions.

The international call for a focus on liberal internationalist approaches rather than state-centric ones inevitably called into question the role and standing of the UN itself. As leading human rights advocate Geoffrey Robertson noted, it was not just the UN's peace operations that were problematic, but its whole organisational structure, based on post-Second World War ideas of state sovereignty and political equality, rather than people-centred human rights:

> It still talks, illogically, of violation of 'state rights', when it is human rights that are being violated. Some of its classic doctrines – sovereign and diplomatic immunity, non-intervention in internal affairs, non-compulsory submission to the ICJ [International Court of Justice], equality of voting

in the General Assembly – continue to damage the human rights cause. (Robertson, 1999, p. 83)

A broader institutional change was heralded in the demands posed by the transformation in UN peacekeeping towards greater military prepared-ness. This meant that the peace operations around the world would have to be increasingly coordinated by regional and sub-regional organisations, which ensured their participants were carefully vetted. The Brahimi Report suggested that 'caution seems appropriate, because military resources and capability are unevenly distributed around the world, and troops in the most crisis-prone areas are often less prepared for the demands of modern peacekeeping than is the case elsewhere' (UN, 2000b, p. 10). The ques-tion of the suitability of many UN member states for taking on the military tasks involved in the new peace operations was also raised in the UK Government Joint Consultative Committee Report on UN Reform, which argued:

> [T]he UN's reaction to human rights abuses or conflict situations has some-times been slow, inconsistent and ill coordinated . . . Those nations with the capacity to support peacekeeping or other operations, whether it be finan-cially, logistically or through the provision of high quality forces and equip-ment, need to respond swiftly and effectively. (UKJCC, 2000, p. 3)

The shift towards a greater stake in peace operations for 'coalitions of the willing' reflected the increased willingness of Western states to undertake peacekeeping tasks independently of the UN. This was highlighted by the launch of NATO's new 'strategic concept', at the Alliance's 50th Anniversary Summit in Washington in late April 1999. US Deputy Secretary of State Strobe Talbott explained:

> 'We must be careful not to subordinate NATO to any other international body or compromise the integrity of its command structure. We will try to act in concert with other organizations, and with respect for their principles and purposes. But the Alliance must reserve the right and freedom to act when its members, by consensus, deem it necessary.' (Simma, 1999, p. 15)

Lord George Robertson, Secretary General of NATO, argued that the organisation needed an enhanced military capability precisely to take on 'non-Article 5 crisis management operations', actions not related to

NATO members' self-defence and therefore neither defined nor limited in geographical scope by the NATO Charter (Littman, 1999, p. vii). NATO's lead was being followed by the European Union's common security and defence policy, which was concerned less with collective defence than developing the capacity for peacekeeping intervention abroad in situations where NATO declined to get involved (Ulbrich, 2000). The decline of the UN as the central peacekeeping institution was highlighted by the fact that, by 2000, 77 per cent of UN troops were contributed by developing countries, and no developed country contributed troops to the most difficult UN missions in Sierra Leone or the Democratic Republic of the Congo, while the major powers, like the US, UK, France and Germany, contributed sizeable forces to NATO-led operations (UN, 2000b, p. 18).

Ominously, for the future of the UN as the key institution in upholding international peace and security, the Brahimi Panel argued that political consensus in the Security Council has been a barrier to effective mandates and action:

> As a political body, the Security Council focuses on consensus-building, even though it can take decisions with less than unanimity. But the compromises required to build consensus can be made at the expense of specificity, and the resulting ambiguity can have serious consequences in the field...While it acknowledges the utility of political compromise in many cases, the panel comes down in this case on the side of clarity, especially for operations that will deploy into dangerous circumstances. (UN, 2000b, p. 10)

The panel suggested that maintaining the principle of political consensus would hamper more militarised peacekeeping, in which case it would be better for the Council to refrain from mandating such a mission. The UK government was also in favour of change and advocated that the UN should 'reassess the circumstances under which a veto can be used' (UKJCC, 2000, p. 4).

At the same time as the restrictions on intervention were being lifted the focus on peaceful, diplomatic resolutions to crises was also being challenged. During the Cold War, long-term conflict prevention attempted to reinforce political solutions, usually through diplomatic initiatives. As the Brahimi Panel noted: 'Such preventive action is, by definition, a low profile activity; when successful, it may go unnoticed altogether' (UN, 2000b, p. 2). The softly-softly diplomatic approach was eschewed for the more public approach followed traditionally by NGOs. The UN Secretary General argued that one solution to the root cause of conflict was the promotion of human rights and that 'the best preventive strategy in this context is transparency: "naming and shaming"' (UN, 2000a, pp. 45–6). The task of 'naming and shaming' countries meant that 'civil society actors had an enormous role to play', alongside states and international bodies, in gathering information and publicising abuses.

According conflicts with a higher political profile involving 'naming and shaming' generated publicity for the problems of vulnerable people but the Secretary General also recognised potential problems in that this framework 'might encourage secessionist movements deliberately to provoke governments . . . in order to trigger external interventions' (UN, 2000a, p. 48). The double-edged nature of the liberal internationalist approach in this area reflected both the potential dangers in politicising UN peace operations and the clear contrast between a liberal internationalist approach, which tended to internationalise conflict situations, and the former approach, which prioritised local solutions based on consensus between the parties. The rolling back of restrictions on peacekeeping intervention and problematisation of consensual diplomatic solutions set up the context in which the internationalisation of peace processes led inevitably to the transformation of international peacekeeping and its extension and formalisation in the new tasks of international peacebuilding.

THE REFORM OF PEACE OPERATIONS

In the first 40 years of the United Nations, 13 peacekeeping operations were authorised, most of them to monitor ceasefire lines. After 1990 another 20 operations were mounted, involving 75,000 troops by 1994, at an annual cost of $3.6 billion. By 2000, some 35,000 troops were being deployed in 14 countries. But the change was not just a quantitative one it was also qualitative. 'While traditional peacekeeping had focused mainly on monitoring ceasefires, today's complex peace operations are very different' (UN, 2000a, p. 48). By 2000, UN peace operations were no longer purely military. They were more complex, also seeking to modify the political, economic and social spheres, through strengthening political institutions and broadening their base, ensuring sustainable development, and engaging in education, media and civil society work. This shift from a narrow military focus meant that peacekeeping was increasingly becoming just one aspect of a more extensive process of peacebuilding. Peacebuilding was more civilian than military in content, 'a hybrid of political and development activities targeted at the sources of conflict' (UN, 2000b, p. 8). The following sections outline the changes advocated by the UN Millennium Assembly to the main aspects of peace operations: negotiations, peacekeeping, peacebuilding.

Peace Negotiations

Prior to the 1990s, a UN peace operation began once the parties to a conflict had negotiated a settlement and then asked the UN to monitor and assist the implementation of it. By the mid-1990s, the UN was much less likely to come in at such a late stage of the process. Whereas, in the past, the assumptions of sovereignty and political independence meant that any settlement had to accord with the wishes of the parties, the assumption shifted to not trusting the conflict parties to design an adequate settlement without external guidance. Peace was no longer to be settled between conflict parties but was to be a matter of international management: 'Although peace negotiators (peacemakers) may be skilled professionals in their craft, they are much less likely to know in detail the operational requirements of soldiers, police, relief providers or electoral advisors in United Nations field missions' (UN, 2000b, p. 10).

Knowledge of the complex needs of UN peacebuilding missions and the implementation framework of human rights concerns was held to be beyond many state negotiators focusing on the traditional task of bringing the parties in conflict to an agreement on the cessation of hostilities. The Brahimi Panel requested that any peace agreements which were to be implemented by the UN must be drawn up under UN guidance, with the UN having 'adviser-observers present at the peace negotiations' and ensuring that 'any agreement be consistent with prevailing international human rights standards' (UN, 2000b, p. 10).

This approach was directly influenced by criticisms of the UN and international community attempts at mediation in the conflicts during the 1990s, where many commentators felt that too much credibility was often being given to local leaders. Leaving peace negotiations to regional representatives was felt to be giving international legitimacy to warlords and ethnic cleansers. Many commentators had criticised the need for negotiations at all. If the UN was serious about protecting the rights of vulnerable people it should have the political will to impose a solution. Thus, Hugo Young argued in *The Guardian* that the 'allies' should not commit themselves to a negotiated settlement on Kosovo as this 'for all Clinton's sound-bite pieties, will be a deal and not a victory' (Young, 1999). The influential media NGO, Radio Free Europe/Radio Liberty, argued that the war over Kosovo was disappointing because it resulted in a 'Saddam Hussein peace', leaving Milosevic in power and failing to continue the war to take over the running of Serbia (RFE/RL, 2000). Daniel Goldhagen similarly suggested that war for unconditional surrender was the only viable solution for Serbia: 'As with Germany and Japan, the defeat, occupation and reshaping of the political institutions and prevailing mentality in Serbia is morally and, in the long run, practically necessary. With an ally-occupied Serbia...peace and eventually prosperity could come to the region' (Goldhagen, 1999).

Once the stakes had been raised by the view of people-centred goals, which internationalised the domestic political arena, previously out of bounds to international policymaking, it was difficult for advocates of these aims to accept peace deals around the negotiating table. The problem with the liberal internationalist approach of ensuring that any peace settlement guaranteed the rights of the most vulnerable, including rights of refugee return, restitution, war crimes trials and so forth, was that there could be little tendency towards compromise or negotiation (Anon, 1996, p. 256; D'Amato, 1994). Aryeh Neier, President of the New York-based Open Society Institute, argued that the human rights movement 'needs to develop the argument that the promotion of human rights should not be weighed against competing concerns' (Neier, 1996). Any compromise between the parties was often labelled as 'appeasement' or condemned for condoning the gains of 'ethnic cleansing' (Garton Ash, 1999; Goldhagen, 1999). The removal of peace processes from a process of negotiation to the imposition of a rights-based settlement, regardless of context, could only lead to conflict rather than peace, as could be seen from the breakdown of the Rambouillet talks over Kosovo (Chomsky, 2000; UKFAC, 2000, Para 56; Falk, 1999, p. 855).

The requirement that peace processes be internationalised inevitably led to the involvement of international actors in the final peace settlement and therefore to their engagement in or oversight of post-conflict peacebuilding requirements. Thus the transition to more internationalised forms of conflict settlement had the unintentional by-product of generating new demands and responsibilities for international actors and facilitated the conflation of peacebuilding with statebuilding (as considered in the next chapter).

Peacekeeping

In the past, the UN, which had been invited in by the parties, would have been forced to withdraw if renewed conflict broke out. Peacekeeping meant deploying monitors and lightly armed forces between ex-combatants once there was a peace to keep, not imposing peace on the parties. By 2000 this was no longer seen to be adequate to protect the vulnerable from the risks of conflict. The UK government argued: 'We firmly believe that the doctrine of peacekeeping, which evolved in the 1950s in the context of interstate conflict, is no longer valid' (UKJCC, 2000, p. 8). The consensus that UN peacekeeping mandates be extended to protect civilians in armed conflicts, and the demand that UN troops or police 'who witness violence against civilians should be presumed to be authorized to stop it', established a very high threshold of expectation and necessitated the deployment of much larger military resources (UN, 2000b, p. 11). The UN Brahimi Panel proposed that ensuring peace mandates were enforced 'means bigger forces, better equipped and more costly, but able to pose a credible deterrent threat, in contrast to the symbolic and non-threatening presence that characterizes traditional peacekeeping' (ibid, p. 9). The panel therefore suggested:

> Rules of engagement should not limit contingents to stroke-for-stroke responses but should allow ripostes sufficient to silence a source of deadly fire that is directed at United Nations troops or at people they are charged to protect and, in particularly dangerous circumstances, should not force United Nations contingents to cede the initiative to their attackers. (Ibid, p. 9)

Although peacekeeping was being conflated with the civilian tasks of peacebuilding, the actual peacekeeping component itself was becoming more coercive. A foreign policy based on protecting human rights rather than upholding international peace inevitably involved greater military capacity. There was also greater acceptance that participating states should be willing to accept casualties on behalf of the mandate (UN, 2000b, p. 9). Michael Walzer argued that Western governments 'cannot panic when the first soldier or the first significant number of soldiers, like the eighteen infantrymen in Somalia, are killed in a firefight' (cited in

Wheeler, 1997, p. 12). Nicholas Wheeler suggested that 'the duty of moral guardianship requires state leaders to spend treasure and shed blood in the name of human solidarity' (ibid.). Rearmament had support from across the political spectrum, particularly from humanitarian NGOs who advocated a much greater international role for the Western military. A 1997 ActionAid UK briefing paper argued that UN forces should 'not just dish out relief in proportion to needs, but also dish out criticism (advocacy) or military bombardment in proportion to human rights wrong doing' (cited in Weiss, 1999, p. 8). Oxfam's 1998 submission to the UK Select Committee on Defence called for much greater military commitment abroad: 'We have developed quite firm views on what does and does not constitute an appropriate role for the military...Oxfam's starting point is that Britain should have a substantial role to play' (UKSCD, 1998, Para 91). It was on these grounds that the radical advocates of the people-centred approach took over from the conservative right as the biggest advocates of increased military spending (Gray, 2000; Lloyd, 1999; AFP, 1999).

Peacekeeping was also being transformed in another direction. The UN argued that the traditional neutrality of the 'Blue Helmets' should be abandoned:

> Impartiality for such operations must therefore mean adherence to the principles of the Charter and to the objectives of a mandate that is rooted in those Charter principles. Such impartiality is not the same as neutrality or equal treatment of all parties in all cases for all time, which can amount to a policy of appeasement. In some cases, local parties consist not of moral equals but of obvious aggressors and victims, and peacekeepers may not only be operationally justified in using force but morally compelled to do so. (UN, 2000b, p.9)

For the Brahimi Panel, the former position of equal treatment of all parties 'can in the best case result in ineffectiveness and in the worst may amount to complicity with evil' (ibid, p. ix). This repeated the critique of human rights advocates, like Michael Ignatieff, who condemned the UN's intervention in Sierra Leone in the New York Times:

> To keep the peace here is to ratify the conquests of evil. It is time to bury peacekeeping before it buries the UN...Where peace has to be enforced

rather than maintained, what's required are combat-capable warriors under robust rules of engagement, with armour, ammunition and intelligence capability and a single line of command to a national government or regional alliance ... [T]he international community has to take sides and do so with crushing force. (Ignatieff, 2000)

This militarisation of peacekeeping ran counter to the traditional role of the UN. As Michael T. Corgan, a former NATO planner, noted: 'We have to recognize that peacemaking essentially involves war. You must be able to convincingly threaten full combat even if it doesn't come to that, and you incur many of the costs of a war' (cited in Radin, 2000). The Brahimi Panel recognised 'that the United Nations does not wage war' (UN, 2000b, p. 10). This meant that peacekeeping would be increasingly shifted from UN control to that of NATO or other 'coalitions of the willing': 'Where enforcement action is required, it has consistently been entrusted to coalitions of willing States, with the authorization of the Security Council under Chapter VII of the Charter' (Ibid, p. 10).

As was seen over Kosovo, once the threat of force was used to apply pressure to the parties, the conflict became internationalised and there was pressure to apply force to maintain international credibility. The UK government Select Committee on Defence noted that 'the very act of introducing British forces into a situation transforms any crisis from the UK's perspective into something more fundamental, because, if nothing else, the safety and reputation of the UK's Armed Forces are then at stake' (UKSCD, 1998, Para 104). Once a conflict, like that of Kosovo, was internationalised, it was qualitatively transformed: '[I]t is not only the security of Europe, in its widest sense that is at risk in Kosovo. So too is the credibility of NATO in its newly developing role, and so too is the effectiveness of the United Nations' (UKSCD, 1998, Para 95). Rhetorically Western leaders still upheld the UN Charter's primary aim of protecting humanity from 'the scourge of war' (UKJCC, 2000, p. 3). Yet military intervention was becoming far from an 'option of last resort'. The militarised peacekeeping mandates designed to be able to deploy overwhelming force inevitably raised expectations and placed UN and NATO credibility on the line more often. Despite the rhetorical repetition of the agreement to use force only as a last resort, the UK government asserted 'the threat of it may be needed at an early stage in a conflict' (UKJCC, 2000, p. 6).

Peacebuilding

Until the end of the Cold War, UN peace operations for the most part had no direct peacebuilding mandates to build the 'foundations of something that is more than just the absence of war' (UN, 2000b, p. 3). This new programme was part of a liberal internationalist framework in which the human rights component of a peace operation was seen as critical to its long-term effectiveness (UN, 2000b, p. 7). The Brahimi Panel defined peacebuilding as including, but not limited to: rebuilding civil society; strengthening the rule of law, through police restructuring and judicial and penal reform; improving the human rights situation by monitoring, educating and investigating abuses; democratic development including election and media regulation; tackling corruption; HIV/AIDS education and control; and promoting conflict resolution and reconciliation (UN, 2000b, p. 3).

Under these broad-ranging powers of international regulation, the UN panel emphasised the importance of the reform and restructuring of the penal and judicial system in post-conflict societies, and the need to make available international judicial experts, penal experts and human rights specialists. The panel also suggested a 'doctrinal shift' in the role of civilian police in peace operations (UN, 2000b, p. 7). In the past, this role was a monitoring one, documenting behaviour and by their presence attempting to discourage unacceptable behaviour. This was now seen as a 'somewhat narrow perspective' more akin to old peacekeeping needs than to peacebuilding (ibid.). Instead, the panel report proposed that the UN police should reform, retrain and restructure local police forces and have the capacity to take over their role if necessary, responding to civil disorder. It also suggested that the UN drew up a 'justice package' with an interim legal code to avoid the difficulties of establishing 'applicable law'. This would address the problems of Kosovo where the UN was formally working under Federal Yugoslav law but allowed their appointed judges to overrule it while NATO troops and UN police initially worked according to their own conflicting national laws.

The panel also emphasised the danger of seeing the first post-war elections as the end of the peacebuilding process. It warned that 'elections merely ratify a tyranny of the majority' until democratisation and civil society-building processes have been completed and a 'culture of respect for human rights' has been established (UN, 2000b, p. 7). Because of the perceived lack of legitimacy of post-conflict governments, elected or not, the panel suggested that the economic reconstruction programme should be kept under UN control, with no direct aid or investment, as the UN 'should be considered the focal point for peacebuilding activities by the donor community' (UN, 2000b, p. 8). These extended peacebuilding mandates were taking the UN into new areas of direct political and social regulation, where the mission goals were much less clear than in traditional politically neutral mandates.

THE CASE OF BOSNIA

Foremost in the minds of the UN was the recent ratification of the first peacebuilding experiment that extended the ad hoc remits to that of a permanent protectorate, in Bosnia-Herzegovina, in December 1997, following the 1995 Dayton Peace Agreement and the 1996 state-level elections. The Bosnian experiment was then repeated with the granting of peacebuilding protectorate powers to the UN in Kosovo and East Timor in 1999. The Dayton Agreement of 1995 was unlike any other peace treaty of modern times, not merely because it was imposed by powers formally external to the conflict, but because of the far-reaching powers given to international actors, which extended well beyond military matters to cover the most basic aspects of government and state. The majority of annexes to the Dayton Agreement were not related to the ending of hostilities, traditionally the role of a peace agreement, but to the political project of constructing a liberal constitutional state in Bosnia: 'reconstructing a society' (Bildt, 1996a).

The demarcation of international peacebuilding as a distinct policy arena was thus a direct consequence of the internationalisation of the peace settlement, which gave international actors temporary authority to ensure that the peace agreement was fully implemented in the new state. Peacebuilding had now properly come of age. The contention of this book is that the crisis of international peacebuilding only began to become apparent once international actors assumed indefinite powers rather than merely mandates of a temporary and time-limited nature. The level of international responsibility for the outcomes of the peace settlement was such that international actors came face to face with the contradictions and limits of external rule. While it was one thing to advocate liberal institutions and legal frameworks as the solution to problems, attempting to impose or enforce them was quite another.

Reconstructing Bosnian society was undertaken in the same interventionist spirit as Dayton itself. Carl Bildt, the first international High Representative for the new state, described the Dayton Agreement as 'by far the most ambitious peace agreement in modern history' (Bildt, 1996b). It was 'ambitious' because, under the guise of a negotiated peace settlement, it sought to build a liberal constitutional state – a state which was not a product of popular consensus or popular involvement and was seen by many Bosnians as an external imposition. The marginalisation of the people of Bosnia from their own political system by external powers was summed up in Bildt's observations on the new constitution (Annex 4 of the Dayton Agreement, GFA, 1995): 'No-one thought it wise to submit the constitution to any sort of parliamentary or other similar proceeding. It was to be a constitution by international decree' (Bildt, 1998, p. 139).

Although often presented as a peace agreement rather than a framework for the reconstruction of Bosnia, the civilian annexes comprised five-sixths of the Dayton accords and involved a wide range of activities in which international actors, coordinated by the Office of the High Representative, were mandated to temporarily play key coordinating roles (Gow, 1998, p. 169). For this reason, the state-level elections, to be held within nine months of the signing ceremony, were initially seen to be crucial for restoring ownership over the new state to its citizens. Under the Dayton Agreement there was to be a year of internationally supervised transition, during which there would be elections and the establishment of the political institutions of the new state, which were to be elected and directly accountable to the people (see further Chandler, 1999, pp. 43–51).

The planned year of internationally supervised transition to self-governing democracy was due to end with the election of state and entity bodies in September 1996, symbolising 'the democratic birth of the country' (PIC, 1996, Para 27). Thus the Bosnian protectorate developed in an ad hoc way out of the extended peacekeeping mandates whose supervisory powers were due to end with the first state-level elections. Although these bodies were elected under internationally supervised and ratified elections, the transitional international administration was prolonged for a further two-year 'consolidation period' and then, in December 1997, extended indefinitely.

While international peacekeeping was being extended and militarised, the core of the mandates were always their emergency or exceptional status. Peacebuilding developed in response to the limits of peacekeeping, as an extension of international military capacities to the regulation of the civilian sphere, but this process was never one that was fully thought through and was led more by events on the ground than by clear processes of decision-making. The extension of the time-limits for international withdrawal from Bosnia and the creation of new mandates for international agencies, coordinated by the ad hoc international grouping, the Peace Implementation Council (PIC), was justified initially by the ambiguous wording of the Dayton Agreement itself but later by increasingly subjective 'interpretations' of the mandate by the High Representative, including innovative reference to the 'spirit of Dayton'. Under the Dayton Agreement, Annex 10, Article 5, the High Representative had the 'final authority in theatre regarding interpretation of this Agreement'.

The Dayton Agreement provided little guidance for understanding the extension of international mandates or the mechanisms of international administration over the new state. This was because the agreement was ostensibly a treaty between the regional parties and not formally a treaty between the international agencies and the government of Bosnia-Herzegovina. The Dayton Agreement was rigid where it concerned the limits to Bosnian self-rule but extremely flexible in relation to the powers which international actors could exercise over this nominally independent state. As Paul Szasz noted, the Dayton Agreement was 'merely a part of total arrangements to bring peace to Bosnia' (Szasz, 1996, p. 304). According to the international constitutional lawyer, closely involved in the development of Dayton:

> Explicitly mentioned or merely implied by those texts are a host of other agreements or arrangements, which are to be concluded ... by or within the numerous international organisations assigned various roles by these texts, and which may take the form of bilateral or multilateral executive agreements, resolutions of the [United Nations] Security Council or decisions of NATO, the OSCE ... and other organisations ... [E]vidently the parties to the GFA [General Framework Agreement] and the ancillary agreements could not bind these external actors ... nor, of course, are these external actors precluded from taking steps not foreseen in these texts. (Szasz, 1996, p. 304)

This flexibility was later exemplified by the extension of the OHR's powers. The High Representative explained this process as one that had no fixed limits: 'if you read Dayton very carefully...Annex 10 even gives me the possibility to interpret my own authorities and powers' (Westendorp, 1997). The pattern of ad hoc and arbitrary extensions of international regulatory authority was initially set by the PIC itself as it rewrote its own powers and those of the High Representative at successive PIC meetings. The most important of these were the initial strategic six-monthly review conferences: at Florence, in June 1996; Paris, in November 1996; Sintra, in May 1997; and Bonn, in December 1997.

At the Sintra meeting, in May 1997, a new package of measures to ensure co-operation with the High Representative was announced, including the capacity to pursue deadlines announced by the PIC and enact measures in the case of non-compliance (PIC, 1997a, Para 92). These measures included visa restrictions on travel abroad for 'obstructive' Bosnian representatives as well as economic sanctions targeted at a local level and the capacity to curtail or suspend any media network or programmes which contravened 'either the spirit or letter' of the Dayton Agreement (PIC, 1997a, Paras 35; 36; 70). At the Bonn PIC summit, in December 1997, these measures were extended to give the High Representative the power to directly impose legislation, giving international officials both executive and legislative control over the formally independent state. The OHR was now mandated to enact 'interim measures' against the wishes of elected state, entity, cantonal and municipal elected bodies. These decrees were to remain in place until formally assented to by the respective level of government. The 'Bonn powers' also enabled the High Representative to dismiss elected representatives and government officials held to be obstructing the OHR's task of implementing the Dayton Agreement (PIC, 1997b, XI, Para 2).

The shift to the permanent protectorate Bonn powers in 1997 marked the start of the 'twenty years' crisis' of peacebuilding, placing the international community in direct control of the political and constitutional processes of Bosnia-Herzegovina, setting the template for Kosovo and East Timor and facilitating the confidence that international regimes could be imposed in post-conflict Afghanistan and Iraq. It should also be highlighted that the extended mandates, laid down at Bonn, were qualitatively different from earlier extensions to the OHR's powers: the new mandates granted by the PIC, to itself, for the purpose of overseeing the state, were also made indefinite (PIC, 1997b, XI, Para 1). International withdrawal and the ceding of sovereignty and policymaking powers to Bosnian institutions was now to be dependent on an ill-defined set of 'benchmarks' to be determined by the PIC at a time of its own choosing (PIC, 1998, Para 108). Since December 1997, successive High Representatives have grasped the opportunities unaccountable power has provided, using them to impose legislative measures against the will of elected bodies and to sack hundreds of Bosnian public officials, from members of the Presidency and entity prime ministers down to municipal civil servants.

By the end of 1997, the PIC and the OHR had accumulated an array of powers unimaginable in 1995 when the Dayton Agreement was signed. Yet, despite the new mandates and the indefinite extension of the power to impose legislation and to dismiss non-compliant officials, it was rapidly apparent that the international peacebuilders seemed to be running out of ideas. The international bureaucracy increasingly appeared to be running the country with little purpose or legitimacy. The war over Kosovo, and the more interventionist approach of the European Union to the region which followed, finally provided the international administrators with a new source of legitimacy in the discursive framework of 'peacebuilding-as-statebuilding' (Kemp and van Meurs, 2003, pp. 63–4) (discussed in the following chapter). This legitimacy was to come not from any new attempt to involve or engage with the people of Bosnia, but from further problematising the capacities of Bosnian people on the basis that they were undermining their own 'sovereignty' and through enrolling the support of the European Union in guiding the small and economically impoverished state to the goal of EU membership.

CONCLUSION

Today's pragmatic international consensus argues that international peacebuilding was a discrete policy misunderstanding based on an erroneous theory of statehood. This could not be further from the truth, in fact, it is vitally important to place the development of these policies in the broader context of the changing understanding of international relations and sovereignty. The discourse of peacebuilding was closely aligned to a much broader post-Cold War shift away from the international state order of sovereign equality. On one hand, the understanding of international peace itself was transformed with the extension and militarisation of international peacekeeping away from consensual policymaking to active intervention in conflict. On the other hand, the shift away from the sovereign order of non-intervention opened up the new sphere of international peacebuilding as the internationalisation of the domestic political sphere of post-conflict states.

By 2000, the UN argued that internationalised peacebuilding responsibilities were all encompassing, going well beyond the promotion of conflict resolution and reconciliation to include rebuilding civil society, strengthening the rule of law, police restructuring, judicial and penal reform, monitoring human rights, election and media regulation, and tackling corruption. The next chapter considers in more detail the shift away from the high point of international peacebuilding as protectorates to discourses of peacebuilding-as-statebuilding, which attempted to shift the burden of responsibility back to the people and societies themselves.

CHAPTER 4

Peacebuilding as Statebuilding

INTRODUCTION

Practically as soon as international protectorates had been established in the late 1990s in Bosnia-Herzegovina, Kosovo and East Timor, peace-building discourses sought to roll back from international responsibilities. Peacebuilding was not to be associated with protectorates for peace but with a new process, that of statebuilding – strengthening 'sovereignty' rather than undermining it – on the basis of the development of liberal institutional mechanisms of conflict management. This was the dominant framework for the international regulation of non-Western states in the 2000s. This chapter seeks to examine the development, content and consequences of the 'peacebuilding-as-statebuilding' discourse. Locating peacebuilding as a response to the consequences of the 1990s decade that militarised and internationalised the issue of peace, it engages with changing theoretical approaches to state sovereignty, which redefined sovereignty as state capacity rather than as political independence; recasting intervention as strengthening sovereignty rather than undermining it. Peacebuilding interventions increasingly appeared not as external coercion but as an internal matter of administrative assistance for 'good governance' or 'institutional capacity-building'. The consequences of this move are also considered and it is suggested that 'peacebuilding-as-statebuilding' in non-Western states without self-government resulted in the institutionalisation of weak states which had little relationship with their societies and lacked legitimate authority.

© The Author(s) 2017
D. Chandler, *Peacebuilding*, Rethinking Peace and Conflict Studies,
DOI 10.1007/978-3-319-50322-6_4

'Peacebuilding-as-statebuilding', the development of international regulatory mechanisms aimed at strengthening liberal institutional frameworks, was a pressing international policy concern, considered central to global security, by the early 2000s. According to Francis Fukuyama, this was 'one of the most important issues for the world community' that had 'risen to the top of the global agenda' (Fukuyama, 2004, pp. ix–xi). Robert Rotberg argued that peacebuilding had 'become one of the critical all-consuming strategic and moral imperatives of our terrorized time' (Rotberg, 2004, p. 42). As the 2002 US National Security Strategy stated: 'America is now threatened less by conquering states than we are by failing ones.' (NSS, 2002, Section 1)

In the mid-2000s it seemed that no international policy or strategy document could be complete without the focus on peacebuilding-as-statebuilding as a key objective: in August 2004 the US government established a statebuilding department, the Office of the Coordinator for Reconstruction and Stabilization; in February 2005 the UK Government's Strategy Unit report *Investing in Prevention: An International Strategy to Manage Risks of Instability and Improve Crisis Response* viewed statebuilding as a key part of its 'partnerships for stability' agenda (UKPMSU, 2005); in March 2005, at the High Level Meeting of the OECD Donor Assistance Committee in Paris, the Ministers of Development of OECD countries agreed to a set of 'Principles for Good International Engagement in Fragile States' with a 'focus on state-building as the central objective' (OECD, 2005, p. 8); the same month the Commission for Africa report, welcomed the fact that more than a quarter of bilateral aid to Africa was already channelled directly into state capacity-building (CfA, 2005, p. 136); in September 2005 the UN world summit agreed on the establishment of a proposed Peace-Building Commission to coordinate international activity in this area (UN, 2005, Paras 97–105).

The focus on state capacities and institutions seemed to herald a shift away from the late 1990s when new, more interventionist, norms were heralded which challenged the fundamental rights of state sovereignty – those of self-government and non- intervention. These rights took their clearest institutional form in the UN Charter framework of international law that emphasised the rights of peoples to self- government (Article 1.2), the sovereign equality of member states (Article 2.1), and the principle of non-intervention – outlawing the threat or use of force (Article 2.4) (UN, 1945). Throughout the Cold War, successive judgements of the International Court of Justice upheld these rights to self-government and denied the existence of any legitimate grounds for external intervention, even on the basis of 'humanitarian' or 'human rights' justifications (see Chandler, 2002a, pp. 157–66).

After the end of the Cold War, as considered in the previous chapter, the focus appeared to shift to an emphasis on the rights of individuals, often posed as a liberal internationalist counter to the 'realist' doctrine of the rights of states. States were no longer seen to be the primary security referent and state sovereignty was not considered to be an absolute barrier to external intervention. Following extended intervention in Iraq, to protect the Kurds and Marsh Arabs after the 1991 Gulf War, and external military intervention for humanitarian purposes in Somalia (in 1992–1993) and Bosnia (1993–1995) the high point of this new liberal internationalist focus on individuals rather than states was the NATO-led international intervention over Kosovo in 1999.

With the shift to peacebuilding-as-statebuilding, the state was once more at the centre of security concerns. It now appeared that states, particularly those that had been marginalised by the world economy or weakened by conflict, could no longer be ignored or isolated. In the aftermath of 9/11 – where the failure of the Afghan state to control its borders and the activities of its citizens was held to have opened the way for Al Qaeda's operations – the state was no longer viewed from a mainly negative perspective. Non-Western states now appeared less obviously as objects of opprobrium and were more likely to be fêted by international institutions and leading Western states, offering peacebuilding programmes of liberal institutional support to enable poverty reduction, capacity-building, democratisation, and good governance.

This chapter examines the vision of the state that was placed at the centre of international peacebuilding policymaking. The following section puts the peacebuilding discussion in the context of a response to the 1990s decade of internationalisation and military 'humanitarian' intervention on the basis that state sovereignty was no longer a vital consideration. Further sections then lay out specific problems which highlight the corrosive nature of the policy practices in this area: firstly, that the redefinition of sovereignty, central to the peacebuilding-as-statebuilding framework, facilitated the erosion of ties linking power and accountability, enabling international interveners to distance themselves from the policies they promoted; secondly, that (as will be explored further in the next part of the book) these policies did not work. States without the capacity for self-government were weak and lacking in legitimate authority. The policy agenda focused on bureaucratic, administrative mechanisms, which institutionalised divisions between the West and the non-West and were unable to overcome the social and political divisions of post-conflict states.

From Peacebuilding Protectorates to Statebuilding

The discussion of peacebuilding as statebuilding – of international mechanisms to capacity-build liberal institutions in post-conflict and conflict-prone states – seemed, at face value, to herald a return to traditional frameworks of International Relations. This chapter suggests that this focus on a familiar political form should not obscure, what was, in effect, a radical transformation of the mechanisms of international regulation. Analysts agreed that states were not what they used to be. As Fukuyama noted, 'for well over a generation, the trend in world politics has been to weaken stateness', this trend had been particularly marked since the end of the Cold War (Fukuyama, 2004, p. 161). It was only in the context of uncertainties over the role and purpose of the state that the novel processes at the heart of peacebuilding-as-statebuilding as a set of policy practices can be fully grasped.

It would seem that states were losing their capacities rather than gaining them. For many commentators, this was clearly a positive shift (Archibugi et al., 1998; Linklater, 1998; Rosenau and Czempiel, 1992). Across the board of social theory and especially in critical theoretical approaches in the discipline of International Relations, states had increasingly been cast as problems rather than solutions. Charles Tilly's work was regularly drawn on to argue that states were merely government-run 'protection rackets' based on the repression and exploitation of their citizens in the interest of criminal or self-interested elites (Tilly, 1985). Poststructuralists drew on the work of Foucault to argue that Clausewitz's famous dictum should be inverted to reveal the illegitimacy of the liberal democratic state and understand 'politics as the continuation of war by other means' (Foucault, 2003). David Campbell, Mary Kaldor and others argued that it was the state-orientated perspective of the international community that encouraged many post-Cold War conflicts, such as the Bosnian war (Campbell, 1998; Kaldor, 1999).

In this context, the focus on the state, rather than on alternative forms of international governance might seem to be an unexpected development. Some commentators explained this by suggesting that the new focus on state capacity was a reaction against the 'humanitarian intervention' policies of the 1990s which were held to have underestimated the importance of states for maintaining international stability (e.g. Malone, 2005, p. xv). One example of interventionist policies, often held to have been counterproductive in this context, was that of international aid provision which bypassed state institutions establishing parallel bureaucracies and encouraging a brain drain from the underpaid state sector (see Ghani et al., 2005, p. 10). The Commission for Africa report argued that peacebuilding and statebuilding policies should:

> ...stand in marked contrast to the approach in the 1980s and much of the 1990s, when aid was often used to try to compensate for poor governance, simply ignored governance issues, tried to force policies on reluctant countries, or aimed primarily at advancing the economic or political interests of the donor. (CfA, 2005, p. 94)

Several commentators highlighted that the result of 1990s humanitarian and human rights interventions had been the 'sucking out' of state capacity as core state functions had been taken over by UN agencies, international institutions and international NGOs, undermining the legitimacy and authority of non-Western states (Fukuyama, 2004, p. 139; Ignatieff, 2003; ESI, 2005, p. 10).

With the end of the Cold War, there rapidly developed increasingly interventionist regimes of international regulation, clearly exposing claims of international sovereign equality and in the process forcing Western powers and international institutions to account for the outcomes of these regulatory practices. Once relations of sovereign equality were openly brought into question through aid conditionality and human rights intervention, the question was sharply posed of Western responsibility. This was most strikingly raised in the Balkans, where individual Western states, and the EU, UN and other international institutions played a major role in overseeing the fragmentation of the Yugoslav state, making key decisions on recognition and republic boundaries. The result of this process of being drawn directly into conflict prevention was the unwieldy international protectorates of Bosnia, since 1995, and Kosovo, since 1999, which left intervening institutions exposed (so much so that the UN was opposed to assuming responsibilities in Afghanistan). With 9/11 and the likelihood that new Western responsibilities would be acquired through 'regime change', there was even greater pressure to develop new approaches which could help distance the West from the consequences of interventionist policies.

There was little doubt that international policy intervention in the 1980s and 1990s tended to bypass or reduce the non-Western state's administrative and political institutional capacity: through giving coercive powers of conditionality to international financial institutions which imposed fiscal regimes cutting the state's role in the economy and service provision; implementing discrete projects run independently by international agencies and NGOs; or by dictating policy outcomes through tying aid to donor goods and services. However, the key element of these interventions was their overtly external and coercive nature. The relations of authority were transparent; nowhere more so than in aid conditionality where international financial institutions specified detailed policies that the recipient countries had to accept. It was clear that, in these cases, non-Western governments, particularly those in Africa, were more accountable to international donors than to their own people (highlighted in CfA, 2005, p. 92).

Bearing this context in mind, this chapter suggests that the focus in the 2000s on peacebuilding in non-Western states had less to do with the desire for strong non-Western states, or a new found confidence in non-Western governing elites, than a desire on the behalf of Western states to avoid direct accountability for peacebuilding interventions, which threw up as many problems as they answered. The fact that peacebuilding-as-statebuilding was not driven by the need to enable the autonomy of non-Western states was highlighted by the strong consensus, among those engaged in the field, that 'strong' states were deeply problematic; that state capacities should not include the traditional 'right to do what they will within their own borders'.

Zartman, for example, argued that 'weak/soft' states were no worse than 'hard/brittle' states – while weak states could not exercise adequate authority over the domestic arena, 'strong/hard/brittle' states exercised too much authority and tended to marginalise other voices from civil society (Zartman, 2005). Rotberg agreed that there was a 'special category of weak state: the seemingly strong one' and that the number of states in this category had grown rapidly in the 1990s (2004, p. 5). States that were resistant to external engagement in their affairs, which clung to traditional ideas of 'Westphalian sovereignty, referring to the exclusion of external actors from domestic authority configurations' were now seen to be problematic (Krasner, 1999, p. 9; see also; Fearon and Laitin, 2004; Krasner, 2004; Keohane, 2002, 2003). In fact, reading the capacity-building literature it was difficult to isolate exactly what was meant by claims that states were being 'capacity-built' by external interveners. The first thing that becomes clear is that the aim was not to create states as classically understood, as self-governing, independent and autonomous political subjects.

This chapter argues that the early 2000s discussion of peacebuilding as a renewed attention to institutional structures – 'bringing the state back in' – in the policy discussions of post-conflict fragility, can be better understood as a radical extension of the practices of the 1980s and 1990s which internationalised the domestic policymaking sphere of non-Western states (e.g. Straw, 2002). The key difference, with the overtly 'interventionist' approach of the 1990s was that the emphasis was now on the non-Western state rather than those states and institutions doing the intervening. The transition away from justifying and holding intervening powers to account was presaged by the International Commission on Intervention and State Sovereignty (ICISS) *Responsibility to Protect* report, published in December 2001, and formulated prior to 9/11.

In this widely cited report, the Commission proposed a shift in language away from the 'human-centred' framework of a 'right to intervention' and towards a 'state-centred' framework of the 'responsibility to protect'. Whereas the 'right of intervention' put the emphasis on the international interveners to justify and legitimise their actions, the 'responsibility to protect' sought to avoid this 'attention on the claims, rights and prerogatives of the potentially intervening states' (ICISS, 2001a, p. 16). The 'responsibility to protect' sought to off-load responsibility onto the non-Western state at the same time as these states increasingly lost their policymaking authority.

The ICISS report successfully set out to 'shift the terms of the debate' and facilitated the evasion of any clarification of the competing rights of state sovereignty and of those of intervening powers, by arguing that state rights of sovereignty could co-exist with external intervention and peacebuilding-as-statebuilding. The report spelt out that, in its view, 'sovereignty then means accountability to two separate constituencies: internally, to one's own population; and internationally, to the community of responsible states' (ICISS, 2001b, p. 11). As the Commission co-chairs noted, this shift changed 'the essence of sovereignty, from control to responsibility' (Evans and Sahnoun, 2002, p. 101). The major implications that this shift had for accountability (a power which is accountable to another, external, body clearly lacks sovereign authority – the capacity for self-government) were consistently played down by the report's authors

and academic commentators. Robert Keohane, for example, disingenu-
ously argued that the ICISS report was not at all 'devaluing' sovereignty,
merely that it was 'reinterpreting' it, to bring the concept more into line
with the modern world (2003, p. 276).

Rather than the 1990s debate, where international intervention was
posed in terms of a clash of competing rights – the 'right of intervention'
against the 'right of state sovereignty' – by the mid-2000s the language
was one of 'shared responsibilities' and 'new partnerships'. Where the
non-Western state was the subject of overtly coercive external intervention
it was now more likely to be the focus of supportive, empowering, and
capacity-building practices and new modalities of surveillance. The product of this change was the enthronement of the peacebuilding-as-
statebuilding discourse as the framework for discussing international
security through the mechanism of new forms of intervention in non-
Western states.

This shift in the language of the Western projection of power reflected
both the new relations of subordination with the end of the bi-polar world
and at the same time the desire of Western institutions to reject direct
accountability and distance themselves from the direct management
of 'zones of instability'. The peacebuilding-as-statebuilding framework
sought to obfuscate and confuse relations of power and accountability
which stood clearly exposed in the 1990s as a fundamental clash of rights.
The *Responsibility to Protect* report, in emphasising the responsibilities
of the non-Western state, heralded the shift towards peacebuilding-as-
statebuilding as a policy of both intervention and avoidance. The contradictions involved in this process were highlighted in the irony that states
were alleged to being 'built' at the same time as they increasingly lost the
traditional attribute of sovereignty: self-government.

STATES WITHOUT SOVEREIGNTY

Sovereignty in International Relations signified political and legal autonomy: constitutional independence. It was a legal concept which was
unconditional and indivisible. As Robert Jackson summarised:

> [It is] legal in that a sovereign state is not subordinate to another sovereign
> but is necessarily equal to it by international law…Absolute [uncondi-
> tional] in that sovereignty is either present or absent. When a country is
> sovereign it is independent categorically: there is no intermediate condition.

Unitary [indivisible] in that a sovereign state is a supreme authority within its jurisdiction. (Jackson, 1990, p. 32)

Prior to decolonisation in the last century, the sovereign state form was only one of several kinds of international status. Under European colonialism territorial entities took the form of 'colonies', 'protectorates', 'mandates', 'trust territories' or 'dominions' (Jackson, 1990, p. 33). What these various forms had in common was formal legal subordination to a foreign power; they were a denial of sovereignty. There was nothing inevitable or natural about the sovereign state form or about its universalisation in the twentieth century, in the wake of World Wars One and Two (see Wight, 1979, p. 23; Morgenthau, 1970, pp. 258–61).

Few people engaged in the field argued that international peacebuilding in post-conflict situations was a framework for the creation or support of traditional sovereign entities. This could be seen clearly in practice in the cases of international engagement in Bosnia, Afghanistan, the handing over of 'sovereignty' in Iraq, and moves to make Kosovo an independent state in the mid-2000s, and more broadly in the UN and G8 proposals for state capacity-building in Africa. The sovereign state forms were held up but sovereignty was being redefined (or 'unbundled' in Stephen Krasner's phraseology; see Krasner, 1999), emphasising the importance of the legal shell of the state form while abandoning its political content of self-government and autonomy.

This was done in three ways. Firstly, by redefining sovereignty as a variable 'capacity' rather than an indivisible right; legitimising a new hierarchy of variable sovereignty and undermining the UN Charter principle of sovereign equality. Secondly, by redefining sovereignty as a duty or responsibility rather than a freedom; legitimising external mechanisms of regulation, held to enhance 'sovereignty' despite undermining the traditional right of self-government or autonomy. Thirdly, by exaggerating the formal importance of international legal sovereignty; this formal shell then facilitated the repackaging of external domination as 'partnership' or 'country ownership' and the voluntary contract of formally equal partners.

SOVEREIGNTY AS CAPACITY?

The most important challenge to traditional conceptions of sovereignty was the conflation of the formal political and legal right to self-government (an absolute quality) with the question of state capacity (a variable quantity), usually formulated in terms of 'good governance'. The conception of sovereignty as a capacity, rather than as a formal legal right to self-government and international legal equality, created a structure of a 'continuum' of sovereignty or a hierarchy of sovereignty where some states were considered to be more sovereign than others. This approach was famously developed by Robert Jackson, with his conception of 'quasi-states' (Jackson, 1990). For Jackson, the sovereignty granted to post-colonial states was artificial. Not because they were often still under the influence of their former colonial rulers, but because many of these states did not have the capacity to regulate and control their societies to the same extent as states in the West. For Jackson, these states possessed de jure sovereignty, formal international legal rights, but lacked de facto sovereignty, the capacity to govern domestically.

This idea of the 'unbundling' of sovereignty into its different attributes was popularised by Stephen Krasner in his 1999 book *Sovereignty: Organized Hypocrisy*. In his later work, he focused on sovereignty as a 'bundle' of three separate attributes: 'domestic sovereignty', the capacity of domestic governance structures; 'Westphalian/Vattelian sovereignty', i.e., self-government or political autonomy; and international legal sovereignty, formal juridical independence (2004, pp. 87–8). Krasner used the problem of weak capacity to argue that self-government should not be a barrier to international intervention. Whereas in the 1990s intervention would have been posed as a conflict between human rights (or the right of intervention) and the right of state sovereignty (self-government and autonomy), in Krasner's terminology there was no conflict with sovereignty because human rights would be protected if governments possessed adequate governing capacity ('domestic sovereignty'):

> Honoring Westphalian/Vattelian sovereignty...makes it impossible to secure decent and effective domestic sovereignty...To secure decent domestic governance in failed, failing, and occupied states, new institutional forms are needed that compromise Westphalian/Vatellian sovereignty for an indefinite period. (Krasner, 2004, p. 89)

The discovery that the equality of sovereignty hid the inequality of state capacities was not a new one. The same problem, although to a lesser extent, was present in domestic politics, where equality at the ballot box or under the law in liberal democracies did not necessarily ameliorate social and economic inequalities between individuals. In the domestic context, of course, relatively few people would have argued that these inequalities meant that formal political and legal equalities should be abandoned. In the international sphere, the existence of vast inequalities of power was one of the reasons that state sovereignty, held to be unconditional and indivisible, was the founding principle of international society. It was only on this basis, of formally upholding the equality and autonomy of states and the sovereign rights of non-intervention, that post-colonial societies could be guaranteed the rights to self-government. UN General Assembly declarations during the Cold War regularly asserted that differences in state capacity could never be grounds for undermining the rights of state sovereignty.

The affirmation that differences in capacity were no justification for the unequal treatment of sovereign equals was confirmed most notably in the UN General Assembly Declaration on the Granting of Independence to Colonial Countries and Peoples of 14 December 1960 (Resolution 1514 (XV)) which proclaimed that: 'all peoples have the right to self-determination; by virtue of that right they freely determine their political status and freely pursue their economic, social and cultural development' and that 'inadequacy of political, economic, social or educational preparedness should never serve as a pretext for delaying independence'. This was passed in the General Assembly by a vote of 89 to 0, with 9 abstentions. Even the colonial powers were unwilling to reject it (Jackson, 1990, p. 77).

By associating sovereignty with a sliding scale of 'capacities', rather than political and legal rights of equality, not only was a new international hierarchy legitimised but intervention was framed as supporting 'sovereignty' at the same time as it was undermining the rights of self-government. This inversion of the concept of 'sovereignty' was formulated in the clearest terms in the UK Overseas Development Institute (ODI) working paper report 'Closing the Sovereignty Gap'. In this report, by Ashraf Ghani, Clare Lockhart and Michael Carnahan, sovereignty was understood in functional rather than political or legal terms:

> The consensus now emerging from global economic, military and political institutions signals that this gap between de jure sovereignty and de facto sovereignty is the key obstacle to ensuring global security and prosperity. The challenge is to harness the international system behind the goal of enhancing the sovereignty of states – that is, enhancing the capacity of these states to perform the functions that define them as states. Long-term

> partnerships must be created to prepare and then implement strategies to
> close this sovereignty gap. (Ghani et al., 2005, p. 4)

Here sovereignty was no longer conceived of as a right to self-government.
Sovereignty was merely a capacity that could be 'enhanced' or, presumably,
'weakened'. The conflation of external intervention for the purposes of
'capacity-building' with enhancing state sovereignty and independence
was central to the peacebuilding-as-statebuilding discourse. In Africa,
where state capacity was held to be a fundamental concern for external
powers engaged in supporting a multitude of empowering projects, head-
lined by the UN's Millennium Development goals, these governance interventions went furthest (CfA, 2005, Chapter 4; UNMP, 2005).

If sovereignty was defined as the capacity of non-Western states for
'good governance', there seemed to be little wrong in external institutions
implementing strategies for long-term engagement in these societies in
order to enhance their 'sovereignty'. In fact, governments that resisted this
external assistance were, in the Orwellian language of international peacebuilders, accused of undermining their own sovereignty. The key to the
success of this conceptual conflation was not in its legitimisation of external intervention (already accepted in the 1990s) but in its portrayal of
external regulation as somehow empowering or strengthening non-
Western states. Here was potentially a virtuous circle for peacebuilding
powers, one that was not possible in the direct protectorates established by
peacebuilding interventions of the 1990s: without formal protectorate
powers, sovereignty could be upheld formally and the more intervention
there was the more the target state could be held responsible and accountable for the consequences of peacebuilding policies and outcomes.

Sovereignty as Responsibility?

The second shift articulated by the advocates of peacebuilding as empowerment was the assertion that post-conflict or conflict-prone non-Western
states had the 'responsibilities' of sovereignty rather than the rights of
sovereignty. What these 'responsibilities' consisted of was not held to be a
decision made solely by the citizens of a state or their representatives, but in
'partnership' with external bodies. Rather than being a barrier to external
interference, sovereignty became a medium through which non-Western
states and societies became integrated into networks of external peacebuilding regulation. International regulatory mechanisms of intervention were

legitimised, firstly through the role of international institutions in deciding the content of the 'responsibilities' of sovereignty, and, secondly, through holding states to external account for 'failings' in the exercise of sovereignty (now discussed in the language of responsibility/capacity).

Sovereignty as 'responsibility' enabled a new consensual or 'partner-ship' approach to peacebuilding. Non-Western states were in a poor position to resist new international mechanisms of regulation which came replete with carrots of international aid, trade privileges, debt for-giveness or integration into international organisations, in return for external support for peacebuilding governance reforms and institutional capacity-building. Peacebuilding as 'sovereignty-building' involved non-Western states being firmly embedded in international institutional frame-works, over whose decision-making processes they had little influence. For the UK's ODI, the focus on strengthening sovereignty entailed a much more interventionist role by international peacebuilding institutions:

> We define a sovereignty or state-building strategy as . . . the alignment of the internal and external stakeholders . . . In order to design and implement state-building strategies, the operation of the current international system must be reorientated towards a model where partnership and co-production of sovereignty becomes the aim of both national leaders and international partners. (Ghani et al., 2005, p. 13)

This 'co-production of sovereignty' followed the peacebuilding strategies adopted by the European Union towards Balkan states from 2000 onwards where international partnerships enmeshing applicant states in a network of international institutional processes were coordinated through the Stability Pact, the Stabilisation and Association Process, the Community Assistance for Reconstruction, Development and Stabilisation programme, and the 'European Partnership' process. The prospect of future EU membership was explicitly offered to Albania, Bosnia, Croatia, Macedonia and Federal Republic of Yugoslavia at the Feira European Council in June 2000. At this point the EU shifted away from peacebuilding as external conditionality and towards peacebuilding-as-statebuilding in the Balkan region, initiating a project of 'reforming and reinventing the state in South Eastern Europe' (EWI/ESI, 2001, p. 18).

This shift from external relations of aid and trade conditionality to 'partnership' in domestic governance was symbolised by the dropping of the term 'Balkans' by international institutions, as too 'negative' and 'hegemonic' and its replacement by 'South Eastern Europe' symbolising that this was a joint project of partnership, addressing 'European problems' with 'European solutions' (see, for example, Balkanologie, 1999; Hatzopoulos, 2005). The EU argued that it was well placed to assist these states in developing governance capacity which was identified as not just their main barrier to progress but also an area where the EU held a vital 'comparative advantage' and could 'provide real added value' (EC, 2001, p. 9). This engagement in domestic policymaking was held to have 'both pedagogical and political' benefits for the target states (EU, 2001). Although talking up the partnership between international institutions, the EU and target states; the peacebuilding-as-statebuilding process was directed through close cooperation between the EU and international financial institutions which together provided 'an effective means of focusing authorities' minds on essential reforms and of engaging with them in a sustained way to secure implementation' (EU, 2001, Para IIIc).

From 2000, the concept of peacebuilding-as-statebuilding through international partnerships to enhance governance capacities increasingly replaced external pressures. Where the incentive of European membership was not available a wide range of other governance partnerships were established around acceptance that the core security problem of non-Western states was that of state capacity and that the solution lay with the shared 'responsibilities' of both the non-Western state and international institutions. The general rule of thumb was that the greater were the inequalities at play, in the relationship between non-Western states and international institutions, the more grandiose was the language of partnership. As would be expected, it was in relation to Africa that the rhetoric and reality were most out of step. Here the language was of 'African leadership' and an entirely 'new kind of partnership' not based on inequality and hierarchy but 'mutual respect and solidarity' (CfA, 2005, p. 17). The UN Millennium Development Goals (MDG) project, following and extending the 'country ownership' approach of the interventionist Poverty Reduction Strategies, required that states engaged in far-reaching governance reform and opened up every area of domestic policymaking to international scrutiny and involvement. The 'responsibilities' or 'leadership' or 'ownership' lay with the domestic state but their partners (or joint 'stakeholders', in the language of the ODI authors) decided the policies:

> The host country should lead and own the effort to design the MDG strategy, drawing in civil society organisations; bilateral donors; the UN

specialized agencies, programs, and funds; and the international financial institutions, including the IMF, the World Bank, and the appropriate regional development bank. The contributions of the UN specialized agencies, programs and funds should be coordinated through the UN Country Team, and the UN Country Team should work closely with the international financial institutions. (UNMP, 2005, p. 53)

Policy 'coherence' was the new buzzword for peacebuilding as external capacity-building; this coherence was gained from closely tying international aid to new institutional frameworks of regulation and monitoring. In effect, this transformed external assistance for peacebuilding from being a subject of International Relations, between states, to one of domestic politics, of management and administration. This radical transformation in the relationship between non-Western states and international institutions was highlighted forcefully by the Commission for Africa report which stressed that it was: 'not simply recommending throwing money at the problems' but a 'fundamental change in the way in which aid works' (CfA, 2005, p. 94).

Once international financial institutions had a more direct role in the internal governance mechanisms of non-Western states, aid was much less likely to be based on overt external regulation in the form of external conditionality. Graham Harrison usefully highlighted the 'post-conditionality' regimes of international financial institutions in states like Tanzania and Uganda, where the influence of external donors was better conceived not as a 'strong external force' but as 'part of the state itself', through direct involvement in policymaking committees (Harrison, 2001, p. 669; see also, Harrison, 2004). The undermining of sovereign autonomy and the enmeshing of subject states in international institutional frameworks fundamentally blurred the lines of accountability and control and the relationships of power behind these mechanisms. The relationship between Western institutions and non-Western states was a highly coercive one that forced these states to cede their sovereign powers to external institutions; the fiction of 'partnership' then relied heavily on an exaggeration of the importance of international legal sovereignty.

INTERNATIONAL LEGAL SOVEREIGNTY?

By the mid-2000s, despite the new interventionist consensus and the international peacebuilding attention given to 'failing' states and the lack of governance capacities in 'zones of instability', there was surprisingly little support for the return of international protectorates and direct external administrations. Only a small number of commentators argued that states should, in fact, be 'allowed to fail' and more capable neighbours allowed to directly govern these territories (e.g. Herbst, 2004), or that the UN Security Council should establish new international trusteeships (Helman and Ratner, 1993).

Intervening powers and international institutions seemed to have a particularly strong desire to preserve the formal trappings of sovereignty. The contradictory desire to intervene but also to avoid responsibility was most sharply posed in questions of military intervention, such as post 9/11 'regime change' in Afghanistan and Iraq. Few acts are as fundamentally undermining of sovereignty as the external removal of a state's government. Yet, no sooner had intervening actors destroyed sovereignty than they were talking up its fundamental importance and pledging to restore authority to local actors at the soonest possible moment. Peacebuilding-as-statebuilding was the process of negotiating these contradictory drives towards intervention and away from responsibility for outcomes.

Leading US policy advisers and international think tanks were increasingly singing from the same hymn sheet, suggesting that international peacebuilding should no longer be seen in the old ways. The policy context meant that the old restrictions on international intrusion no longer existed. In the absence of Cold War rivalries between competing Great Powers, external intervention no longer needed to be overtly recognised in the undermining of sovereignty and open return to trusteeships and protectorates. In fact, the maintenance of formal sovereignty was at the heart of new approaches to 'neotrusteeship' (Fearon and Laitin, 2004), 'pooled sovereignty' (Keohane, 2002), or 'shared sovereignty' (Krasner, 2004). In the words of Krasner:

> Shared sovereignty would involve the engagement of external actors in some of the domestic authority structures of the target state for an indefinite period of time. Such arrangements would be legitimated by agreements signed by recognized national authorities. National actors would use their international legal sovereignty to enter into agreements that would compromise their Westphalian/Vatellian sovereignty [self-government/autonomy] with the goal of improving domestic sovereignty [governing capacity]. One core element of sovereignty – voluntary agreements – would be preserved, while another core element – the principle of autonomy – would be violated. (Krasner, 2004, p. 108)

The key difference between new forms of external peacebuilding – 'neo-trusteeship' or, even more user-friendly, 'shared sovereignty' – and traditional notions of a trust or protectorate was that the subordinated territory would formally be a contracting legal equal. International legal sovereignty was maintained while political autonomy – self-government was to be given up. The Bosnian peace agreement at Dayton in 1995 was the classic example of the voluntary surrender of sovereignty; the permanent 'neo-trusteeship' after 1997 was formally legitimised not through war and intervention or through international legal agreement (the UN Security Council's blessing was bestowed retrospectively) but through the signature of the Bosnian parties (Chandler, 2005b).

Law and reality no longer coincided when considering the location of sovereign power and authority (Yannis, 2002, p. 1049). Kosovo, for example, was formally part of the state of Serbia-Montenegro, but again the lack of fit between the formal location of sovereignty and external mechanisms of regulation made discussions of final status hard to resolve as decision-making authority lay neither with the elected Kosovo government in Pristina nor the Serbian government in Belgrade. Afghanistan and Iraq had the juridical status of independent states despite their dependence on the political and security role of the US. The artificial nature of these regimes was highlighted by the fact that their governments' writs seldom extended outside the protected security zones of the capitals. The restrictions on the Iraqi interim government's authority meant that the formal transfer of Iraqi sovereignty from the US-led Coalition Provisional Authority to an Iraqi government in June 2004 did not reflect any substantial change in the relations of state authority (see, for example, Klein, 2005).

International peacebuilding regimes led to an increasing number of states without sovereignty. States existed on paper, in terms of juridical status, for example, as members of the United Nations, with national flags, and maybe their own currencies, but not as independent political subjects capable of self- government. As Robert Keohane argued:

> We somehow have to reconceptualize the state as a political unit that can maintain internal order while being able to engage in international co-operation, without claiming the exclusive rights ... traditionally associated with sovereignty ... The same institutional arrangements may help both to reconstruct troubled countries that are in danger of becoming 'failed states', and to constrain the autonomy of those states. (Keohane, 2003, p. 277)

He suggested that peacebuilding-as-statebuilding could establish the 'institutional arrangements' which were capable of taking responsibility for maintaining order ('domestic sovereignty') but without giving rise to rights of self-government ('Westphalian sovereignty'). He recommended an exit strategy for Kosovo, for example, where there was a shift from existing trusteeship status, which could be called 'nominal sovereignty', to 'limited sovereignty' with external powers able to override domestic authorities, to a final stage of 'integrated sovereignty' where the state was locked into international institutions able to override domestic authorities (Keohane, 2003, pp. 296–7). This would have resolved the problem of Kosovo's independence as it would never achieve independence beyond the purely formal trappings of statehood: 'Westphalian sovereignty . . . is simply bypassed in the movement from limited to integrated sovereignty' (ibid, p. 297).

His proposals were strikingly similar to those advocated by the International Commission on the Balkans. The Commission's April 2005 report, *The Balkans in Europe's Future*, talked about Kosovo's 'independence without full sovereignty', to be followed by 'guided sovereignty' with 'reserve powers' for the EU and a final stage of 'full and shared sovereignty' (ICB, 2005, pp. 18–23). Here peacebuilding-as-statebuilding was held to be able to build a new type of state; one that had 'sovereignty' but was still in essentially the same position as it was when it was formally a protectorate. The difference being that formal accountability had been shifted back to the non-Western state.

James Fearon and David Laitin suggested a similar approach, arguing that a return to traditional forms of sovereignty was not the solution, but instead that the transfer of power in cases of post-conflict intervention and regime change should be 'not to full sovereignty but rather as a state embedded in and monitored by international institutions' (2004, p. 42). Krasner argued the point even more openly in his support for the concept of 'shared' sovereignty, which similarly used 'sovereignty' as a means for enabling external regulation. Here, international legal sovereignty would allow post-conflict states to enter into 'partnerships' that informally violated their sovereign rights:

> For policy purposes, it would be best to refer to shared sovereignty as 'partnerships'. This would more easily let policymakers engage in organized hypocrisy, that is, saying one thing and doing another. Shared sovereignty or partnerships would allow political leaders to embrace sovereignty, because

these arrangements would be legitimated by the target state's international legal sovereignty, even though they violate the core principle of Westphalian/Vatellian sovereignty: autonomy ... Shared sovereignty or partnerships would make no claim to being an explicit alternative to conventional sovereignty. It would allow actors to obfuscate the fact that their behaviour would be inconsistent with their principles. (Krasner, 2004, p. 108)

It was this 'obfuscation' of the maintenance of international legal sovereignty that enabled international institutions to present themselves as facilitating partners in a shared peacebuilding project rather than as coercive external powers. Robert Cooper, focusing particularly on the enlargement policies of the European Union, described this as a new conflict-free 'postmodern' or voluntary' form of imperialism (Cooper, 2003). Mark Leonard argued that unlike the old imperialism based on conflict and overt subordination, the EU was completely transforming states from the inside, rather than ruling them from above, for example: 'Europe is changing all of Polish society, from its economic policies and property laws to its treatment of minorities and what gets served on the nation's tables' (Leonard, 2005, p. 6).

The more 'sovereignty' was voluntarily shared between target states and international institutions, coercive external conditionality was exchanged for internal forms of 'enhanced surveillance' through the peacebuilding reporting mechanisms generated by the good governance requisites of openness and transparency enforced by international institutions (CfA, 2005, p. 376). Policy advisers could no doubt see the gains to be made in enabling Western governments to talk about peacebuilding and strengthening sovereignty and accountability in non-Western states, while avoiding accountability for their actions and policy prescriptions. However, while sovereignty could be 'unbundled' as a heuristic device there was little evidence that conceiving the non-Western state in purely administrative and bureaucratic terms, as a conduit for external policy, was necessarily a recipe for success. States without sovereignty were not easy to 'capacity-build'.

PHANTOM STATES AND FRAGILE EMPIRES

States that were not designed to be independent political subjects in anything but name were a façade without content. States without sovereignty may have had technically sound governance and administrative structures on paper but the atrophied political sphere hindered attempts to peacebuild post-conflict societies and overcome social and political divisions. The states created, which had international legal sovereignty but had ceded policymaking control to international institutions, were phantom states because their lack of self-government prevented them from being recognised or legitimised as embodying a collective expression of their societies. The states of Afghanistan, Iraq, and Bosnia, for example, may have had formal sovereignty and elected governments but their relationship of external dependency meant that the domestic political sphere could not serve to easily legitimise the political authorities or cohere their societies. This form of peacebuilding-as-statebuilding was, in fact, no less corrosive of the authority of the non-Western state than earlier policies which sought to bypass or marginalise the state.

Bosnia in the mid-2000s became a clear example of this type of peacebuilding. Once the European Union took over a larger role through the accession process, a new type of 'state' was built precisely through this process of distancing power and formal accountability. To all intents and purposes Bosnia was a member of the European Union; in fact more than this, Bosnia was the first genuine EU state where sovereignty had in effect been transferred to Brussels. The EU provided its government; the international High Representative was an EU employee and the EU's Special Representative in Bosnia and had the power to directly impose legislation and to dismiss elected government officials and civil servants.

However, even if the High Representative's office had been closed-down, as had been discussed intermittently, this would have made little difference as EU policy and 'European Partnership' priorities dominated the legislative agenda and were overseen through the EU-supported office within the Bosnian state, the European Directorate for Integrations (see, for example, EU, 2005). The EU also ran the police force, taking over from the United Nations at the end of 2002, and the military, taking over from NATO at the end of 2004, and managed Bosnia's negotiations with the World Bank. One look at the Bosnian flag – with the stars of the EU on a yellow and blue background chosen to be in exactly the same colours as used in the EU flag – demonstrated the Bosnia was more EU-orientated than any current member state (Poels, 1998). However, the EU distanced itself from any accountability for the power it exercised over Bosnia; formally Bosnia was an independent state and member of the United Nations and a long way off meeting the requirements of EU membership.

After many years of peacebuilding-as-statebuilding in Bosnia there was a drastic separation between power and accountability (see Chandler, 2005a). This clearly suited the EU, which was in a position of exercising control over the tiny state without either admitting it into the EU or presenting its policy regime in strict terms of external conditionality. Bosnia was neither an EU member nor did it appear to be a colonial protectorate. Bosnia's formal international legal sovereignty gave the appearance that it was an independent entity, voluntarily asking for external EU assistance with state capacity-building. Questions of aligning domestic law with the large raft of regulations forming the EU aquis appeared as ones of domestic politics. There was no international forum in which the contradictions between Bosnian social and economic demands and the external pressures of Brussels' policy prescriptions could be raised.

However, these questions were not ones of domestic politics. The Bosnian state had no independent or autonomous existence outside of the EU 'partnership'. There were no independent structures capable of articulating alternative policies. Politicians were subordinate to international institutions through the mechanisms of governance established which gave state bureaucrats and administrators the final say over policymaking. The Bosnian state was a phantom state; but it was not a fictional creation. The Bosnian state played a central role in the transmission of EU policy priorities in their most intricate detail. The state here was an inversion of the sovereign state. Rather than representing a collective political expression of Bosnian interests – expressing self-government and autonomy – 'Westphalian sovereignty' in the terminology of peacebuilders or statebuilders – the Bosnian state was an expression of an externally-driven agenda.

The more Bosnia became the subject of external peacebuilding-as-statebuilding, the less like a traditional state it became. Here, the state was a mediating link between the 'inside' of domestic politics and the 'outside' of International Relations, but rather than clarifying the distinction it removed the distinction completely. The imposition of an international peacebuilding agenda of capacity-building and good governance appeared internationally as a domestic question and appeared domestically as an external, international matter. Where the sovereign state clearly demarcated lines of policy accountability, the state without sovereignty blurred them. In fact, accountability for policymaking disappeared with the removal of the traditional content of state sovereignty.

In this context, domestic politics had no real content. There was very little at stake in the political process. For external peacebuilders, the subordination of politics to bureaucratic and administrative procedures of good governance was a positive development. In functional terms they argued that sovereignty, and the political competition it brought with it for control of state power, was a luxury that post-conflict states could not afford. Keohane argued that many non-Western states were 'troubled societies' plagued by economic, social and ethnic divisions, which meant that elections could be highly problematic 'winner-take-all' situations. In these states, unconditional sovereign independence was a curse rather than a blessing and conflict could be prevented by enabling 'external constraints' on autonomy in exchange for institutional capacity-building (Keohane, 2002, pp. 755–6; also Paris, 2004, pp. 187–94).

Post-conflict states, such as Bosnia, stood in desperate need of a political project that could engage with and recohere society around a shared future-orientated perspective (see also Bickerton, 2007). What Bosnia received was external regulation which, in effect, prevented the building of genuine state institutions which could engage with and represent social interests. Phantom states were an inevitable product of the technical, bureaucratic and administrative approach exported by international peacebuilders. Where weak or post-conflict states stood in need of socially engaging state-based projects of development and transformation they were subject to external forms of domination which, as will be analysed in the next part of the book, were uniquely unsuited to the task.

International peacebuilders sought to focus on legal, administrative and bureaucratic institutional processes rather than engaging with populations with programmes of social and economic inclusion. 'Good governance', 'transparency' and alignment with the EU *acquis communitaire* stood in as a weak substitute for any collective process of political engagement (see, for example, Leonard, 2005, pp. 36–45). Even the international financial institutions, such as the World Bank and the International Monetary Fund were encouraged to drop earlier aspirations towards development and economic growth and to focus more narrowly on non-Western state frameworks of transparency and accountability (CfA, 2005 p. 374).

CONCLUSION

Peacebuilding-as-statebuilding sought to address the crisis of peacebuilding as it emerged in the late 1990s. This crisis was brought on by the extension of international peacekeeping into new militarised forms of 'humanitarian intervention' and internationally-driven peace settlements giving international actors sovereign authority in post-conflict states. These new internationalised forms of governance and supervision were initially established on an ad hoc basis but were put at the centre stage of international policymaking as the international community oversaw the wars of the break-up of the former Yugoslavia. These peace interventions resulted in the establishment of international peace protectorates starting in Bosnia in 1997.

Initially the Bosnian protectorate developed on an ad hoc basis and was the basis for UN supervised regimes in Kosovo and East Timor. The promise that peacebuilding-as-statebuilding held out was that of managing these powers and enabling a shift away from direct protectorates, relieving Western elites from the need to legitimise and clearly articulate the new hierarchy of domination revealed by the collapse of the UN Charter framework of state sovereignty and non-intervention. International actors engaged in peacebuilding sought to deal with the problem of having direct regulatory authority through attempts to back away from their claims of external sovereign power. The impasse of peacebuilding is the story of international attempts to negotiate a retreat from international responsibilities. This crisis shaped peacebuilding in the 2000s as peacebuilding-as-statebuilding; on the one hand, responsibility was shifted on to domestic actors, while on the other, the attempt to impose or develop liberal institutional frameworks continued to reproduce the gap between the 'internationals' and the 'locals'. This impasse is the subject of the next part of this book.

PART III

The Peacebuilding Impasse

CHAPTER 5

Civil Society Building

INTRODUCTION

This chapter and the following one address the two central policies of peacebuilding-as-statebuilding, following the formalisation of peacebuilding as the externally managed construction of liberal institutional frameworks for sustaining peace. Both focus mainly on the experience of Bosnia, where the author was closely involved in the study of the development of new peacebuilding approaches. The case studies are used heuristically to tightly draw out the limitations of peacebuilding as an externally managed exercise and to highlight the highly illiberal nature of these external interventions, seeking to engineer and manipulate the domestic political process. The following chapter engages with attempts to socially and politically engineer Bosnian society through the formal institutional framework of the rule of law, this chapter focuses on the informal institutional engagement in attempts to shape and influence civil society organisations and activities.

For many commentators, the construction of civil society in post-conflict states was considered a precondition for the development of consolidated peaceful and democratic institutions. Nowhere was this more the case than within Bosnia-Herzegovina, where ethnic and nationalist identification indicated a deeply politically segmented society. To challenge this segmentation, international institutions provided financial and technical support to a growing civil society sector based on non-governmental organisations. In fact, the first symptom of the crisis of

© The Author(s) 2017
D. Chandler, *Peacebuilding*, Rethinking Peace and Conflict Studies,
DOI 10.1007/978-3-319-50322-6_5

peacebuilding in 1997 was the formal establishment of a Democratization Branch within the Organization for Security and Co-operation in Europe (OSCE). Democratisation implied that rather than the first state-level elections demonstrating democracy in the new state, the problem of the elections and the victory of nationalist parties was a manifestation of the opposite: the lack of democracy.

The formalisation of a peacebuilding protectorate, in 1997, required a discourse of legitimacy on the basis that Bosnia was not ready for self-government and required 'democratization'. The United Nations Secretary General noted 'democratization' was 'predominantly a new area' for the UN, nevertheless it was already seen as 'a key component of peacebuilding', addressing the 'economic, social, cultural, humanitarian and political roots of conflict' (UN, 1996, Paras 13; 46). Democratisation was broadly defined by the UN to constitute a 'comprehensive approach' covering the broad range of new peacebuilding priorities: the 'top-down' international regulation of elections, institutional development and economic management, accompanied by 'bottom-up' assistance to develop a democratic political culture through civil society-building (UN, 1996, Para 124; see also; UN, 1995b, Para 13). Democratisation grew rapidly as a policy area, legitimising international peacebuilding at the same time as problematising those being 'peacebuilt'. In 1997, the first budget of the OSCE Democratization Department was a little over US$1 million and consisted solely of voluntary contributions; by 1999 the budget had risen to over US$4 million and was being financed through the regular mission budget (du Pont, 1999, p. 304).

Civil society development was generally viewed to involve support for the associational sphere of interest groups that stood between the private sphere of the family and market economy and the public sphere of the state and government. A richly pluralistic civil society, generating a wide range of interests, was held to mitigate polarities of political conflict and develop a democratic culture of tolerance, moderation and compromise (Diamond, 1994; Seligman, 1992; Cohen and Arato, 1992; Keane, 1988). The main focus of civil society-building was often local non-governmental organisations (NGOs) seen as capable of articulating needs independently of vested political interests and involving grass-roots community 'voices'. The UN's web-site incorporated nearly 2,000 documents referring to 'civil society', while the Secretary General's *Agenda for Development* Report explained that:

A vigorous civil society is indispensable to creating lasting and successful development... Locally based NGOs, in particular, can serve as intermediaries and give people a voice and an opportunity to articulate their needs, preferences and vision of a better society... in countries where civil society is weak, strengthening civil society should be a major purpose of public policy. (UN, 1994, Par. 107)

In the late 1990s and 2000s, the discussion of civil society-building as a priority for the consolidation of peacebuilding was sharply focused by the democratic transitions of eastern Europe and the conflict in former Yugoslavia (see, for example, Gallagher, 1995; Fine, 1996; Sztompka, 1996; Rau, 1991; Gellner, 1994). It was often viewed that the wars of Yugoslavia's dissolution were the product of an ethnic segmentation, that reflected a lack of civil society and led to a failed transition to democracy (for example, Burg, 1997; Denitch, 1996; Ferdinand, 1997; ICB, 1996; Woodward, 1995, Chapter 5). In Bosnia-Herzegovina, war resulted in thousands of casualties and nearly half the population becoming displaced or refugees, and was only brought to an end by forceful United States (US)-led international intervention. In December 1995, the Dayton Peace Agreement was signed. This created an independent Bosnian state divided between two separate entities, the Muslim (Bosniak)-Croat Federation, occupying 51 per cent of the territory, and the Serb-held area, Republika Srpska (RS), occupying 49 per cent.

For the Dayton Peace Agreement to hold, many commentators argued that civil society development was central to the democratisation and peacebuilding process. Without civil society, economic reconstruction aid was said to have little impact on political and social division within Bosnia. Leading analysts thus argued that European Union funding of over US$2,500 per head to residents of Muslim and Croat-divided Mostar had done little to reduce tensions and that US aid to Bosnia, amounting to US$1,200 per head by 1998, was creating dependency and acting as a disincentive for Bosnians to resolve problems (Deacon and Stubbs, 1998). There was similar disillusionment with the political sphere. Influential commentators stated that 'elections without civil society will not produce democracy', and that elections in Bosnia were 'deeply flawed', legitimising nationalist elites responsible for the war and division (see, for example, Denitch, 1996, p. 210; Gallagher, 1997; Woodward, 1996, p. 35; Kaplan, 1997, p. 58).

While 'top-down' economic and political interventions were often seen to perpetuate social segmentation and ethnic nationalism, 'bottom-up' support for the sphere of civil society was held to have an empowering and transformative content. For example, Ian Smillie, author of an influential CARE Canada report on NGOs and civil society-building in Bosnia, argued:

> Rebuilding tolerance and pluralism in Bosnia and Herzegovina is perhaps more important than anywhere else in the former Yugoslavia. It is important because without it, the Dayton Accord ... and the hope of a united Bosnia and Herzegovina will be lost ... Accountability, legitimacy and competence in public life are the key, and these can only be achieved through the active participation of the electorate, buoyed by a strong, plural, associational base, by a web of social, cultural and functional relationships which can act as a 'societal glue' and as counterbalance to the market and the state. The alternative for Bosnia and Herzegovina ... is paternalism, exploitation, corruption, and war. (Smillie, 1996, p. 13)

Dialogue Development, preparing the 1998 European Union PHARE Civil Society Development Programme for Bosnia, stated:

> The strong emergence of a Third Sector in the form of civil society in Bosnia will be instrumental in the gradual emergence of a pluralistic and democratic society ... NGOs are ... destined to play an important role in this post-conflict situation as they have a vast potential for transcending the faultlines of society through the creation of new partnerships and alliances. They can moderate and mediate in addressing the relevant needs of society, not always within the realm of the state. (DD, 1997, Annex 1, p. 1)

The OSCE mission in Bosnia was restructured at the end of 1996 to enable it to carry out a more long-term approach to democratisation, focusing on the challenges of creating or restoring civil society in the region. This perspective was informed by the consensus that peace and stability in Bosnia was 'still very much dependent on the development of a democratic civil society' (OSCE, 1997a, p. 3). The first monthly report of the OSCE mission's Democratization Branch outlined the institution's view of the obstacles to civil society development. The obstacles listed were all connected to the incapacity of the Bosnian people in general, or specific sections of them, to act and think in a manner suited to meet the 'challenges' of democratisation.

For the Bosnian elites, the problem was seen to be a lack of technical and organisational abilities. These incapacities were highlighted by the people involved in building local NGOs (LNGOs) in RS, who 'continue to struggle for funding, programme ideas and the acquisition of administrative skills', and in leaders of opposition parties more broadly, because 'even though the number of political parties is increasing, they are only now beginning to receive training on how to enlarge their popular appeal' (OSCE, 1997a, p. 3).

While the skill-shortages of the elites could be overcome by training and aid, the other obstacles, located at the level of Bosnian society in general, were seen to be more long-term. First, the problem of an ethnic mentality: 'the passive acceptance of prejudices [which] must be overcome for real and psychological barriers to inter-ethnic reconciliation to be dismantled'. Secondly, the problems stemming from a lack of awareness of the workings of a democratic society, which meant that it was difficult to make informed choices at elections: 'The elections served as the basis for the establishment of democratic institutions, yet more efforts are required to increase citizen's awareness of the working and roles of their authorities, the rule of law, and democratic rule and procedures' (OSCE, 1997a, p. 3).

The barriers to LNGOs and civic groups empowering communities were either viewed as technical problems, which the Bosnian elites were seemingly unable to grasp, or as deeper problems of Bosnian culture. This approach sidelined the fact that the citizens of Bosnia and the former Yugoslavia had extensive higher education provision, an historical record of inter-ethnic tolerance and understanding and a relatively high level of involvement in local political and civic life (see Heath, 1981; Bertsch, 1973; Bougarel, 1996; McFarlane, 1988; Seroka, 1988, 1989). This chapter therefore highlights the framework of thinking which forced international peacebuilding into an impasse in the late 1990s. It rapidly became clear that the peacebuilding-as-statebuilding perspective was problematic in that it paid attention solely to the incapacities of Bosnian citizens, resulting in a lack of attention given to failings within international peacebuilding practice itself.

Experience on the ground in Bosnia indicated that the top-down approach of international regulation and the bottom-up approach of empowerment and civil society development had conflicting impacts on Bosnian society, rather than the complementary one assumed by the proponents of extended internationally-led peacebuilding. If it was the case that the comprehensive nature of international mandates acted to constrain the emergence of civil society initiatives, then the extension of external regulation paradoxically made international with-drawal problematic and lead to the reproduction of institutional fail-ings, rather than facilitating the creation of a stable self-governing democracy.

BUILDING CIVIL SOCIETY

The focus on civil society, going beyond the governing institutions of the country, gave the international community a much broader remit of involvement in Bosnian affairs by extending the role of the OSCE under Dayton. Annex 3 of the Dayton Peace Agreement, the Agreement on Elections, gave the OSCE the authority to 'lay the foundation for repre-sentative government and ensure the progressive achievement of demo-cratic goals throughout Bosnia and Herzegovina' (GFA, 1995). Under the broader interpretation of the 'spirit of Dayton' this was now seen to include the promotion of civil society through support for the work of Bosnian NGOs and civic groups (Woodger, 1997).

This wider remit facilitated the development of a separate Democratization Branch, a unique step for an international institution. The OSCE Democratization Programme in 1997 was designed to bring the international community into a closer relationship with grass-roots groups and associations which could provide a counterpoint to the politics of the governing authorities and nationalist parties; through this, opening political debate and creating new opportunities for alternative voices to be heard (OSCE, 1997g). As Jasna Malkoc, the Senior Coordinator for Democratization/NGO Development explained to me at the time: 'Establishing NGOs is a first principle for democratisation. NGOs are vital for the reconstruction of civil society. Political parties deal with majorities. It is important to address issues without thinking about mino-rities and majorities'.

The OSCE strategy for encouraging political participation was under-stood to be a three stage process: first, identifying targeted individuals or groups who were open to external support and influence; secondly, pro-viding training and building a civil society agenda within these groups; and thirdly, mobilising active NGOs as political voices in the domestic and international environment.

Targeting

The Democratization Branch worked through the extensive OSCE field presence strategically placed to play a key role in identifying individuals and groups for peacebuilding initiatives. Based in the field, the Democratization Officers had the role of assessing which groups were most open to OSCE influence and to then develop strategies in relation to them. The OSCE strategy had a regional approach because the receptiveness to external intervention and support was dependent on the vagaries of the local political situation. In the Federation part of Bosnia there were many active NGOs, partly because of the influx of foreign donors and partly because the political climate was more receptive to external influence. The OSCE felt that in many urban areas in the Federation there was a 'diverse and vibrant NGO community' (OSCE, 1997a, p. 5). The climate had been less receptive in RS, with the Banja Luka area being the centre for NGO activities and parts of Eastern RS having virtually no NGOs.

The strategy was to integrate the 'more developed', politically active, NGOs into the broader OSCE perspective and, under OSCE 'facilitation', for them to link up with groups and individuals in areas with 'less developed' NGOs and a low NGO presence. In the Tuzla region experienced LNGOs were encouraged to expand their networks to give the OSCE new areas of influence (OSCE, 1997d, p. 4). In areas with little organised NGO presence, the OSCE had to trawl for prospective partners. Staff in Banja Luka, for example, created a workshop on proposal drafting for NGOs with plans to travel outside the city to the surrounding areas. In Velika Kladusa, a targeted area where the OSCE was concerned about the 'clear dearth of local initiatives', the OSCE-organised seminars on 'How to Establish an NGO', which targeted teachers, students, political party representatives, women, intellectuals and local journalists, to enable them to 'form a clearer idea of what fields NGOs work in, their legal status, and funding possibilities' (OSCE, 1997c, p. 6).

The target groups for developing networking and community-building initiatives were essentially those that the OSCE felt it could influence. Within this, the more social weight a group had, the better was its perceived qualification. Elite groups, such as lawyers, journalists, religious leaders, teachers, academics and intellectuals were therefore of great importance to civil society building. Outside this, the OSCE attempted to establish links with groups that were either excluded from the mainstream political processes, in need of funding and resources, or unhappy with their current situation, such as self-help initiatives including women's groups, youth associations, and displaced persons' associations.

Any activity that could be undertaken in a cross-entity form, and thereby become a potential challenge to ethnic segmentation and division, was likely to be supported. The OSCE's interest was not so much in the activity itself but in locating people who were willing to organise around alternative political focus points to the majority parties. However, the OSCE feared that being up-front about its aims could put off potential supporters: 'When groups focus on non-political matters they have an optimal chance of making gains' (OSCE, 1997a, p. 4). The Democratization Branch monthly report for March 1997 demonstrated this in relation to sponsorship and other information: 'While promoting inter-ethnic tolerance and responsibility is the main goal of confidence building, events this month show how this is sometimes easiest done when it is not an activity's explicit goal' (OSCE, 1997b, p. 4).

Developing a Peacebuilding Agenda

Regardless of the humanitarian aid or information needs that an NGO was initially established to meet, it was expected to participate in cross-entity forums and training and to become part of the NGO lobbying network dominated by the more openly political 'civic groups'. The OSCE involvement with LNGOs had a directly political goal:

> The goal of the NGO development work is to assist LNGOs [to] become self-sufficient, participatory, and actively involved in working on behalf of their communities. The kind of LNGO projects which most closely reach this aim, offering a new political voice to citizens, are those which focus on advocacy and are willing to tackle actual political or social issues. As more and more LNGOs accept the responsibility of implementing these kinds of programmes, they gradually strengthen Bosnia's civil society. (OSCE, 1997a, p. 5)

There was no hiding the feelings of frustration that the officers of the OSCE had for the LNGOs, which they saw as 'less developed' because they were concentrating on needs, as opposed to becoming part of a political opposition. Their willingness to use their influence to alter the approaches and goals of LNGOs also could not be denied. The following extract from a Democratization Branch monthly report clearly illustrated the support and guidance available from the OSCE:

> In areas where LNGOs are barely developed, as a start they implement humanitarian-type programmes which seek to satisfy basic needs. Over the past month, local groups identified in Eastern Republika Srpska (excluding Bijeljina) correspond to this. As true civil actors however, LNGOs must do more; otherwise they will be providing temporary solutions to what remains long term problems. An early step was taken [when] the Helsinki Committee Bijeljina started monitoring and investigating human rights abuses in mid-1996... In the Bihac area [of operations], the Centre for Civic Co-operation (CCC) in Livno has gradually gone with OSCE support from a humanitarian LNGO working with children to one which seeks to increase awareness about human rights and democracy. (OSCE, 1997a, p. 6)

The OSCE women's development work demonstrated how this process worked. Reporting on the OSCE-organised Mostar Women's Conference, in March 1997, it was noted that nine women currently living as displaced persons in RS attended. The OSCE was disappointed that while the Federation women were willing to organise politically, the women from RS clearly had not grasped the OSCE's agenda:

> ...while the Federation women appeared poised to work on joint activities, those from the RS seemed more keen on fulfilling their immediate personal wish of visiting Mostar. Whether the RS participants recognize that working with other Mostar women they have a chance of addressing some of the deeper underlining obstacles to freedom of movement and return, is thus likely to determine future conferences' success. (OSCE, 1997b, p. 3)

The work with women's organisations seemed to have some success as the OSCE noted that 'women are increasingly finding ways to take on political roles, even though frequently outside of political parties' (1997b, p. 5). The report noted that in Bihac a women's NGO was reportedly keen to organise a radio broadcast on elections related issues with OSCE support and that women's groups in Mostar were considering a similar initiative. The women's groups most active in political activity so impressed the OSCE that: 'In the coming months OSCE staff may consider encouraging these women to become electoral monitors... This is a step towards preparing civic groups to take on bigger responsibilities in the political process' (1997b, p. 5).

The OSCE also ran the election process and the regulations of the OSCE-chaired Provisional Election Commission allowed for citizens' organisations as well as political party representatives to monitor the electoral process, after receiving accreditation from a Local Election Committee. From the OSCE's perspective this was 'an important chance to involve a greater number of actors in the political process' (1997e, p. 3). Of course, the new actors involved in this process were those that had already been carefully hand-picked by the OSCE itself. As the Mostar strategy report advised: 'Field Officers and the Regional Centre should begin identifying local partners who could benefit from poll watching training' (OSCE, 1997f, Para IIb). Democratization Officers had been instructed by the OSCE Democratization Branch to facilitate training for these groups, with the assistance of the US-funded National Democratic Initiative and the Council of Europe (OSCE, 1997e, p. 3).

For the OSCE, the sign of successful civil society-building was when the new LNGOs began to act as political actors in their own right. The third monthly report of the Democratization Branch celebrated the success of their work in northern RS, where 'local NGOs are independently addressing more and more sensitive political subjects' (1997c, p. 6). Examples included an internationally-financed inter-entity roundtable, initiated by the Forum of Citizens of Banja Luka, entitled 'The Legal Aspects of Return for Refugees and Displaced Persons' and the establishment of preliminary contacts between a new Doboj NGO and displaced persons in Zenica. The OSCE was full of praise for the two NGOs which were raising an issue that it saw as a major part of its own agenda: 'The fact that the two groups are addressing the politically sensitive issue of return points to their ability to take on the kind of independent stance necessary in any democratic society' (OSCE, 1997c, p. 6).

The Voice of Civil Society

The directly political impact of this NGO work could be seen in initiatives like the Citizens' Alternative Parliament and the Coalition for Return, actively supported by the OSCE-backed NGOs. The Citizens' Alternative Parliament (CAP) was a network of Bosnian NGOs which the OSCE saw as strengthening and coordinating the work of NGOs in Bosnia. To strengthen the impact of the CAP the OSCE intended to focus on developing the 'member organizations' commitment and capabilities of taking action in their regions' (OSCE, 1997a, p. 6). The OSCE's work with displaced persons' groups was designed to feed in with the activities of the Coalition for Return (CFR). The CFR was an association of more than 40 refugee and displaced persons groups from Bosnia, Croatia, Serbia and Germany.

In advance of the September 1996 elections, Deputy High Representative Steiner had already raised the prospect of refugee associations being used to put pressure on political parties 'from below'. In July he had promised that: 'In the future we will aim to include representatives of refugee associations in our meetings in order to speed up the work of the authorities on both sides which has so far been very slow' (OHR, 1996a). The decision to form the CFR was taken at the Office of the High Representative (OHR), following the nationalist parties' success in the September 1996 polls (ICG, 1997, p. 9; OHR, 1997a). The Deputy High Representative discussed plans to establish the association with representatives from associations of displaced persons and refugees and gave full support for the formation of a strategy planning group to liaise directly with international organisations and the relevant authorities. The CFR, meeting under the chair of the OHR then worked to encourage return and to raise the profile of the issue with international organisations. In December 1996, the CFR decided to extend its remit to the directly political questions related to the issue of return and to develop an integrated approach to reconstruction and economic recovery.

By February 1997, this political role was extended to developing information and aid networks calling on displaced persons and refugees to vote for candidates committed to the issue of return in the forthcoming municipal elections. The Deputy High Representative then sought to promote the CFR as a popular 'grass-roots movement' and, in July 1997, at its first meeting not organised and chaired by the OHR, the CFR finally came of age as an independent organ of civil society (OHR, 1997b). It then requested observer status for the municipal elections and equal partnership with elected political representatives in negotiations on donations and reconstruction implementation projects.

THE LIMITS OF CIVIL SOCIETY DEVELOPMENT

International attempts to ensure that the 'different voices' in Bosnia were heard by the outside world involved giving support to a variety of groups and organisations within Bosnia which attempted to challenge the political domination of the main political parties. Groups such as Circle 99, the Tuzla Citizens' Forum, the CAP and the CFR were actively supported by many international funders and had logistical and training support from the OSCE Democratization Branch.

However, as the OSCE Reporting Officer, Sabine Freizer, explained: 'The central problem we have is how to encourage participation'. It seemed surprising that these groups with an international reputation should have problems involving Bosnian people in their work, especially as they were alleged to represent a grass-roots movement for a different voice to be heard. Adrien Marti, the Coordinator for Political Party Development, explained the problem of the lack of popular support for the citizens' groups:

> The Citizens' Alternative Parliament, the Shadow Government and the Coalition for Return are basically the same 20 people when you scratch the surface a little. There is really no depth to this. The nationalist parties have a lot of good and respected people, they play on people's fears but also deliver security and a feeling that you can live normally. They are also much closer to the average person than the elitist Sarajevans. The overqualified Yugoslavs are seen as elitist, whereas the HDZ, SDS and the SDA [the leading political parties] have members and supporters on the ground facing the same problems as you.

When asked why (if there was so little support within Bosnia for the approach of these groups) the OSCE considered it a priority to assist their development, Marti's response was: 'They need the money to make them more efficient. But it should be up to the public at the end of the day. I think there is a balance, the public wants the nationalist parties for security, but they also want an opposition'.

The problem with this approach was that the opposition was, in this case, one that was not chosen by the electorate but by the OSCE and other international agencies. Jens Sorenson noted that:

> The local NGO sector is primarily the creation of an urban middle class, which has been squeezed in the social transformation in the new republics. With polarization increasing... as the ethnic states reward supporters of the ruling party, what remains of the politicized middle class can find a new niche in NGOs. Here the distinction between NGOs as social movements or as service providers becomes unclear. (Sorenson, 1997, p. 35)

Zoran Jorgakieski, the OSCE Democratization Branch Coordinator for Dialogue and Reconciliation, expanded on the problem:

> These groups are all run by intellectuals but they have very little influence. During the war they stayed aside and withdrew from politics. These are the people we have to focus upon. They are a minority, but the best, the cream of Bosnian intellectual society. They have good relations with their colleagues across the Inter-Entity Boundary Line. They are top intellectuals, you can't expect ordinary people to understand them. The language they use is too complicated. People doubt they are good patriots.

There was a large gap between the civil society associations funded and supported by the OSCE, and other international peacebuilding institutions, and Bosnian people. For the OSCE and the international community, this gap demonstrated the lack of a democratic culture in Bosnia. While few people were actively involved in civil society associations, leaving them predominantly middle-class based, the main nationalist parties still easily attained the majority of the votes in elections. In response to this gap, Adrien Marti advised some of the new civil society groups which became established as political parties before the September 1997 municipal elections, to abandon electoral competition after the local polls and become NGOs instead: 'They have no chance as political parties', he argued, these 'groups would have much more influence as NGOs and lobby groups than as political parties with 0.001 per cent of the vote'.

There was little evidence that this civil society strategy was helping to challenge support for the nationalist parties or to overcome ethnic segmentation and division in Bosnia. The OSCE Democratization Branch, in its attempts to celebrate cross-community cooperation and turn this into an alternative political voice, unfortunately tended to politicise, and consequently problematise, everyday activity that organically contributed to confidence building. While thousands of people crossed the Inter-Entity Boundary Line every day, to work, shop, see relatives, or go to school, this was seen as everyday life going on and making the best of the situation (USDoS, 1997, Section 2d). The people whose lives involved cross-entity cooperation did not necessarily want to turn everyday survival into a political movement.

The moment these actions were politicised, they became an implicit threat to the status quo and created a backlash to a perceived threat that did not exist previously. As an experienced Senior Democratization Officer related: 'I'm surprised they tell us anything anymore. Inter-entity contacts are very common with businesses etc. If I was a businessman I wouldn't report it, not just for tax reasons – no one pays tax anyway – but because it just creates problems'. The OSCE Youth and Education Coordinator explained that the teachers she worked with had not wanted attention to be drawn to them and had told her not to park her OSCE car near to their houses. Similarly, people were much more willing to use the cross-entity bus-line once the OSCE licence plates were removed (USDoS, 1998, Section 2d). People wanted to cross the Inter-Entity Boundary Line, and in some cases to return to their pre-war homes, but without drawing attention to themselves and without their actions being seen as threatening the security of others. Returns that were organised spontaneously had much more success than internationally enforced return under the threat of sanctions that both angered and raised the fears of current residents (Amnesty, 1996; ICG, 1997, p. 13).

Ironically the more support that was given to the 'grass-roots' civil associations by the OSCE, the less effective they tended to be. The unintended consequence of creating civil society NGOs that were reliant on external support had been that they were never forced to build their own base of popular support or take on and challenge the arguments or political programmes of the nationalists. Guaranteed funding and the ear of international policymakers, the Citizens' Parliament and other favoured groups in fact prevented or impeded the development of an opposition with roots in society. As Jens Sorensen noted, the reliance on external funders tended to fragment society rather than create a pluralistic exchange of political opinions (Sorensen, 1997, p. 35). Because the funding of civil society NGOs was portrayed as apolitical assistance to democratisation and peacebuilding, this led to a variety of projects and NGOs being funded with no overall strategy. Instead of building bridges within a society as political parties would have to, in order to aggregate support around a political programme, these NGOs relied on outside funding and therefore had no need to engage in discussion or create broader links to society.

INTERNATIONAL REGULATION AND CIVIL SOCIETY DEVELOPMENT

The points raised above about the democratic status of raising unelected minority groups over political parties elected by majorities, and the dangers of downplaying the electoral process of discussion and debate, highlight general questions over the democratic deficit created by international peacebuilding regulation which attempted to shape the political process. However, consideration of the specific context in which civil society-building was being promoted in Bosnia demands a further clarification of these questions. While commentators often wrote of the need to develop Bosnia-specific programmes of civic capacity-building, they rarely considered the broader context of their work (for example, Smillie, 1996, p. 10). Discussion tended to focus on the problems faced by local civic groups without consideration of the impact of the post-Dayton international administration, nor of its legitimation through a denial of Bosnian people's capacity for self-rule.

The advocates of civil society democratisation strategies were undoubtedly correct in their assertions that democracy was about more than holding elections every few years, and in their emphasis on the need for the consent of the governed, the accountability of policies to the electorate, the opportunity for participation in decision-making, and for the decision-making process to be transparent. In Bosnia there were elections but Bosnian society lacked all the above factors. However, before assuming that greater international attention was necessary for the promotion of NGOs, it would have been worth taking a step back to consider the democratic framework in Bosnia.

Following the 1995 Dayton Peace Agreement, Bosnia underwent a process of internationally imposed peacebuilding. This process had been implemented by the major international powers, including the US, Britain, France, Germany and Russia, under the co-ordination of the Peace Implementation Council. The plans drawn up by this body had then been implemented by leading international institutions, such as the UN, North Atlantic Treaty Organization, OSCE, Council of Europe, International Monetary Fund, World Bank and the European Bank for Reconstruction and Development, under their own mandates, creating a network of regulating and policymaking bodies (see the previous chapter; also Szasz, 1996, p. 304). Coordinating the civilian side of this project had been the OHR for Bosnia, the state's chief administrator with the authority to make and enforce law at both state and entity levels and to dismiss obstructive Bosnian officials.

Dayton initially established this interlocking network of international policymaking forums as part of a one year transition to Bosnian self-government. The Dayton Agreement assumed that with state and entity elections, run under OSCE auspices in September 1996, the external international administration of the state would come to an end. Guarantees of long-term stability were built in to the Bosnian constitution which gave key regulating powers to an IMF-appointed director of the Central Bank and to European Union-appointed judges as final arbiters of law through the Constitutional Court. Other Dayton annexes gave the international community further regulating powers through the establishment of key commissions run by international appointees from the UN, OSCE, Council of Europe and European Bank for Reconstruction and Development (GFA, 1995; see also Chandler, 1999).

Within a few months of the Dayton settlement the Peace Implementation Council (PIC) began to consider the prospects of extending the international peacekeeping process and, by June 1996, was already discussing a two-year 'consolidation period', duely ratified by the PIC in December 1996. The High Representative was mandated to draw up two 12-month policy 'action plans' to be ratified and reviewed at six-monthly PIC meetings. This meant that the newly-elected state and entity governments were reduced to little more than rubber-stamps for predetermined international policies. There was little opportunity for the elected politicians to negotiate their own compromises on issues. Any opposition was met with the threat to cancel donors meetings and the World Bank and IMF refusal to release reconstruction aid. In December 1997, just one year into this extended consolidation period, the international administration of Bosnia became an open-ended international commitment, with no clearly defined point at which even the limited Bosnian self-government, promised by Dayton, could be realised.

This extended process of international peacebuilding involved a 'top-down' approach to democratisation. Governing representatives at municipal, canton, entity and state levels had little choice but to follow international policy at the threat of being dismissed from their posts or having sanctions imposed. This process extended from the tripartite Presidency, from which the Serb member, Momcilo Krajisnik, was threatened with dismissal in October 1997, to the municipal level where the September 1997 election results were only ratified by the OSCE, not in relation to any electoral irregularities but on the basis of policies pursued by elected representatives once in post. This level of external regulation even extended to the international take-over of the state-run television station in RS and the High Representative deciding the national flag of the new country.

While the Bosnian politicians were fully accountable to the international community, there were no mechanisms making international policymaking accountable to the Bosnian people. The International Crisis Group (ICG) acknowledged this 'credibility gap', and their response to it served to highlight the diminished nature of democracy in Bosnia under Dayton. The ICG argued that:

> Respect for Bosnian authorities and basic notions of reciprocity argue for at least the degree of transparency necessary for the Bosnian authorities and people to understand the basis for decisions, and the decision-making processes, that so affect them. If the point of the international encampment in Bosnia is to 'teach' democracy, tolerance and good governance to the Bosnians then there is no better way to start than by example. (ICG, 1996, p. 17)

In this case, democratic accountability was reduced to 'transparency'. 'Teaching democracy' ended up as a call for international institutions to make widely available their future plans and policy goals for the region. This did little to alter the fact that the Bosnian people had no active role in decision-making and were instead reduced to the role of passive onlookers. This level of international regulation gave little opportunity for elected representatives, let alone the general public, to voice their concerns or make any input into policymaking. In a society where even elected officials and judges had to be instructed in what the laws of their own country were, and were compelled to rely on international institutions to provide translations and guidance for them, it was unsurprising that people outside the political elites felt excluded and marginalised from the policymaking process (OSCE, 1997h, p. 3, 1997i, p. 2). The guarantee of a measure of autonomy and political self-government for the three ethnic constituencies, all of whom were minorities in the new state, promised by Dayton, was never delivered.

Far from international peacebuilding rebuilding links between communities, the division between the two entities was increased through differential international treatment. For example, the US re-trained and re-equipped a separate Federation army, and turned down RS calls for military integration. At the same time, economic aid and reconstruction projects were concentrated narrowly within the Federation, with the weaker RS economy receiving less than two per cent of the reconstruction aid in 1996 and less than five per cent in 1997. Limited political autonomy for the two entities, promised by Dayton to grant security to minorities fearful of domination in the new state, was similarly under-mined by international regulation.

Within the Federation the formal divisions of power at cantonal and entity level did not facilitate self-government, instead policy at all levels was imposed from the top-down through the US and UN co-chaired Federation Forum. Concerns of the Bosnian Serbs for equal treatment were little assuaged by international policy: including what was gen-erally perceived as a selective anti-Serb bias in The Hague war crimes tribunal; international community prevention of links with Serbia, allowed under Dayton; the extension of direct international rule over Serb-claimed Brcko; the overruling of the RS Constitutional Court and imposition of new Assembly elections; the international take-over of entity media prior to the 1997 elections; and a new government established through international intervention, which excluded the party which gained the most votes (see OHR, 1997d: Kelly, 1998; O'Connor, 1998).

The lack of security caused by the still-born nature of the self-government proposed under Dayton appeared to be the major barrier for the cross-entity civil society groups funded by the international community. As long as basic political security was lacking from the Dayton framework, and there was no guarantee that entity borders or rights to land, housing or work could be assured, opposition parties and civic groups were seen by many as a potential threat to the status quo which was guaranteeing peaceful coexistence. The OSCE Democratization Branch had no man-date to question Dayton, or the tensions resulting from this lack of autonomy, and therefore dealt with symptoms rather than the under-lying problems. This led to seeing the problems as lying with Bosnian people rather than the framework imposed by external powers. Once the Dayton framework was taken out of the picture, Bosnian concerns about security were interpreted by OSCE officers as either a result of nationalist propaganda, war trauma or ethnic prejudice against other Bosnian groups.

CIVIL SOCIETY AND DEMOCRACY

The impetus behind the reorganisation of the OSCE Bosnia Mission and the establishment of the OSCE Democratization Branch was the inter-national community's decision to extend the peacebuilding mandates of the international institutions following the elections at the end of 1996.

It was only after this decision, in December 1996, that the creation of civil society became a central issue in Bosnia (see USDoS, 1996; PIC, 1996). The focus on civil society legitimated a unique situation. The September 1996 elections were held to have been democratic, and to have met the standards set by the OSCE for the recognition of the results, yet they were also declared to be not democratic enough to allow self-rule. A Democratization Branch information document explained this apparent contradiction:

> In the biggest event since the signing of the Dayton Accords, Bosnia's citizens chose for themselves a legitimate democratically elected system of government in September, 1996...Accordingly the first foundations have been laid for Bosnia to become a democracy. Yet even though elections are essential for the creation of a legitimate democratic state, they are not enough to ensure that democracy in Bosnia prevails. It is a mistake to see elections as the endpoint of democratization. They are in fact an early stage of what remains by definition a long term process. (OSCE, 1997j)

Many commentators would agree that elections can only be part of the broader democratisation process; however there would appear to be a problem in asserting that democracy must be consolidated or democratisation completed before self-government and electoral accountability are permitted. The focus on civil society development thereby served to avoid confronting this problem by moving the focus away from the fact that internationally-made policy was being externally imposed on Bosnian institutions. This new grass-roots approach was welcomed as a long-term international commitment to democratic transition, but it could, of course, also be seen as expressing a more disillusioned approach to the prospects of democracy in Bosnia.

The success of the nationalist parties came as a shock to international peacebuilding actors who had assumed, prior to the September 1996 elections, that tighter international regulation over the political process would enable popular opposition groups to gain a hold on power. Their universally poor showing created a strong air of pessimism about the future of a united Bosnia (Kasapovic, 1997, p. 120). This disillusionment with the choice expressed through the ballot box, resulted in a much more negative view of the capacities of the Bosnian people themselves. The solidification of the peacebuilding project was based on this negative response and disillusionment rather than a sign of the hold of liberal universalism. The impasse of peace-building, of attempting to 'democratize' or 'liberalize' Bosnian society was already a product of this hierarchical and elitist gaze, which failed to accept the genuine voice and needs of society as democratic. The shift from the ad hoc extension of international peacekeeping to peacebuilding-as-statebuilding was already deeply 'illiberal'.

For example, Duncan Bullivant, Spokesman for the High Representative, argued that 'Bosnia is a deeply sick society, ill at ease with even the most basic principles of democracy' (*Washington Post*, 1997). For Christian Ahlund, the OSCE Director General for Human Rights: 'Elections are just the first primitive stage of democracy. Political parties are still a pretty blunt form'. He saw the OSCE's role as a 'peda-gogic' one of informing Bosnian people about international standards and 'telling them what democratization is all about'. This view was supported by a Senior Democratization Coordinator: 'Political parties are a new appearance. People don't know how to cope and neither do their leaders, they have no political programme. People just follow the flock. It is the same with the independent parties, people vote for them just because they are the alternative'.

The disparaging attitude towards ordinary people, 'the flock', was not even diminished when they voted for opposition parties because it was assumed that they were not capable of making an independent judgement. The widespread acceptance of this perspective amongst the NGO-building community was illustrated by the Helsinki Citizens' Assembly organiser in Sarajevo, who explained that the people had no democratic experience and were used to 'living under a strong hand', and that this lack of democratic education had to be challenged through NGOs 'teaching people how to behave and to know right from wrong'. She told a joke to illustrate the problem her NGO faced: 'The opposition party leader asks the peasant why he is not going to vote for him. The peasant says that he will vote for him. The opposition leader asks "when?". The peasant says "when you get in power"'.

Often the analogies about democracy tended to involved uneducated peasants as the symbol of ordinary people. One of the leading officers of the Democratization Branch went further, to the extent of seeing Bosnian people not supportive of civil society initiatives as caught up in the back-ward ideology of feudalism. At the OSCE in Sarajevo, Jasna Malkoc, one of the activists whose ideas lay behind the initiation of the Democratization Branch, openly explained that democratisation would be a long process of changing the culture of the majority of the Bosnian people in order to 'implement the concept of individualism':

> The lack of democratic values stems from the divisions of the Austro-Hungarian Empire which instilled individualistic ideas. Areas outside the Empire had feudalist systems which continued as communist structures. Serbia is feudalist, Croatia is individualist. Bosnia is in-between and the division is between urban, individualist areas and peasant, feudal areas. For example, Banja Luka [in Republika Srpska] is urban and is influenced by the West and Croatia.

A similar perspective, which emphasised the long-term problems of civil society construction, was the psycho-social approach, also pursued by the Democratization Branch. Using this framework, one of the main barriers to building civil society in Bosnia was seen to be psycho-social problems. Much or even most of the population was adjudged by many peacebuilders to be unable to see the gains of a civil society approach, due to the impact of their part as victims or as passive supporters of human rights violations during the war (Mimica, 1995, p. 22). This approach put psycho-social work at the centre of strategies for peacebuilding because: 'These persons may offer special resistance to confidence-building, dialogue and reconciliation efforts due to the victims' mistrust, isolation, demoralisation and anger. Due to symptoms of victimisation, they are also less likely to be willing to take on new responsibilities as active members of civil society' (OSCE, 1997a, pp. 7–8).

Even its advocates admitted that this work was 'entering new territory' where 'not much theory exists' in relation to psycho-social projects (Agger and Mimica, 1996, pp. 27–8). However, these doubts did not figure highly for the Democratization Branch, their Semi-Annual Report stated categorically that 'trauma symptoms have become an obstacle to the implementation of the General Framework Agreement for Peace and the development of pluralistic society in Bosnia' (OSCE, 1997k, p. 15). Central to the OSCE Democratization Branch's approach was the understanding that the Bosnian people, 'damaged' or 'traumatized' by the war and the transition from one-party state regulation, were not capable of acting independently or making choices between 'right and wrong'. This approach was not universally popular with the OSCE Democratization Officers, some of whom mentioned in confidence the dangers of a gap between democratisation in theory and in practice:

> 'It is easy to get patronizing. Bosnian society pre-war was highly developed, it was not the civil society of the West, but these people were not illiterate, or not cultured, or not developed, just different';
>   'Democratization is not a good term – it is like teaching them how to behave – naturally people are sensitive to this. A lot of people are educated, they know theory, and they know right and wrong';
>   'Civil society and democratic values existed – Bosnia had a multi-cultural society, good nationalities policy and progressive policies regarding women'.

However, those that felt awkward with the approach of their superiors did not feel it was possible to express this easily within the organisation: 'There is no discussion about what democracy is ... big principled questions you have to leave out and try to find a corner, an area where you can do good work'.

Taking over the language of empowerment from the psycho-social counselling work being developed in the war, the new focus of the senior officials within the Democratization Branch was on the capacity of individuals for democracy as opposed to that of governments. This meant that the broader framework of political and economic regulation was ignored. If anything, the Democratization Branch work of civil society-building from the bottom-up was perhaps more invidious to peacebuilding and democracy than the enforced international administration, because it implicitly assumed that Bosnian people were 'damaged' and incapable of rational choice. Once the capacity of Bosnian people as rational political actors was negated, whether this was understood as due to feudalism, to ethnic identity or to war trauma, there was little reason for the international administration of the new state to be seen as temporary or 'transitional' in the short-term, or for self-government and democracy to be seen as preferable.

At the end of the day, the civil society approach to peacebuilding not only failed to build support for political alternatives, it also provided carte blanche for the international administrators to override democratic processes, on the grounds that Bosnian voters were not responsible enough to have the rights granted to citizens in Western states. As Klaus Kinkel openly confirmed, in December 1997, the international community had little hesitation in moving to make decisions contrary to the will of the Bosnian people (OHR, 1997e). The implication of this approach was the end of formal democracy, of legitimacy through accountability to the electorate. Democracy was redefined as its opposite, adherence to outside standards not autonomy and accountability. High Representative Carlos Westendorp illustrated the new logic of this reversal of democratic accountability when overruling elected Bosnian representatives on the grounds that in his opinion: 'They have a wrong perspective. They are not serving their population properly' (OHR, 1997c).

Conclusions

This chapter has suggested that attempts to directly engage in society to build support for the international peacebuilding project were counterproductive. There was a link between the low level of support for civil society alternatives to the leading political parties and a lack of democracy in Bosnia. However, the relationship between civil society and democracy was very different from the one suggested by the advocates of greater international support for NGO-led civil society-building strategies.

There was little disagreement that the lack of security was the main political resource of the leading nationalist parties (Woodward, 1996, p. 83; Boyd, 1998). However, the extent of international regulation over Bosnian life, the denial of self-government at local and state level, and the inability of Bosnian political actors to negotiate their own solutions, and thereby give their constituents a level of accountability for policymaking, perpetuated a political climate unconducive to the development of political alternatives. For civil society to have the space to develop, and for alternative opinions to gain a broader audience, the basic questions of political self-government and security for entity borders would have to be settled. As long as there was no assurance that existing rights to land, homes and employment would not be put to question through international administrative decisions, taken above the heads of Bosnian people, the leading nationalist parties remained secure and civil society alternatives marginalised.

With the indefinite extension of international mandates over Bosnia there was little prioritisation of self-government. The OSCE's Democratization Branch had no way of assessing whether their civil society development strategy had only limited success due to the impact of extended international regulation or because of purely local factors which were immune to international democratisation initiatives. According to Siri Rustad, Deputy to the Head of Mission for Democratization:

> It is difficult through the [OSCE] activities to measure the overall democratic level of the country. We can't say for definite that any particular activity in itself has changed anything. We propose a set of different activities but then measure them on other levels – the running of institutions, the role of NGOs, the views of the Peace Implementation Conference etc. We don't have a broader theoretical approach at all. That's how the Mission works – its concerned with practical results.

The lack of any way of accounting for the success or failure of civil society-building projects meant that the assumption of leading OSCE officers that there were long-term cultural barriers to democracy was never an issue. Once extended democratisation mandates ignored political power and relations between political elites and the international community and instead focused on ethnic segmentation and civil society, assessment became a subjective exercise in the measurement of attitudes and culture. The lack of progress in peacebuilding only reinforced the idea that the people were too backward or traumatised to be able to cope with political choices. The solution then was not to question the theoretical framework that informed the approach of top-down imposition and bottom-up empowerment, but to tinker with the programmes and call for more resources. As the process continued, a vicious circle – the impasse of peacebuilding – was created, in which the Bosnian people were seen to be less capable of political autonomy and the international community appeared ever more necessary to guarantee peaceful and democratic development.

CHAPTER 6

The Institutionalist Approach

Introduction

Peacebuilding-as-statebuilding was informed by the institutionalist approach: the belief that external experts can help to provide the institutional scaffolding which would form the preconditions for successful peacebuilding. This approach of external institution-building was developed in Bosnia first, then expanded to Kosovo and East Timor and, to all intents and purposes, reached its highpoint with the discussions over governance reform in Iraq in 2003, where many policymakers turned to the Bosnia and Herzegovina experience for lessons in peacebuilding. The key lesson advocated at this point by international officials was the prioritisation of the 'rule of law' rather than the focus on political processes and elections. It was held that while regular elections merely reinforced the dominance of political elites hostile to reform, internationally imposed legal changes could galvanize the peacebuilding process. This approach was captured well in the work of Roland Paris who reflected the impasse of peacebuilding in advocating 'Insitutionalization before Liberalization'. For Paris, holding elections would be problematic if the institutional framework of democracy, markets and the rule of law were not in place beforehand (see, Paris, 2004).

As considered in the previous chapter, the impasse of international peacebuilding was driven by its core discursive construction of Western institutional capacity-building on the basis of the lack of capacities of post-conflict or conflict-prone populations. The more international

© The Author(s) 2017

D. Chandler, *Peacebuilding*, Rethinking Peace and Conflict Studies, DOI 10.1007/978-3-319-50322-6_6 peacebuilders sought to build peace over the heads of the peoples and societies they worked within, the more problems and barriers to peace appeared (problematising the withdrawal or pulling back of international troops and resources) and the more incapable local populations were seen to be. This chapter analyses the limits of this perspective and the impasse constituted, through focusing on three areas of legal activism in Bosnia-Herzegovina: constitutional change, property return and employment laws. It highlights that the 'rule of law' approach, in seeing legal or administrative solutions as a short cut to addressing political problems, fetishised the legal framework at the same time as it marginalised the political sphere. Rather than more coercive external involvement in the form of pressures for more legislation and better law enforcement, the experience of Bosnia highlighted the need for greater levels of political legitimacy, a need that contradicted the logic of the 'rule of law' approach.

THE LESSONS OF BOSNIA AND HERZEGOVINA

In 2003 as questions were raised about the US-led coalition's preparations for post-war transition to self-government in Iraq, the need to learn the lessons from the Bosnian experience of post-conflict peacebuilding was frequently raised. In the US and British press, the voice of the (at that time) international High Representative for Bosnia, Lord Paddy Ashdown was one of the loudest, questioning why we were 'seemingly endlessly condemned to re-inventing the wheel when it comes to peacekeeping?' (Ashdown, 2003a).

The key lesson for Iraq, according to Ashdown, was that of 'the overriding priority... of establishing the rule of law' (2003a; see also, 2003b). Ashdown attributed the slow progress made in Bosnia to the fact that, initially, the international administration focused on working with political representatives rather than on imposing a comprehensive legal framework: 'This, above all was the mistake we made in Bosnia... It is much more important to establish the rule of law quickly than to establish democracy quickly. Because without the former, the latter is soon undermined. In Bosnia, we got these priorities the wrong way round' (Ashdown, 2003a). According to Ashdown, the international administrators were slow to learn that when it comes to peacebuilding, 'the process is sequential'; a 'bitter price' was paid in failing to understand 'the paramount importance of establishing the rule of law as the foundation of democratic development'. That price was allegedly still being paid in facing the impasse of peacebuilding in Bosnia, an impasse Ashdown believed to be caused by entrenched political opposition to peacebuilding reforms:

> Now we are starting to win this battle for the rule of law in Bosnia. But it is tough, because we are fighting an entrenched enemy that reaches into every corner of politics, government and the state. And it is much tougher than it would have been if we had made the rule of law our number one task in the first year rather than in the sixth. (Ashdown, 2003a)

Bosnia was not the only example where political extremism, criminal profiteering, corruption and regional patronage networks were seen to have undermined international peacebuilding initiatives (see, for example, Kaldor, 1999, pp. 6–9; Shaw, 1999; Duffield, 2001). In his pre-departure press conference in December 2000, Bernard Kouchner, the senior UN official in Kosovo, said the 'lesson of Kosovo' was that 'peacekeeping missions need to arrive with a law-and-order kit made up of trained police, judges, and prosecutors and a set of draconian security laws' (Smith, 2000). Following the experiences of international peacebuilding regimes in Bosnia and Kosovo, the continuing instability and the 'light footprint' of the international community security forces in Afghanistan added to fears that current peacebuilding strategies had been inadequate (see, for example, Ignatieff, 2003; Chesterman, 2002b). There was widespread concern that the breakdown of law and order in Iraq following the collapse of the Saddam regime would result in a 'criminalization' of the Iraqi state or in a new outbreak of ethnic and religious strife which could leave large areas of the country in chaos (Smith, 2003; USIP, 2003).

The argument for the sequencing of the rule of law before rolling back the authority of the international peacebuilding projects was at the heart of calls for peacebuilding reforms. The influential 2000 Brahimi panel report on UN peace operations suggested that: 'These missions' tasks would have been much easier if a common United Nations justice package had allowed them to apply an interim legal code to which mission personnel could have been pre-trained while the final answer to the "applicable law" question was being worked out' (United Nations, 2000b, Para 81). Since then, other reports concurred about the need for a rapid introduction of a judicial package supported by effective military forces that could quickly subdue armed opposition, perform basic constabulary tasks, and ensure that civilian law enforcement officers and administrative officials could perform their functions in an atmosphere of relative security (for example, USIP, 2003; King's College, 2003).

By the early 2000s, there was a consensus among international policy-makers that peacebuilding could be 'sequenced' with 'the rule of law' establishing the basis for reconstruction and democratic elections. This 'more muscular' approach to peacebuilding, held to be necessary to deal with criminalised or fragile post-conflict states, where social democratic forces had been marginalised through authoritarian rule, conflict and the privatisation or fragmentation of social networks, was applied to Bosnia under Ashdown's administration (*Washington Post*, 2002). This perspective suggested that the US–British transitional authority in Iraq should concentrate on imposing their control over the territory and ensuring the success of 'an exercise in state building from outside on a scale that has never been attempted before' rather than handing over power 'prematurely' to Iraqi representatives (Hutton, 2003). Transition to Iraqi rule prior to establishing the framework of the 'rule of law' would, in this scenario, leave the path open for power to be consolidated by elites with no interest in peacebuilding, for example, those with links to the previous Ba'athist regime or to fundamentalist religious groupings with support from neighbouring states.

This chapter analyses how the approach of prioritising the 'rule of law' merely heightened the impasse of international peacebuilding, through having the unintended consequence of creating further instability and fragmentation through delaying a political framework capable of giving people a say in the running of their country. 'Rule of law' regulation through the prioritisation of law above the political sphere could not compensate for, or overcome, the political problems involved in peace-building and post-war reconstruction. In Bosnia, international policy, which sought to marginalise the sphere of politics, institutionalised the ethnic and regional divides rather than overcoming them. Progress in the 'rule of law' was promoted by the Office of the High Representative (OHR) as demonstrating the major improvements made under international administration, despite the continued political division of the small state.

This chapter uses the example of Bosnia heuristically to illustrate that the gap between the internationally imposed laws and the politically expressed will of Bosnian society, at the heart of the justification for externally imposed legislation, created a 'rule of law' impasse. This impasse is drawn out below, in examples which illustrate that the attempt to privilege law above politics in fact weakened and discredited the 'rule of law' rather than strengthening it. First, while the imposed laws may have appeared to be very impressive achievements on paper, they did not necessarily reflect or encourage an improvement in practice. Second, and more importantly, the development of the 'rule of law' through the external imposition of legislation undermined the process of consensus-building necessary to give post-conflict populations a stake in the peace-building process.

The following sections consider briefly three areas of legislation publicly justified as necessary to undermine the power of political forces held to oppose post-war reconstruction. In each of these cases the 'rule of law' was developed and imposed over the opposition of Bosnian political representatives. The areas have been selected on the basis of their prominence in international reports on progress in the region. They are: first, the imposition of new constitutional changes that sought to marginalise the governing influence of the main nationalist political parties; second, the imposition of housing legislation allowing refugees and displaced people to return to their pre-war homes; and third the imposition of public sector job allocations, particularly in the police force, in proportion to the pre-war 1991 census figures.

'THE RULE OF LAW' AND POLITICAL REPRESENTATION

In September 2000, the constitutional court of Bosnia ruled that the general principle of political equality of the three constituent peoples should hold throughout Bosnia and both the political entities, the Bosniak–Croat Federation and the Serb-dominated Republika Srpska (RS). This decision, which affected the entity constitutions, was pushed through by the three non-Bosnian, internationally appointed, judges but with the support of only the two Bosniak judges. The two Serb and two Croat judges opposed the ruling.

Already clearly politically divisive, this general ruling on principle was then used by the international administration to radically reshape the political framework. In January 2001 the High Representative issued a decree creating two constitutional commissions, which met to discuss specific textual proposals for constitutional change, already drawn up by an international taskforce (OHR, 2001a; ESI, 2002a, p. 2). The Mrakovica–Sarajevo 'Agreement on the Implementation of the Constituent Peoples' Decision of the Constitutional Court of Bosnia and Herzegovina' was finally imposed by the OHR in March 2002 (OHR, 2002a). Although signed by representatives of the United States and the European Union, the Agreement was not supported by Bosnian representatives despite its perceived constitutional importance as 'an addendum to the Dayton Agreement' (Bisenić, 2002). The new constitution was imposed by three decrees requiring constitutional changes in the two entities and reforming the election laws. According to the then High Representative, Wolfgang Petritsch, imposition was necessary: 'I'm not going to allow . . . nationalist parties . . . to prevent them from taking effect. As a guarantor of the Mrakovica–Sarajevo Agreement, I simply cannot accept the continuing obstruction on the side of these nationalistic dinosaurs. I cannot allow the prospect that these . . . parties could hold the citizens of this country hostage' (OHR, 2002b).

The implications for the governments of both the entities were extensive. Section II, covering the distribution of key political posts stated:

> PM and Deputy Prime Ministers may not come from the same constituent people. Out of the following positions not more than 2 may be filled by representatives of any one constituent people or of the group of Others: 1) Prime Minister 2) Speaker of the House of Representatives/Republika Srpska National Assembly 3) Speaker of the House of Peoples/Council of Peoples 4) President of Supreme Court 5) President of Constitutional Court 6) Public Prosecutors. Presidents of Entities – the President shall have two Vice- Presidents coming from different constituent peoples. (OHR, 2002a, Section 7274#2)

Of the six most important positions in RS only two, or one-third, could be held by Bosnian Serbs. This was held to be a major step forward for democratising the Serb entity because the governing representatives would be dominated by non-Serbs although the majority of the population were Serb. Section III of the Agreement covered in greater detail the 'minimum representation in the government of the Federation of Bosnia and Herzegovina and of the Republika Srpska', stating:

> The RS Government (Prime Minister and 16 ministers) shall be composed of 8 Serb, 5 Bosniak and 3 Croat ministers. One Other may be nominated by the Prime Minister from the quota of the largest constituent people. There shall be additionally a Prime Minister who shall have two Deputy Prime Ministers from different constituent peoples selected from among the Ministers; and the Federation Government (Prime Minister and 16 ministers)

shall be composed of 8 Bosniak, 5 Croat and 3 Serb ministers. One Other may be nominated by the Prime Minister from the quota of the largest constituent people. There shall be additionally a Prime Minister who shall have two Deputy Prime Ministers from different constituent peoples selected from among the Ministers. (OHR, 2002a, Section 7274#3)

The new framework radically transformed the governments of Bosnia, particularly in RS. For Petritsch, the use of the law to implement drastic reforms to the peace settlement was immensely pleasing. He stressed 'that never ever in the three years of my mandate in Bosnia and Herzegovina have I experienced a feeling of such profound relief and satisfaction' (OHR, 2002a). On paper the three main nationalist parties lost their power and control; governments at both the entity and state level were based on multi-ethnicity rather than votes. The October 2002 elections demonstrated the apparent necessity of adopting this strategy of using the law to reshape Bosnian politics. Representatives of the three main nationalist parties, the SDA (Stranka Demokratska Akcija – Party of Democratic Action), SDS (Srpska Demokratska Stranka – Serbian Democratic Party), and the HDZ (Hrvatska Demokratska Zajednica – Croatian Democratic Community), won the Bosniak, Serb, and Croat seats in the three-member Bosnian Presidency. At the state level, and in the elections for the entity parliaments, the HDZ, SDS and SDA were the leading parties in their respective ethnic constituencies, yet were restricted to minority positions in ruling authorities.

The manipulation of election and constitutional laws produced a situation where the results of the elections had no relationship to the expressed will of Bosnia's citizens at the ballot box. It was not just at the level of entity governments that multi-ethnic political representation was imposed from above, regardless of the ethnic composition of the electorate. At the local level of municipal government and at cantonal level in the Federation the constitutional amendments were used to break the hold of majority political parties elected to power where there was a clear ethnic majority. Representation on the basis of the population census of 1991, rather than on the basis of existing constituents, meant that in some towns the representatives of the leading political party or even the town mayor lived outside the town, in some cases many miles away, or even in another entity (ICG, 2002a, p. 26; Sokolović, 2003). This heightened political tensions and raised questions over the legitimacy of policy made by people who did not have to live with the consequences of their decisions.

The imposition of constitutional arrangements that sought to ameliorate the influence of nationalist political parties did little to strengthen the Bosnian political framework. Institutions which were run by politicians elected on few votes, and who had little connection to the people whose lives they were regulating over, had little political legitimacy and were unable to secure wider support for the political settlement (see Chandler, 2002b). While the constitutional changes produced governments that looked good on paper, they institutionalised and perpetuated the problems which they sought to address. The fact that these institutions were dependent on international administrators to appoint them and oversee their operation meant they perpetuated divisions and external dependencies.

As long as the political settlement was dependent on external regulation, the questions of ethnic insecurity and uncertainty over the future remained. Rather than the nationalist parties losing credibility their support was cemented by international manipulation of the political process (Bieber, 2001; ICG, 2001). The use of the 'rule of law' to reform the political process merely resulted in the undermining of Bosnia's political institutions. With growing cynicism over the political process, there was little surprise that only just over half the population wished to vote in the elections of October 2002 (OHR, 2002d).

THE LAW ON PROPERTY RETURN

Annex 7 of the Dayton Peace Agreement, Article 1(1), stated that: 'All refugees and displaced persons have the right freely to return to their homes of origin. They shall have the right to have restored to them property of which they were deprived in the course of hostilities since 1991 and to be compensated for any property that cannot be restored to them' (GFA, 1995). The issue of property return to displaced people and refugees had been held to be a central part of the struggle to enforce the 'rule of law' against the sectional interests of the main political parties. According to many international policymakers, refugees and displaced people were up against the self-interest of political elites in two ways:

> Bosnians wishing to return to areas where they will be a minority population face a double barrier. Nationalists in their former home-towns work to impede their return through administrative obstruction, intimidation and violence, more often than not with the connivance of local (and higher)

authorities. Furthermore, the nationalist elites who rely on these derasci-
nated populations as reservoirs of support also work to prevent their return.
(DPI, 2002, p. 12)

For the international community, imposing the 'rule of law' meant
'squeezing' the 'opaque corrupt political and criminal networks' and
'help[ing] uproot the deadwood that had no interest in Bosnia func-
tioning for its citizens – of any ethnicity' (DPI, 2002, p. 12). In
November 1998 the international community acted to impose legislation in the Federation insisting that the right to repossess pre-war
property took precedence over any rights that local authorities had
granted to the current occupant. In April 1999 similar laws were
imposed in RS (see OHR, 1998, 1999). These laws were later
strengthened and harmonised by the High Representative. The implementation of property legislation met with resistance throughout
Bosnia and entailed detailed regulation and enforcement by international agencies, including the UN High Commission for Refugees, the
OHR, the Organization for Security and Co-operation in Europe and
UN Mission in Bosnia. The UN International Police Task Force supervised local police to ensure that evictions took place and international
officials took over the running of reluctant local housing offices, setting
quotas to be resolved and overseeing the management on a day-by-day
basis (ICG, 2002a, p. 9; OHR, 2002c). The High Representative also
used his 1997 Bonn–Petersburg powers to dismiss over 30 mayors and
other municipal officials held to have obstructed the implementation of
property laws and the exercise of the right to return. Even with the
international community effectively running local housing authorities
and removing any scope for discretion the solution was not straightforward. This was because property return was a political not a purely legal
question.

Studies of the return situation and the imposition of the property
legislation demonstrated that the imposition of laws was not the same as
refugee return itself. On paper the more coercive international policy
seemed to be paying dividends. By the end of September 2002 it was
reported that 150,000 (62 per cent of applicants) had been successful in
reclaiming their property (ICG, 2002a, p. 1). However, forcing through
property returns in a situation of uncertainty merely resulted in the 'legally
dubious but increasingly common practice of selling off property claims
before they have been realised' or in the legally fine but politically

counterproductive selling of the property, often to the family which were the former occupants (Heimerl, 2002).

Although the imposition of property legislation against the will of local authorities was promoted as a key example where the 'rule of law' protections of human rights and equal treatment had taken precedence over Bosnian political will, there was little accounting for the success of this policy on the ground. According to the International Crisis Group: 'No international organisation or government agency has precise figures on how many Bosnians, after reclaiming their houses or flats – or receiving reconstruction assistance – then decide to sell or exchange them and relocate elsewhere. Both anecdotal evidence and classified advertisements in the newspapers suggest that the practice is widespread' (ICG, 2002a, p. 11).

In fact, the OHR was happy to connive in the artificial conflation of 'law' and 'reality' in order to give the impression of progress. In July 2001 the High Representative decreed an end to the two-year moratorium on re-sale in the Federation (OHR, 2001b). After the decree, applications for repossession from refugees 'shot up', the motivation being for sales rather than return (ICG, 2002a, p. 11). Along with not keeping figures distinguishing permanent return from selling or exchanging property, the High Representative was willing to compromise on permanent return in order to boost the success of property law implementation.

The majority of the property law returns were implemented for socially owned apartments in urban areas rather than private property in rural areas. This gave a misleading impression because it was precisely urban municipal properties that were most likely to be exchanged or sold. Permanent return was most often centred on villages because in the towns economic opportunities were scarce, while in the rural areas economic survival was helped through a reliance on subsistence agriculture (ICG, 2002a, p. 10). Even if property sold or exchanged is excluded, many of the properties returned were not occupied by their legal owners and either left vacant or rented out. Media in Sarajevo reported that as many as 10,000 repossessed apartments in the canton remained empty, representing half the properties repossessed. In Dvar about 500 Serb owners of repossessed and privatised flats signed rental agreements allowing displaced Croats to stay on. Similar arrangements existed in Foca where Bosniaks repossessed their flats but rented them out to displaced Serbs.

Often even where property figures did represent actual returns, the level of return was only a partial one, and did not represent a return to pre-war patterns of integration. In many cases where there was return to pre-war housing, the figures were misleading as only part of the family returned, particularly older family members while school-age children were likely to remain in or be sent back to their 'majority' areas (ICG, 2002a, p. 11). In cities such as Prijedor and Sarajevo, survey results indicated that many people who returned continued to commute to work in the places where they were formerly displaced (ICG, 2002a, p. 2).

The 'rule of law' perspective, as imposed by international administrators, attempted to impose a return to the pre-war situation. After four years of war and eight years of living apart, many people had made new lives for themselves, either in Western states, neighbouring states or in other parts of Bosnia. Former sociology professor at Sarajevo University, Dzemal Sokolović, argued that the demographic map could never be put back to 1991. Refugees and those displaced – with new opportunities elsewhere in Bosnia or new national citizenship status in Switzerland, Canada or Sweden – could not be expected to return to their previous lives in Bosnia and, of course, the war dead (estimated at between 30,000 and 250,000) would never return (Sokolović, 2003). While the international community provided support for the return of refugees, it had been left to municipal authorities to look after the needs of displaced persons who did not want to return to their pre-war housing. This section of society was the most vulnerable group in society, with only tenuous rights to welfare and housing. The imposition of property laws contributed to these social and economic tensions, causing a secondary displacement of people on a large scale with more than 150,000 families vacating claimed property and another 100,000 facing eviction. Their care fell to local authorities already under tremendous financial strains (ESI, 2002b, p. 14).

However, from the perspective of the international administrators, any attempt to respond to new needs created by population changes brought about by the war and economic and social transition was problematised and seen as preventing a return to the 1991 ethnic balance. Local authority attempts to address the needs of displaced people living within their area were perceived to be criminal actions designed to shore up the gains of ethnic cleansing (see also Mani, 2002). The distribution of building plots, construction materials, business premises and commercial estate to displaced persons was seen as problematic as this 'cemented' ethnic cleansing, as did the provision of employment.

Many local authorities had been building new housing, something which would normally be seen as positive in the post-war situation. However, new construction was seen as questionable because it inevitably reinforced the post-war status quo. In Pale, Sokolac, Srpska Ilidza and Srpsko Novo Sarajevo thousands of new houses and flats had been built to meet the needs of Serbs displaced from the Federation. RS municipalities previously linked to Sarajevo had been particularly active in building commercial enterprises – hotels, cafés and other businesses on socially owned land. Those involved in authorising and supplying these projects were investigated by OHR staff. In April 2000 the OHR issued an edict banning the use of socially owned land without explicit OHR permission. In order to build on free land, the authorities had to petition the OHR for a waiver on the grounds that its use was 'non-discriminatory and in the best interests of the public' (OHR, 2000). A year later, the OHR wrote to all municipal authorities informing them that the waiver system also applied retrospectively to all transactions since 6 April 1992, throwing into question 96 per cent of land transactions made over this time (ESI, 2002b, pp. 3–9).

Petritsch and his successor Ashdown sacked town mayors and other municipal officials for the crime of making land allocations without adequate permission (ICG, 2002a, p. 13). Yet the OHR was ill-equipped to deal with the enormity of the new powers of decision-making it had awarded itself, covering over 53 per cent of the country's territory, since all urban land, 90 per cent of forests and 10 per cent of agricultural land was socially owned (ESI, 2002b, p. 3). Even welfare policies, such as giving low-interest loans to war veterans and the families of those killed, in order to purchase flats in new blocks, were criticised. All these policies were held by Bosnia's unaccountable rulers to perpetuate current ethnic imbalances rather than encourage a return to pre-war housing allocations (ICG, 2002a, p. 12).

The gap between the Bosnia of the 2000s and pre-war Bosnia continually brought out the problematic nature of international 'rule of law' enforcement. When elected representatives responded to the wishes of the electorate they were held to be pursuing criminal interests or to be 'cementing ethnic cleansing'. The biggest problem with the imposition of the 'rule of law' and focus on the imposed policy aims of the international administrators, rather than political solutions negotiated by Bosnians themselves, was that it was very difficult for society to move forward. There was an open threat that opposition to international regulation would be criminalised along with solutions aimed at enabling people to look forward and establish new lives. Ashdown argued that 'we've invented a new human right here, the right to return after a war', by which he meant not post-war return to one's country but to reclaim and return to one's own home (ICG, 2002a, p. 39). The 'human right' to put the pieces back together to the pre-war status quo was not one that had been decided upon by the people of post-war Bosnia (nor one insisted upon by the Dayton Agreement itself which, under the constitutional rules of Annex 4, explicitly guaranteed the 'right to liberty of movement and residence', GFA, 1995). Across the political parties, regardless of ethnicity, there was a recognition that land allocation policies to displaced people was essential to facilitate returns and restore a sense of security to all ethnic groups (ESI, 2002b, p. 30). However, arguments for the rule of politics, on behalf of those living in Bosnia, rather than the 'rule of law', on behalf of the international bureaucracy, were rejected by the international administration, and Bosnian calls for a new census to be held were condemned for seeking to legitimise post-war population shifts.

LAW ON EMPLOYMENT IN PUBLIC INSTITUTIONS

One of the most widely praised legal developments was the Mrakovica– Sarajevo Agreement of March 2002, referred to above. Section IV of the Agreement covered: 'proportionate representation in all public authorities, including courts' and states:

> Constituent peoples and members of the group of Others shall be proportionately represented in public institutions in the Federation of Bosnia and Herzegovina and in Republika Srpska...As a constitutional principle, such proportionate representation shall follow the 1991 census until Annex 7 is fully implemented. (OHR, 2002a, Section 7274#4)

In this context, the figures and claims of success for multi-ethnic policing were particularly significant because Bosnian police forces were the only public institution that the international community had systematically sought to integrate prior to the new constitutional ruling.

In restructuring agreements signed with the Federation in 1996 and RS in 1998, the UN set down quotas for the recruitment of 'minority' officers. In the Federation, forces were meant to reflect the pre-war national composition of each municipality; in the RS the quotas were less exacting (ICG, 2002b). As of March 2002 there were 307 non-Serb police officers in RS and 633 Serbs and 'Others' in the Federation. The RS police academy had 562 non-Serb cadets who had graduated or were in training and the Federation academy had 516 Serb cadets (ESI, 2002a, p. 5).

The UN Mission in Bosnia (UNMIBH) had responsibility for police reform until the end of December 2002 when the EU assumed responsibility. Former head of the UN mission, Jacques Klein, argued that the police reforms made little difference:

> Initially, it was assumed that the rule of law could be achieved solely by reforming the police. The thin slice of the international mandate given to UNMIBH in 1996 was confined to non-executive police reform and restructuring... Consequently, there is an imbalance between the components of the rule of law. Local police and corrections personnel have reached a baseline of professionalism and democratic policing. All other elements, namely: courts, judges, prosecutors, legal codes, the rules of evidence and criminal procedure, and witness protection, still require radical reform and restructuring. (Klein, 2002)

Klein's comments indicated the limits of seeking to address the question of post-conflict peacebuilding through the imposition of new laws. The broader problems with the legal system in Bosnia revealed that the question of rights was intimately tied to broader questions of social, political and economic transformation which could not be addressed by the swoop of the administrator's pen and sending round a few policemen (see Pugh and Cooper, 2004, Chapter 5).

However, it could be argued that even Klein exaggerated the achievements made in this area. The International Crisis Group argued that the numbers were misleading and that few of the ethnic minority police officers were experienced officers of a high rank (ICG, 2002a, p. 16). Those that did take employment in areas dominated by another nationality often ended up marginalised and sidelined by not being issued with weapons or badges, prevented from participating in investigations or being assigned to menial jobs such as parking attendant (ICG, 2002a, pp. 17, 28, 2002b, p. 41). Studies into police reform in Bosnia suggested that the top-down imposition of ethnic quotas, while impressive on paper, was not sustainable in the absence of international pressure (Celador, 2002).

Despite the problems with the high profile restructuring of the police along the lines of ethnic proportionality, the international administrators argued that they needed to impose ethnic proportionality across the whole public sector. According to the OHR: 'For Republika Srpska, the Agreement states that Bosniaks, Croats and Others have to fill posts in the public administration, from the municipal level to the entity level, according to the 1991 census. This means 45 per cent of all posts – tens of thousands of jobs' (Stiglmayer, 2002). The High Representative stated that, following the Agreement in the RS: 'We have so many more opportunities now in the administration, in the judiciary. There are literally hundreds, if not thousands, of new jobs that are now being made available for Croats and for Bosniaks' (OHR, 2002b).

The High Representative's claim that jobs in the public sector would be allocated on the basis of the 1991 census was clearly problematic. With unemployment officially at 40 per cent for Bosnia as a whole and a weak private sector (accounting for a mere 35 per cent of GDP), public institutions were the largest employers. Any redistribution of public sector jobs in this context, as the International Crisis Group noted, was bound to 'prove difficult for both practical and political reasons' (ICG, 2002a, p. 38).

The motivation for the law based on the 1991 census was the belief that the distribution of public sector posts needed to be challenged. However the law was not necessarily the best mechanism to do this. In Visegrad, for example, the law insisted that 63 per cent of the posts, in the municipal government and administration, should be held by Bosniaks despite the fact that they made up only around three per cent of the post-war population. Further up the Drina valley the law stated that in Foca 52 per cent of the public sector jobs should go to the Bosniaks, though they constituted only six per cent of the population. On the lower Drina in Zvornik, the Bosniak population of 15 per cent was entitled to 59 per cent of government posts (ICG, 2002a, p. 38).

The 'public interest', as interpreted by international law-makers, was held to dictate that what was relevant for public sector employment was the population census of 1991 rather than the population situation 10 years after the war had ended. When the 'rule of law' insisted that 63 per cent of public sector jobs or of government posts should be preserved for just three per cent of the local population, it was clear that the law would either only be imposed through increasing local antagonisms between ethnic groups or that the law would be ignored, risking economic and political sanctions against the region concerned. Rather than the 'rule of law' guaranteeing the basis for peace and reconstruction, these laws were simply statements of intent arising from the minds of international administrators rather than the needs or interests of those affected by them.

As James Heartfield noted, the tendency to develop policies based on the 'good ideas' of bureaucrats, portrayed their distance from the societies which they sought to regulate (Heartfield, 2002, p. 193). While law-making may seem to be a quick and public show of concern about an issue, the experience of Bosnia indicated that legal 'solutions' with little relationship to the political context would inevitably have little effect or produce unintended consequences. This high-handed approach was pursued by the US–UK 'authority' in Iraq and the reliance on legal edicts to address political problems could be seen in the early administrative 'Orders' of the Coalition Provisional Authority. Chief administrator, Paul Bremer's Order No.1, the so-called 'de-Ba'athification' decree had the effect of threatening tens of thousands of public sector Iraqi professionals in education and the health service with dismissal for membership, contributing little to reconstruction or attempts to win support for the regime among the small Iraqi middle class (CPA, 2003a; Steele, 2003b). Order No.2 dissolved the Iraqi army, making thousands of men unemployed and at a stroke removing the one force best equipped for tackling many of the security tasks (CPA, 2003b).

The 'Rule of Law'?

Even the advocates of the 'rule of law' realised that the external imposition of 'law' had been problematic in Bosnia. For example, the Democratization Policy Institute suggested:

> International experts are poorly poised to craft such sets of laws. The track record of internationals drafting laws for Bosnia is abysmal. Legal experts who parachute into Sarajevo on six-month contracts, have little grasp of the Bosnian context, no understanding of the language, and who don't have to live with the results of their work, have made a mess of attempts to reform Bosnian statutes...The muddle resulting from internationals drafting detailed statutes leaves the Bosnian people understandably feeling like guinea pigs. (DPI, 2002, p. 15)

For the Democratization Policy Institute and other policy think tanks the problem was a technical rather than a political one. Internationals involved in the drawing up of laws were too often more focused on 'high salaries, low expenses and a "per-diem rich environment"', resulting in bad laws (DPI, 2002, p. 15).

The Democratization Policy Institute recognised that there was a gap between the laws imposed and the needs and sensitivities of the society in which they were meant to take effect and argued that this gap could be closed by giving selected Bosnians a larger role in the law-making process. They suggested that these Bosnians could be selected by international officials rather than by political representatives: 'Because the Bosnian political system is broken, OHR should not defer to it...selecting the small group of Bosnians itself' (DPI, 2002, p. 15). This influential policy institute was typical in its response to the impasse of peacebuilding, suggesting that laws should be drawn up by international experts and the OHR, in the light of consultation with local experts, while stressing forcibly that 'politicians should be excluded' (DPI, 2002, p. 15).

For the Institute, the problem with external imposition of the law in the 'public interest' was a technical, not a political one. It was precisely this narrow understanding of both law and politics that was problematic for international peacebuilding administrations such as the one in Bosnia-Herzegovina. No better was promised in Iraq. The US chief administrator hand-picked 25 Iraqi 'representatives' to form a Governing Council, but few of its members represented substantial domestic constituencies and their role was consultative rather than legislative (CPA, 2003c; Clover, 2003; Al-Khafaji, 2003).

The narrow understanding of both politics – which was dismissed as irrelevant to public needs, and of law – which was seen as an off-the-peg external solution, had little in common with the traditional liberal-democratic meaning of the 'rule of law'. The rule of law had historically been understood in relation to the modern democratic framework and in contrast to the rule of bureaucratic regulation or authoritarian repression (Dicey, 1959, pp. 202–3). The 'rule of law' had not meant merely that there was a set of rules and regulations or laws, backed up by the military, police and the courts. It also meant that this framework was predicated on consent, the equality of rights and the autonomy of individuals. It is important to stress the qualitative difference between the classic liberal-democratic approach, which derived rights from self-governing human subjects, and the peacebuilding-as-statebuilding 'rule of law' approach of externally imposing a rights framework outside of the political process of debate and consensus-building.

The central component of all democratic systems of rights or legal systems, and their theoretical starting point, was the individual's capacity for self-government. The subject of the modern law was a person assumed to be a moral agent or self-willing actor. As a rights-bearing subject the person was not simply coerced into accepting the law by forces outside their influence. The law was seen to be freely accepted and to derive from their will. The framework of regulation of the modern democratic system was historically and logically derived from the formal assumption of equal self-governing individuals, responsible and accountable for their actions and capable of rational decision-making. All modern doctrines of the enforcement of contract, the punishment of crime, the election of govern-ments and the state system of international law rested on this core assump-tion (Heartfield, 1996). This can be usefully highlighted by a brief consideration of the different facets of a modern state's 'rights-framework' or legal system.

Civil law was the clearest expression of the derivation of the law from the will of the self-governing subject. In enforcing the law of contract, civil law did not impose an alien or external goal onto individuals. In fact, the civil law only bound individuals to their word; this was an expression of the will of the legal subject as the contract was voluntarily made. There was no compulsion to higher policy goals or ends; the only object of the law was the contract between two equal contracting parties. Criminal law also assumed the equality and free will of the legal subject. The accused was represented at the court in the same way as for breaches of civil law and had the right to defend their interests in court equal to any other citizen. The law was binding on the individual as if it were a contract, although there was no formal contract beyond the assumption of assent to membership of a law-bound community (mythologised in social contract theory). This was clearly only notional assent, but it was through this fiction of consent that the equal rights of defendants before the law were enshrined. In constitutional law, the notional social contract was given content. For all its limitations, the principle of popular sovereignty was a thoroughly radical conception of authority from the people. It argued that the state's authority and legislative legitimacy derived exclusively from the people, rather than any external source, whether this was the 'divine right' of Kings or the 'civilizing' mission of a colonial administration.

This idealised picture reveals the centrality, to all aspects of the modern framework of rights, of the rights-bearing individual with the capacity for self-government. The source of democratic rights and the modern 'rule of law' was the citizen, as an autonomous legal subject, rather than an external body that laid down the law from above. As Hannah Arendt observed, the concept of the 'rule of law', separated from a political framework that involved society in the decision-making process, would inevitably be a hollow one:

> Equality, in contrast to all that is involved in mere existence, is not given us, but is the result of human organisation...We are not born equal; we become equal as members of a group on the strength of our decision to guarantee ourselves mutually equal rights.' (Arendt, 1979, pp. 300–1)

The 'rule of law' approach of international peacebuilders in Bosnia attached little importance to the political sphere and state institutions. The essence of the 'bureaucratic gaze' was the belief that the 'rule of law' could be developed and implemented separately from, and in counterposition to, the political process (see Chandler, 2006c). However, as E. H. Carr noted in his landmark study of international relations (from which this book derives its subtitle), the derivation of modern law from rights-bearing individuals was not merely of historical or philosophical importance:

> Law is a function of a given political order, whose existence alone can make it binding...Law cannot be self-contained; for the obligation to obey it must always rest on something outside itself. It is neither self-creating nor self-applying. 'There are men who govern,' says a Chinese philosopher, 'but there are no laws that govern.' (Carr, 2001, p. 165)

While for Carr 'the ultimate authority of law derives from politics', it was precisely the attempt to separate the sphere of law from that of politics which was the sine qua non of the 'rule of law' approach in international peacebuilding administrations (Carr, 2001, p. 166). The attempt to externally impose the 'public interest', through imposing the 'rule of law' from the top-down, in fact, undermined the creation of any genuine public consensus from the bottom-up through the political process. Removing the process of engagement and participation in the political and legal process gave citizens no sense of ownership of these 'rights' granted by the international administration. The people of Bosnia may have had a legal framework, which institutionalised their rights, but these imposed rights appeared as an oppressive, alien and artificial creation. In the same way, the 'rights' of Iraqi citizens, declared by the US–UK administration, did not appear as rights but as alien impositions and were unlikely to bind society.

If there was any lesson from the extension of international peace-building regulation over Bosnia, it was that high-handed intervention to give priority to the 'rule of law' over the political sphere did little to help overcome insecurities and divisions, while undermining collective political bodies in which Serb, Croat and Bosniak representatives could negotiate solutions. The consequences for Iraq were even more desta-bilising as security depended on isolating support for armed insurgency, which was difficult as long as ruling institutions were seen as an illegitimate foreign imposition. The limitation of the view that the imposition of 'the rule of law' could be a solution to security problems was highlighted by growing instability in Iraq and Afghanistan in 2003 and onwards (see, for example, *Guardian*, 2003) and responses to the bomb at the UN headquarters in Baghdad which resulted in the tragic death of the head of mission, UN Special Representative Sergio Vieira de Mello. In a sad irony, de Mello was one of the few high-level diplomats who had argued that greater political legitimacy could do more to promote security than more law-making or military and police re-enforcements (see Bone, 2003; Steele, 2003a).

CONCLUSION

The institutionalist approach, which developed in the impasse of interna-tional peacebuilding, today stands condemned as utopian and hubristic. However, the impasse was already the result of a retreat from modern liberal understandings of politics and law. The traditional understanding of the 'rule of law' was the rule of constitutionality (Jackson, 1990, pp. 95–8). Law and justice were seen to result from autonomy and self-government. The focus on the 'rule of law' by international peacebuilding administrators was very different from the post-1945 approach when the importance of state sovereignty vis-a`-vis external rule was universally acknowledged. In the late 1990s and into the 2000s, the problematisation of the political process in many sovereign states and the demand for international legislative action in the cause of sustainable peacebuilding seemed to reflect the opposite trend, involving a return to colonial for-mulations (ICISS, 2001b, p. 199).

The international doctrine of peacebuilding-as-statebuilding posited the 'rule of law' in opposition to self-government. Through viewing the political process as problematic, law appeared as an external solution. In the areas considered above, the law was imposed against the will of the population in the belief that the legal framework was the basis on which post-conflict reconstruction and peacebuilding could be shaped and guided. The experience of Bosnia-Herzegovina is a good case study example, highlighting that this legal idealism undermined the political process, the standing of the law and the transition to self-government.

As briefly described above, the imposition of the 'rule of law' in order to enforce political consensus merely served to discredit the political process rather than to give it greater authority, as intended. The universalist nature of this lesson was clear in Iraq in the lack of popular support behind the Iraqis hand-picked to consult with the US and British administration, and the lack of any possibility for locally accountable representatives to take responsibility for reconstruction. Similar unintended consequences occurred with regard to the imposition of specific legislation, which allegedly could not be left to Bosnian politicians, for example, in the areas of housing and employment. The advocates of the 'rule of law' criticised the slowness of political reform in Bosnia for producing 'facade democracy' but the housing and employment laws demonstrated that the top-down imposition of the 'rule of law' could be equally artificial, creating a legal facade of universality while in practice institutionalising ethnic division.

Finally, the danger of prioritising the 'rule of law' above the political process was the risk of unregulated and arbitrary power. This danger was similarly all too apparent in Iraq under US and British administration where there was no constitutional process of appeal for wrongful detention or capacity to challenge the rule of international administrators. Once the rule of law was separated from the democratic process it became the rule of tyranny rather than the rule of justice. Although these projects were promoted in the 'liberal' language of peacebuilding-as-statebuilding, the impetus was far from liberal or democratic. Peacebuilding as capacity-building tended to reproduce and institutionalise international hierarchies, weakening states and leaving little possibility of international exit strategies without undermining the legitimacy of the peacebuilding project itself. Attempts to go beyond this impasse were reformulated in the late 2000s and early 2010s and will be analysed in the next section.

PART IV

Beyond Peacebuilding

CHAPTER 7

The Turn to the Local

INTRODUCTION

The following two chapters consider ways in which thinking about international peacebuilding attempted to move beyond the impasse of peacebuilding-as-statebuilding at the end of the 2000s and shift further towards the pragmatic approach (discussed in the introductory and concluding chapters). As already noted, the crisis of international peacebuilding approaches started in 1997 with the full development of peacebuilding as a separate policy sphere. The first sets of policy reforms merely extended the tasks and remits of international agencies, prolonging the impasse of international peacebuilding as a statebuilding project. It was not until the end of the 2000s that international policy and academic analysis sought to go beyond peacebuilding, pulling back from international transformative aspirations entirely. This shift towards pragmatism is the focus of this part of the book. This chapter concerns the turn to the local, which was closely tied to non-linear understandings of peace as a process less amenable to international intervention. The following chapter extends this analysis to engage with the further development of pragmatic approaches and the rise of discourses of resilience.

This chapter reflects upon the shift away from linear understandings of peacebuilding, which assumed that Western 'blueprints' could be imposed upon non-compliant elites. By the end of the 2000s it was increasingly suggested, in both the policy and academic literatures, that there should be a shift towards 'non-linear' understandings. Rather than focusing upon

© The Author(s) 2017   143
D. Chandler, *Peacebuilding*, Rethinking Peace and Conflict Studies,
DOI 10.1007/978-3-319-50322-6_7

Western policy prescriptions intra-elite bargaining and formal institutional structures, these understandings stressed non-linearity, hybridity, local societal processes and practices and the importance of 'hidden' agency and resistance. This chapter highlights that, while these approaches set up a critique of 'liberal' linear approaches, they tended to reify hybrid, non-liberal or non-linear outcomes as the product of local inter-subjective attachments (still working within a liberal divide between universal solutions and local problems). Because of the continuation of this logic, these criticisms tended to reproduce the voluntarist and idealist understandings of international peacebuilding, locating the problems or barriers to peace and development at the cognitive or ideational level rather than considering the barriers of economic and social context.

By the late 1990s, it seemed as if the internal political processes of problematic states were irrelevant to international policy-making. As we have seen in the previous part of this book (on the impasse of peacebuilding) the problems of peacebuilding in post-conflict interventions were seen as largely technical questions concerned with the export and establishment of liberal institutional frameworks. In this framing, problems of peace were narrowly understood in terms of exporting democracy and good governance. The barriers or limits to success were seen essentially from two inter-linked perspectives: first, concerning the limits of Western will, resources or co-ordination; and second, the illegitimate blockages of local elites concerned to maintain their control of power, patronage and resources. This technocratic approach, to institutional capacity-building and peacebuilding, worked on the basis that local elites were not representative of their societies' needs or interests; elites were seen as illegitimate representatives, influencing society but manufacturing their support through illegitimate means of patronage, media manipulation and corruption (to be challenged through 'top-down' institution-building and 'bottom-up' civil society-building). The assumption was that the populations concerned had real interests in supporting international peacebuilding aspirations for reform and that therefore these reforms would work smoothly once blocking elites were removed, undermined or constrained by the policies of conditionality.

By the late 2000s and early 2010s, approaches that were based on imposing a set of international policy-prescriptions through bargaining, bypassing or constraining local elites were seen in a much more negative light. These approaches were seen to be externally driven, hubristic – in their assumptions that external actors had the right policies and the means to attain them – and as expressing a limited understanding of politics as an inter-elite process of bargaining or co-option, focusing solely on the limited and artificial formal or public political sphere. Approaches which appreciated the limits of the 'linear' approach emphasised that international peacebuilding was not a technical question of application or implementation but a more pragmatic or 'political' question, involving a problematic which was not open to easy calculation and 'elite bargaining'.

The 'non-linear' understanding of the limits to peacebuilding interventions was very different to the civil society-building approach analysed in Chapter 5, which attempted to build unrepresentative NGOs as advocates for institutional policy reform to legitimise international policy. The much more pragmatic 'turn to the local' started neither with international designs and blueprints nor with the problematisation of local actors (seen as lacking capacity) but with the problematic of the local or societal agents and actors and the processes, practices and interrelationships that shaped ideas and understandings. By emphasising the importance of system- and process-based thinking, and the contingent and unknown factors involved in the peacebuilding process, in particular, these non-linear approaches sought to highlight the importance of local agency (often hidden or unrecognised) in resistance to international aspirations (for a discussion of non-linear approaches in the social sciences, see, for example, Jervis, 1998; Richards, 2000; Brown, 1995; Popolo, 2011).

THE BARRIERS OF NON-LINEARITY AND HYBRIDITY

The civil conflicts of the 1990s, unleashed by the collapse of the Cold War divide – which impelled the transformation of Soviet-style regimes in Central and Eastern Europe and the removal of super power clientelism in sub-Saharan Africa – provided the backdrop against which understandings of peacebuilding interventions and their limits developed in linear ways. Perhaps paradigmatic of linear understandings of peacebuilding in terms of compliance with international blueprints was Mary Kaldor's highly influential analysis of 'New Wars'. Using this framing, she described conflicts in ways that constructed a moral divide between the understanding of war and conflict in the West and in the non-West. The binary of old and new war had little to do with the spatial framing of conflict as intra-state rather than inter-state, for example, the US or Spanish civil wars would be construed as old wars rather than new wars (Kaldor, 1999, pp. 13–30). Following Kalevi Holsti's analysis of 'wars of the third kind' (Holsti,

1996, pp. 19–40), Kaldor drew a conceptual distinction where old wars were rational – constitutive of a collective or public interest and politically legitimate – whereas new wars were understood to be irrational – driven by private interest and politically illegitimate. This conceptual divide then enabled her to argue that illegitimate political elites had no right to hide behind the rights of sovereignty and that external peacebuilding interventions were morally necessary and legitimate, casting international interveners as interest-free enforcers of emerging international peacebuilding norms that could be universally applied.

Another leading example of the linear framing of international intervention in the cause of peace, with its implicit liberal telos, was Margaret Keck and Kathryn Sikkink's influential book *Activists beyond Borders* which argued that, to diffuse liberal norms of democracy and human rights, illegitimate state-based or interest-based barriers to communicative interaction needed to be removed (Keck and Sikkink, 1998). The overcoming of barriers, seen to be at the level of state government resistance, was construed in terms of the 'boomerang effect', which allowed the spread of liberal norms as international actors 'removed the blockage' of the narrow interest-based action of repressive regimes, 'prying open space' for domestic civil society actors which were bearers of these democratic aspirations:

> Voices that are suppressed in their own countries may find that networks can project and amplify their concerns into an international arena, which in turn can echo back into their own countries...networks open channels for bringing alternative visions and information into international debate...At the core of network activity is the production, exchange and strategic use of information. (Keck and Sikkink, 1998, p. x)

In these linear discourses, peacebuilding transformation was understood, in a highly voluntarist way, as an act of subjective will rather than a matter of social and economic transformation. It was thereby the task of international institutions and powerful Western states to remove the narrow 'interest' blockages of entrenched power elites, thus freeing the local agency of civil society, understood to be unproblematic. This framing was perhaps most clearly exemplified by those advocating international intervention in the break-up of Yugoslavia, particularly in the Bosnia war 1992–1995, which was one of the key foreign policy focuses of the mid-1990s. It was held that international interveners were acting in the support of local civil society actors in seeking to preserve multi-cultural Bosnia against the machinations of unrepresentative nationalist elites who were acting in their own narrow and criminal interests (e.g. Burg, 1997; Fine, 1996; Kaldor, 1999). Once international intervention had removed the nationalist leaders from power, through prosecutions for war crimes and the oversight of free and fair post-war democratic elections, it was assumed that the population of Bosnia would express their support for universal liberal democratic norms in voting for non-nationalist political representatives.

In these 1990s framings of linearity, formal political processes at the local level were often problematised – for example, in terms of local elite resistance – but these problematic blockages to liberal international norms were understood as amenable to resolution through a combination of top-down international carrots and sticks. Once local elites were removed from power or constrained, it was assumed that the externally drawn-up plans for peacebuilding and institutional reform could continue unhindered. However, these linear liberal interventionist aspirations rapidly dimmed in the mid-2000s – in the wake of policy failures in the Balkans and in other post-conflict scenarios from Afghanistan to Iraq. The understanding of political blockages then shifted from the more easily accessible formal level of local state institutions to concern with the less accessible level of societal relations. With this shift, the emphasis moved from linear ends-based or goal-orientated interventions to understanding the limits to change in the non-linear or 'hybrid' politics of social or everyday practices and interactions.

Rather than being understood to be resisting through the political motivations of self-interest, elites increasingly came to be seen as lacking the capacity or the authority to implement Western policymaking goals. By the end of the 2000s, academic commentary upholding the linear approach, advocating that international actors should assert more leverage over recalcitrant elites, stood as an exception to the general trend in thinking in the post-conflict literature (Zürcher et al., 2013). Critical international relations theorising problematised the Western export of 'liberal peace' and the peacebuilding impasse of 'top-down' frameworks, which ignored local societal influences, stressing instead the need for 'bottom-up' theorising; giving a much larger role to local agency and the spaces and mechanisms which needed to be accessed in order to understand, empower and transform local actors. Rather than focusing on the formal public political sphere of domestic elites, analysts argued that researchers needed to go deeper into the societal sphere, particularly to those actors capable of expressing, influencing and shaping 'grass roots' opinion.

This understanding of 'politics' worked in a very different register to the 'top–down' liberal institutionalist frameworks, which had tended to ignore or 'black box' the societal sphere. In the late 1990s, as post-Cold War experiments of intervention extended their remits, peacebuilding-as-statebuilding approaches envisaged states being constructed on the Western, or 'Weberian', model, focusing on the export of liberal institutions standing above society, assumed to operate independently from social forces. These approaches understood the institutional framework as determining the outcomes of social interaction. International peacebuilding would thereby be assured through the production of a liberal state: through attention to the construction or reform of neutral constitutional arrangements, political party representation, civil service appointments, the army and policing, and the courts and judiciary (see Lemay-Hébert, 2009).

The failure of these 'illiberal' experiments in producing liberal outcomes led to attention shifting to the societal sphere and a critique of institutionalist assumptions regarding state-society relations and the potential universality of the liberal subject. Approaches during the late 2000s reversed liberal institutionalist frameworks, understanding states as operating as products of the societal sphere rather than standing neutrally above it, as if the state was purely a technocratic and administrative body along Weberian lines. Work on the institutional level was increasingly seen to be purely formal and superficial when it came to post-conflict governance for sustainable peace. For non-linear approaches, work purely on the level of elites and state institutions was seen as mistaking a part for the whole and assumed the successful top-down or linear imposition of the end goals of Western peace and democracy promotion.

As Körppen and Ropers noted: 'systemic approaches understand phenomena as an emergent property of an interrelated whole; hence, a phenomenon cannot be fully comprehended by analysing its constituent parts' (Körppen and Ropers, 2011, p. 13). Roger Mac Ginty similarly argued that linear approaches ignored the local relational and contextual aspects; for this reason he deployed the concept of 'hybridisation' to bring clearly into question top–down understandings of temporality and linearity (Mac Ginty, 2011, p. 73). 'Bringing the local back in' thereby indicated a shift from a linear approach to a non-linear or systems approach focused upon societal relationships and interactions at both the local–local level and the local–international level (Mac Ginty, 2011, p. 210). In this way, academic commentators focused on the 'hybrid' outcomes produced by attempts to impose or develop formal liberal institutional frameworks in what was argued to be non- or a-liberal societies (e.g. Roberts, 2008).

These hybrid outcomes ware held to indicate that the 'top-down' shaping of state institutions had little broader social impact and that liberal aspirations were easily undermined or blocked by 'resisting' or counter-vailing societal practices and institutions (e.g. Paris and Sisk, 2009a; Richmond and Mitchell, 2012; Mac Ginty, 2011). Non-linear approaches thereby sought to work at the societal level, focusing on addressing the transformation of societal processes and understanding the social repro-duction of resistances to democracy and peace, allegedly ignored by liberal universalist 'top-down' policymaking (Woodward, 2007).

The problematic of how states could be strengthened through accessing and influencing social or societal processes thereby become positioned at the heart of the peacebuilding problematic (see also Hameiri, 2010; Joseph, 2012). Non-linear approaches sought to highlight how attention to societal processes, instead of the formal institutional frameworks of government, necessitated a different form of interventionary practices and understand-ings. In focusing on the peacebuilding shift to society and societal processes, non-linear conceptions built upon the growing interest in the shift to governance approaches of societal intervention (e.g. Foucault, 2010, pp. 25–40, 2008; O'Malley, 2004; Miller and Rose, 2008; Rose, 1989, 1999; Dean, 2010; Walker and Cooper, 2011; Owens, 2012). This frame-work of governance, and the focus on the ways in which external actors could influence the societal environment in which individuals made choices and took decisions, fundamentally challenged the traditional liberal assumptions on which the division of the public and private spheres were based – the societal sphere became problematised and 'life' became the subject of gov-ernance (see further, for example, Dillon and Reid, 2009; Chandler, 2010).

In this respect, Michel Foucault's work, on shifting liberal governing rationalities and the birth of biopolitics, served as useful starting point for the non-linear analysis of the barriers or 'resistances' involved in the social practices which produced and institutionalised cognitive and ideational understandings. As Foucault indicated, this shift away from state-based, sovereign and disciplinary power to a biopolitical or 'society-centred' approach, constituted 'the population as a political problem' and, within this, focused on the real lives or the everyday of individuals and commu-nities 'and their environment, the milieu in which they live . . . to the extent that it is not a natural environment, that it has been created by the popula-tion and therefore has effects on that population' (Foucault, 2003, p. 245).

It was this inter-subjective 'milieu' that was understood to shape social and individual behavioural choices and to account 'for action at a distance of one body on another' and thereby 'appears as a field of intervention' for governance policymaking (Foucault, 2007, pp. 20–1). In this framework, any external peacebuilding intervention could only operate on society indirectly, through connecting to, understanding and facilitating the inter-subjective processes of societal life itself, rather than through the formal framework of public law in relation to individuals as citizens: 'action is brought to bear on the rules of the game rather than on the players' as Foucault stated in *The Birth of Biopolitics* (2008, p. 260). In this shift, liberal understandings of linear politics with the state (as representing and directing society from above) and the subject (as universal, rational and autonomous) were fundamentally challenged.

THE DISCOVERY OF THE 'LOCAL'

The shift from linear to non-linear understandings and, with this, the shift from the formal sphere of government institutions and elite interactions to a sustained focus on the local or societal level was captured well in the pioneering work of John Paul Lederach. His work was crucial in establishing this approach in the policy literature (e.g. Lederach, 1997). Lederach was the first leading policy-academic to problematise 'top–down' or linear approaches to peace and democracy. Lederach took the emphasis away from international diplomatic agendas and local elites to focus on a societal approach. This approach was also described as a 'relationship-', 'practice-' or 'process-orientated' understanding. In this framework, the role of external actors was to assist in establishing 'infrastructure that empowers the resources for reconciliation from within that society' (Lederach, 1997, p. xvi). In his focus upon 'the experiential and subjective realities shaping people's perspectives and needs', Lederach argued that institutional structures and elite settlements were not the key concern:

> traditional mechanisms relying solely on statist diplomacy and realpolitik have not demonstrated a capacity to control these conflicts, much less transform them toward constructive, peaceful outcomes. Contemporary conflict thus demands innovation, the development of ideas and practices that go beyond the negotiation of substantive interests and issues. This innovation, I believe, pushes us to probe into the realm of the subjective-generationally accumulated perceptions and deep-rooted hatred and fear. (Lederach, 1997, p. 25)

Lederach's approach was to point towards the pragmatic understandings of the 2010s. His key break with existing practices was not merely to reject the focus on state-level elites but to insist that Western policy-conceptions, posed in linear terms of 'conflict management' or 'conflict resolution', were misplaced. Instead of linear thinking of the imposition of external blueprints, he argued that social scientists needed to learn from the new thinking of natural scientists, particularly in physics, where both quantum and chaos theory indicated that the system itself was more important than looking at its individual parts (Lederach, 1997, p. 26). Rather than understanding politics in terms of leaders, elites and political programmes, or 'throwing money at problems', he suggested that societal spaces, practices and processes should become the starting point for transforming social subjectivities (ibid, p. 87). In this focus on societal processes, the concern was with social practices and relationships, rather than the external design or imposition of some alleged 'solution' to conflict (ibid, p. 112).

It is useful to consider how, in this framework, the space of politics – the space of blockages to peace and their removal – shifted from the formal institutional sphere to the informal social sphere. For Lederach, the formal political sphere of elite politics lacked representational legitimacy, not in the 'linear' sense of Mary Kaldor's 'new wars' analysis – where, as we have seen, elites were seen to be criminal and corrupt – but in the sense that elites were no longer understood as 'representative' of, or as fully connected to, society. Local elites were seen to represent the formal machinations of government; elites in this understanding, precisely because of their public visibility, were inevitably conservative upholders of the status quo, dependent on military, political or media power for their standing, and thereby were less connected to society itself (Lederach, 1997, pp. 38–41). For the non-linear, societal or process-based approach it was the social milieus of everyday life that were crucial, not formal politics operating in the rarefied sphere of international-elite diplomacy and negotiation.

The sense of a 'disconnect' between formal political authority and social processes and practices was central to non-linear approaches to peacebuilding. In these framings, international policymakers needed to connect with, to understand and to enable or influence local agency, now seen as key to successful peacebuilding outcomes. For Lederach, the key to peacebuilding was not Western knowledge or resources but local agency: 'The greatest resource for sustaining peace in the long term is always rooted in the local people and culture.' (Lederach, 1997, p. 94). In this framework, locals were foregrounded, not in terms of formal political representation but the social processes and relationships in which they were embedded and reproduced. In which case, the approach to the local was transformed, to 'see people in the setting as resources, not recipients' (ibid). In this way, there was a 'move beyond a simple prescription of answers and modalities from outside the setting' to 'empowering the resources, modalities, and mechanisms for building peace that exist within the context' (ibid, p. 95). There was no quick diplomatic solution to conflicts which could be agreed and somehow imposed from the top-down, rather, it was 'the healing of people and the rebuilding of the web of their relationships' which took centre-stage (ibid, p. 78).

Lederach is worth quoting to gain an understanding of the distinctive nature of 'non-linear' as opposed to 'linear-thinking', regarding the 'infra-politics of peace':

> An infrastructure for peacebuilding should be understood as a process-structure, in the way that quantum theory has proposed. A process-structure is made up of systems that maintain form over time yet have no hard rigidity of structure . . . In more specific terms . . . a process-structure for peacebuilding transforms a war-system characterized by deeply divided, hostile, and violent relationships into a peace-system characterized by just and interdependent relationships with the capacity to find nonviolent mechanisms for expressing and handling conflict. The goal is not stasis, but rather the generation of continuous, dynamic, self-regenerating processes that maintain form over time and are able to adapt to environmental changes. Such an infrastructure is made up of a web of people, their relationships and activities, and the social mechanisms necessary to sustain the change sought. This takes place at all levels of the society. (Lederach, 1997, p. 84, emphasis in original)

Non-linear, systems-based approaches sought to transform social practices and behaviours understood as self-reproducing processes. Understood as systems of societal reproduction, there could be no 'solution' that fixed some settlement. It was a matter of ensuring that societal reproduction through practices and relationships became sustainable at a level at which conflicts could be managed peaceably. As Berghof Director, Hans Giessman noted:

> The inter-linkages of causes, intervening variables and consequences of conflict dynamics are still widely under-researched. In complex conflict scenarios it can be hard to distinguish between causes and consequences,

and the borders between both become fuzzy, if not blurred. Goal-seeking linear approaches will most likely fail in such scenarios ... The actual matter of transforming (violent) conflict into constructive interaction is about people internalising the chances for socialising alternative non-violent patterns of beliefs, behaviour and relations. (Giessman, 2011, p. 8)

While Lederach stressed the need to engage with community leaders with well-established links and reputations, 'chosen not for their expertise or profession, but for who they are in the network' (1997, p. 96), other, more critical, academics argued that societal transformation needed to operate at a deeper level still. Thania Paffenholz, for example, argued for a more comprehensive approach to conflict transformation with greater emphasis on context sensitivity and local agency (Paffenholz, 2012).

This may have seemed a radical departure from dominant theorising but non-linear or systems-based approaches reproduced, and in fact deepened, the voluntaristic or ideational framings of international peacebuilding-as-statebuilding understandings, focusing not on the structuring of economic and social relations but at the level of inter-subjective understandings, spaces and practices. Here, societal problems were addressed at the level of practices, ideas and cognitive frameworks held to produce the problematic reality or problematic responses to the stresses of post-conflict transformation. By shifting 'politics' to society, these approaches opened up 'a new object, a new domain or field' for policy intervention (Foucault, 2008, p. 295): the 'local' (e.g. the 'Local First' development and peacebuilding initiative, launched in November 2012, by Peace Direct and supported by the Overseas Development Institute and linked into the UK Government's Building Stability Overseas Strategy).

In non-linear approaches, the focus of the problematic was the local level, understood as the sphere within which political agency operated in the production and reproduction of barriers to – as well as the facilitation of – peace. This radical understanding, of the societal or informal reproduction of social identities and practices, which could be seen as 'resistance' or as a barrier to international peacebuilding aspirations, was analogous to Louis Althusser's conception of the individual subject as always and already ideologically embedded through its insertion into material social practices (Althusser, 2008, p. 42). He had argued that these social practices were shaped by the 'Ideological State Apparatuses' of religion, culture, the family, communicative media and so on – operating in both the public and private spheres and, through which, cognitive and ideational understandings were continually formed (2008, pp. 17–8). Contra Marx, therefore, individual understandings were not shaped by the real conditions of existence but instead, dominant ideological framings 'represent to them there [through social practices]...the imaginary relation of those individuals to the real relations in which they live' (ibid, pp. 38–9). Imaginary, false or 'ideological' understandings were therefore inescapable 'material' products of the social practices of everyday life, through which subjects were always and already interpellated inter-subjectively (ibid, pp. 47–50). It was here that different 'rationalities' or 'temporalities' were held to be in play, which resisted or contested the linear demands of international peacebuilders.

The local production and reproduction of difference through micro-practices, spaces and relationships was at the heart of non-linear under-standings and the 'embedded' understanding of the subject. Linear peace-building approaches were discursively dependent upon the universal telos of the rational subject, which merely needed to be 'freed', in terms of the removal of elite blockages. The non-linear subject could no longer be 'freed' by peacebuilding interventions, as if the 'blockages' somehow existed outside the subject and its relations and understandings. Thus, there was a shift away from rationalist approaches – which were held to ignore the societal relations shaping cognitive understandings – and atten-tion was paid to the deeper social practices of 'everyday life' shaping cognitive and behavioural choices.

The 'local', 'bottom–up', focus on 'the hidden' processes of the societal sphere focused on this sphere as the problematic barrier preventing better, more effective, more adaptive responses to post-conflict stresses. This ontological framework, focused upon the real lives of local actors and their 'everyday' practices, thereby assumed that social practices were much less open to transformation through external intervention which focused on the formal, public and political sphere. It was through this construction of the 'local' – as self-producing of emergent rationalities and temporalities of difference – that external peacebuilding interventions became inevitably understood to produce non-linear or hybrid outcomes.

THE 'HIDDEN' POLITICS OF RESISTANCE

As long as liberal rationalist approaches to politics were the dominant framework for understanding peacebuilding, the formal political sphere of inter-elite bargaining was seen to be the sphere through which pro-blems could be understood and overcome, for example, by forcing illegitimate elite practices to change through compliance practices, such as conditionality or imposing legal reforms (as considered in the previous chapter). In non-linear, hybrid, approaches there was a very different approach to politics and the space and mechanisms of its action. In these understandings, politics was primarily understood in terms of societal processes held to be self-reproducing. For Coleman et al, for example, politics was seen to operate through social practices in a form that was more analogous to the reproduction of cancer – operating beneath the surface and transforming from the inside – than a clash of political interests or structural contradictions:

> An intractable conflict can be looked upon as a 'malignant' social relation. Cancer works by penetrating the structure of the organism and enslaving essential elements of the body, which then lose their original functions and begin working in the service of the structure of cancer... The richness and multidimensionality of all the processes occurring in a healthy society become entrained in the structure, leaving no opportunity for positive interactions. (Coleman et al., 2011, p. 46)

Here, systems came to the fore, with complex mechanisms of interaction below the surface. In this framework, in the words of EU High Representative for Common Foreign and Security Policy, Javier Solana, 'domestic politics matter' (Solana, 2009). He explained:

> Domestic politics matter because they limit what is achievable... This is never more the case than when the problem is a dispute over the control and legitimacy of the state... In the Balkans and elsewhere, the aim of crisis management has been to create the space for politics to work. But functioning politics is one thing that foreigners cannot provide; only the locals can do that. (Solana, 2009)

Traditional, linear, 'top-down' or technical approaches assumed that the West could bring institutional changes and sustainable peace through the removal of blockages and opening the 'space for politics to work'. By the late 2000s a different understanding suggested that the problem was precisely that of 'politics' itself. 'Politics' in this sense, was not merely a matter of establishing or imposing technical solutions but referred to the area outside of external or Western influence. As the UK government Foreign Office and Department for International Development argued 'politics is central to stability' (BSOS, 2011, p. 16). The British government saw this as a shift from previous approaches of the international community, which merely 'looked for technical fixes to conflict' (ibid). What the West could not easily influence through external interventions apparently was the social space in which 'politics' was now seen to operate. In this space, there were blockages that did not appear to be amenable to Western influence. This was the space in which resistance worked and where 'only the locals' could take responsibility.

It seemed that the discovery of 'hybridity' brought back 'politics'; but not the linear politics of representation, with its linear understanding of state–society interactions. The politics of 'the local' operated in the informal and societal sphere, out of the reach or vision of Western policymakers and 'linear' social theorists. This shift was reflected in Mary Kaldor's view of the increasing importance of 'subterranean politics' where political contestation (in all its xenophobic, populist and emancipatory forms) was seen to operate below the surface. The important point was that, using this framework, social mobilisations and collective activities were re-interpreted as 'public displays of subterranean politics' (Kaldor and Selchow, 2012, p. 8). In these analyses, trying to understand politics through a focus on elites missed the bigger and more important picture, which could only be found through digging deeper and engaging with society itself. Kaldor argued that, with hindsight, this blindspot could be clearly seen in relation to the 1989 'velvet revolutions' of Central and Eastern Europe. Policy and academic analysts were caught blindsided because they were only studying elite and inter-elite relations (ibid, p. 24).

For authors, such as Oliver Richmond, it was precisely here – in the hidden or neglected political agency of the masses – that the impasse of linear, top–down understandings of international peacebuilding-as-state-building could be found:

> How do we know these agencies exist if they are hidden? Where is their empirical proof? An easy response to this counter-critique is because power, state and sovereignty, as well as international blueprints for which IR maintains compliance – an enormous gathering of the power of liberal modernity – have not had their way so far. This has been one of the lessons of modernity … How do the 'powerless' engage in politics and international relations should be its starting question, not whether they do. (Richmond, 2011b, p. 434)

Here, there was no engagement with the economic, social and political structures beyond the reach of local agency, in fact, any such structures were explicitly written out of the picture once the gap between asserted aims and policy outcomes was entirely the product of hidden agency. With the dismissal of social and economic relations all that was left was 'politics'. However, this was no longer politics understood in terms of the rational pursuit of self-interest and as amenable to top-down 'solutions' or 'settlements'. Nor did the return of politics imply a focus on the public politics of the formal sphere of representation. The politics of hidden agencies and resistances operated in the social sphere and was, by necessity, not amenable to traditional liberal political theory, with its episteme of linearity and means-ends relations. This shifting conception of resistance was usefully highlighted by Hollander and Einwohner in their discussion of resistance literature, considering resistance as both political and formal or public as well as stemming from the informal or private sphere of interaction (Hollander and Einwohner, 2004).

James C. Scott has probably had more influence than any other author on this understanding of resistance as manifesting below the surface of formal political processes, for example, through emphasising the importance of access to non-public 'hidden transcripts' – the cognitive and sociological institutional contexts in which shared meanings were produced and transmitted at the local societal level (Scott, 1990). Scott, in his focus on resistance under authoritarian rule, where open political contestation was impossible, articulated a conflation of the political and the social which spoke powerfully to this discourse, through his emphasis on the 'infra-politics' of resistance and his location of political understandings in the spaces, practices and relationships of 'everyday life'.

Scott argued that social science had failed to understand the politics and conflicts of the societies it examined as it had 'focused resolutely on the official or formal relations between the powerful and the weak' (Scott, 1990, p. 13) and, essentially, in focusing on the formal level, was 'looking in the wrong place for political conflict' (ibid, p. 17). He articulated the hidden, subterranean, societal space for politics in the socially embedded practices, relationships and networks of the informal sphere set apart from power (ibid, pp. 151–2). It was the 'infrapolitics' of these relations that provided 'the cultural and structural underpinning of the more visible political action' (ibid, p. 184) and enabled analysts to understand how political conflicts could escalate in ways that social movement approaches or public choice theory failed to (ibid, p. 203).

The blockages of politics thus shifted from the resistance of elites, seen to be easily amenable to international resolution, to the blockages of the 'local' or social sphere that, by their very virtue of being 'hidden', were much less amenable to understanding or to external influence. It was here that Scott's critical anthropology began to resonate with policy understandings of the difficulties of overcoming the barriers of local resistance that did not necessarily take public or formal political forms. Scott's suggestion that 'infrapolitics' was difficult to know or to govern was easily transferred to the policy realm of understanding the blockages that seemed to constitute the impasse of international peacebuilding:

> There are no leaders to round up, no membership lists to investigate, no manifestos to denounce, no public activities to draw attention . . . infrapolitics is . . . the realm of informal leadership and nonelites, of conversation and oral discourse, and of surreptitious resistance. The logic of infrapolitics is to leave few traces in the wake of its passage. By covering its tracks it not only minimizes the risk its practitioners run but it also eliminates much of the documentary evidence that might convince social scientists and historians that real politics was taking place. (Scott, 1990, p. 200)

Non-linear and systems-based approaches appealed increasingly to policymakers as external interventions at the level of formal politics were seen to be ineffective. This understanding was confirmed by academic work exploring the limits of peacebuilding. Elena Semenova, in a survey of Central and East European political elites highlighted the problem, noting that: 'We can't use parties to identify elites. The party system is quite unstable.' (Semenova, 2012) A similar finding was confirmed by Christoph Zürcher from research in post-conflict states where, similarly, there seemed to be a breakdown between political elites and social or political processes: 'We have no idea who really are the power holders in these regions. In post-war contexts we have no clue who these people are. We just don't know.' (Zürcher, 2012) The starting assumption was that local agency, in fact, drew strength from its hidden forms, evading the 'top-down' international peacebuilding gaze. 'Infrapolitics' was no longer analysed as a product of weakness and repression but as an ontological starting point for explaining the impasse of international peacebuilding.

THE REIFICATION OF 'RESISTANCE'

The assertions at play in these understandings of 'politics' operating below the surface and through 'hidden' agencies of resistance were quite astounding. Resistances may be hidden, as Scott's research showed, they may be 'mobile and transitory' as Foucault suggested and may even become 'strategically codified' to 'make a revolution possible', as he further indicated (Foucault, 1981, p. 96) but, as suggested above, resistance could not become the ontological limit to international peacebuilding ideals without the rejection of the importance of structures of economic and social relations. Foucault's much quoted statement on the imbrication of power and resistance had been turned into a reification of resistance as marking the limit to peacebuilding aspirations and linear understandings. In fact, the actual sentence was this: 'Where there is power, there is resistance, and yet, or rather consequently, this resistance is never in a position of exteriority in relation to power.' (Foucault, 1981, p. 95) Power cannot be conceptualised without resistance, without a strategic problematic enabling power to project itself and to 'secure' itself through its operation.

It seemed that (in an entirely opposite reading of Foucault) it was a 'relationship of exteriority' that drove the search for 'hidden agency' in the sphere of the 'local'. This approach was probably best exemplified in the work of Oliver Richmond who argued that International Relations, as a discipline, 'needs a theory of resistance' (Richmond, 2011b, p. 421) and that, along the lines of Scott, the discipline's lack of attention to 'hidden capacity and resistant agency' meant that the limits to peacebuilding-as-statebuilding were ignored. That, in fact, 'hidden resistance' was entirely exterior to liberal power: 'akin to the dark matter of physics, upon which the world itself depends'; forming 'a massive percentage of the scale of all capacity for reform, development, justice, institutions, civil society, rights, needs, peace and emancipation' (ibid, p. 424). It was thereby hidden resistance which explained the limits to external projects of peacebuilding, operating as 'a conglomeration or aggregation of fragmented and hidden everyday forms of resistance', which 'cannot be seen or easily resisted by power' or co-opted by it, yet was capable of agency and 'holds power to account and illustrates the limits of its sovereignty' (ibid, p. 433).

The need for theory to understand 'resistance' was thereby of prime importance; Richmond set out a pragmatic research agenda critical of peacebuilding, in the early 2010s, in this way:

> It has now become axiomatic in several other disciplines that the sum of disaggregated, uncoordinated and fragmented, hidden, disguised and marginal agencies represents a significant totality. It is not homogenous, unidirectional or unilevel, but still it is almost impossible to predict or to

> countermand. It represents decentralized, bottom-up and grass-roots forms
> of identity, culture and legitimacy, and a capacity that disrupts hegemony.
> (Richmond, 2011b, p. 434)

Non-linear approaches, bringing a variety of self-reproducing frameworks
of explanation to bear on the reproduction of cultural and ideational
barriers to peacebuilding success, increasingly came to dominate the academic and policy agendas by the end of the 2000s. Non-linear and hybrid
approaches reflected well the sense of impasse in international peacebuilding. Importantly, they tended to reify or to naturalise these limits as
somehow inherent in the world and beyond the reach of liberal reason
(see, for example, Popolo, 2011, p. 128). The limits of peacebuilding were
therefore understood to be a product of the hubristic linear thinking of
Western modernity rather than economic and social structural problems
eliciting the possibility of social transformation. Resistance articulated as
the limits of liberal aspirations of peacebuilding thereby no longer needed
the transformative political agency of subjects. It was for this reason that
Oliver Richmond suggested that resistant agency was a vital determining
factor, much as the dark matter of space. This agency was resistant onto-
logically, in its inaccessible mode of life or being, regardless of subjective
political actions or demands.

   Once it was understood that resistance, or the impasse of liberal peacebuilding aspirations, was an objective or inevitable aspect of the world,
then it was easy to understand how the academic boom in 'resistance
studies' articulated much lower horizons for peacebuilding interventions
(see, for example, Hollander and Einwohner, 2004; Eschler and
Maiguashca, 2005; Richmond, 2010; Richmond and Kappler, 2011).
Resistance as an objective characteristic of the world beyond the focus of
the linear epistemes of 'liberal' peacebuilding needed no politics. For
example, Michael Hardt and Antonio Negri gave ontological priority to
resistance rather than to power, enabling the 'Multitude' to resist 'Empire'
through the nature of their biopolitical or ontological being rather than
traditional political forms of organisation, which remain trapped in territorial understandings (see Hardt and Negri, 2005, p. 315).

   Drawing upon, and feeding into this shift, complexity and new materi-
alist approaches were able to further dilute understandings of agency and
resistance to suggest that non-human actors could also be seen to 'resist'
and 'undermine' the linear causal assumptions at the base of international
peacebuilding (see, for example, Bennett, 2010; Connolly, 2011; Latour,

2005). Whereas the old 'historical' materialism understood that the structuring of inequalities was amenable to conscious human transformation, the world of agency of the 'new' materialism lacked the framework for structural change. The actor-network framework of Bruno Latour was a good example of this approach, where social explanation needed the 'missing masses' – both human and non-human – whose 'hidden' influence was seen in the uncertainties and contingencies of the world (see Latour, 2005, pp. 241–6).

In this way, non-linear approaches explained the limits of peacebuilding and its linear reasoning as a product of the objective complexity of assemblages or associations of human and non-human actors, in a flat world of 'quasi-objects and quasi-subjects'. Latour's ontology was thus similar to Richmond's in his insistence that the 'dark matter' or 'plasma' of the world, untouched by the social sciences of liberal modernity, was the key to overcoming our 'astronomical ignorance' and the hubristic fantasies created by this. Latour differed mainly in his understanding that this 'vast hinterland' was limited and bordered by the lack of inclusion of both human and non-human actors or agents and also in his more radical challenge to liberal linearity, in his assertion that these excluded agencies were 'not hidden, simply unknown' (Latour, 2005, p. 244, emphasis in original). In this ontology, it was the 'recalcitrance' of being itself that resisted liberal linear framings rather than conscious or intentional political activity on behalf of the subject (Latour, 2004, p. 81).

Conclusion

While Foucault insightfully argued that 'where there is power, there is resistance', this survey of the shift towards non-linear understandings of peacebuilding suggests that the power/resistance binary became a formalistic and reified one, explaining, rationalising and legitimating 'hybrid' outcomes. In reifying peacebuilding outcomes, the transformative aspirations of peacebuilding became muted and dissipated. The analytical focus on the 'local' and upon 'hidden agency' naturalised the understanding that the impasse of international peacebuilding could be explained at the local level by practices that were internally generated or reproduced through local ways of life or modes of being which were understood as 'resistant' to external 'liberal' forms of compliance. While it was understandable that Western assumptions of exporting external 'blueprints' could be criticised as both politically and practically problematic assertions of unaccountable power and that attention was drawn to the importance of local agency and capacity in the face of these moralised frames of understanding, the non-linear discourses of local 'hidden' agency neither created the basis of any genuine understanding of the limits to international peacebuilding nor provided any emancipatory alternative.

In the first place, the power/resistance binary, as applied in the non-linear peacebuilding discourse, provided an entirely voluntarist or idealist understanding of the limits to peacebuilding. The success or failure of peacebuilding goals was determined by a clash of subjective wills, cultures, cognitive frameworks and temporalities. Ironically, the non-linear approach shared much with the 'linear' approach highlighted at the top of the chapter, which assumed that the problem was subjective elite will or understanding rather than the social and economic context. In evading the question of the material social and economic explanations for the limits to liberal universalist aspirations, non-linear approaches, in fact, still shared much with the conservative understandings of peacebuilding-as-statebuilding approaches, popular with the World Bank and the International Monetary Fund, similarly concerned with highlighting the local (rather than international) limits to economic development – understanding these limits to be endogenous, self-produced and emergent on the basis of cultural and ideational differentiation (see North, 1990; IMF, 2005; World Bank, 2002; also Chandler, 2013).

Second, the ontologicial assumptions of non-linear framings tended to problematise the transformative and emancipatory objectives behind peacebuilding itself rather than the problematic imposition of external projects per se. The ontological assumptions of hybrid understandings rested on the privileging of difference, where conflict was understood as an inevitable product of temporal and cognitive clashes between different modes of being, never amenable to the homogenising gaze of 'liberal' linear thinking. In effect, the 'liberal' frameworks for legitimising external intervention, through the telos of the promise of peace, were rejected while the need for external intervention was accepted as long as it took new, more reflective and less liberal or 'post-liberal' forms, which accepted the need to work with the 'hidden' agencies of the local rather than against them.

Third, and perhaps more importantly, from within this framework, peacebuilding interventions could no longer be held to account through highlighting the gap between their legitimating promise and their reality in terms of outcomes. In the world of 'resistance' rather than 'compliance' the limits of Western liberal aspirations were not constructed as the effects of social and economic inequalities, structuring the asymmetries of intervention, but were seen instead to be the product of cultural or ideational choices of 'resisting' or 'recalcitrant' subjects. Peacebuilding interventions working on the ontological basis of hybridity merely institutionalised lower expectations and horizons, allocating responsibility for this to local agency. Failure to achieve transformative goals and the rejection of these goals in going beyond peacebuilding approaches could then be re-presented as success, both in recognising local agency and in rejecting the 'hubris' of the 'liberal' peacebuilding past.

CHAPTER 8

The Rise of Resilience

Introduction

As considered in the previous chapter, by the 2010s, there had been a shift towards critical understandings of international peacebuilding approaches which argued that local culture held the key to the impasse of peacebuilding interventions. In this 'bottom-up' approach, peace, reconciliation, and a 'culture of law' were understood to be secondary effects of sociocultural norms and values. However, these critiques of peacebuilding (the 'turn to the local') remained trapped in the impasse of international peacebuilding-as-statebuilding: the inability to go beyond the binaries of liberal universalism (the liberal telos of building 'peace') and cultural relativism (the understanding of the barriers to 'peace' as an essentialised product of 'difference'). This understanding will be contrasted in this chapter with an analysis of the rise of 'resilience' approaches to intervention – which built on this attention to the particular context of application but moved beyond this impasse through philosophical pragmatism and the positive focus on concrete social practices. This chapter clarifies the nature of this shift through the focus on the shifting understanding of peacebuilding in addressing community conflicts and stresses caused by the failure of 'war on drugs' peacebuilding interventions in the Americas.

The impasse of international peacebuilding became increasingly apparent as institutionalist understandings came to dominate critical debate over peacebuilding interventions by the 2010s. These frameworks were critical of liberal assumptions of the universal autonomous rational subject,

© The Author(s) 2017

D. Chandler, *Peacebuilding*, Rethinking Peace and Conflict Studies, DOI 10.1007/978-3-319-50322-6_8 drawing attention to ways in which the subjects of peace interventions were non- or a-liberal and socio-culturally embedded (see, for example, Paris, 2004; Richmond, 2011a; Mac Ginty, 2011; Newman et al., 2009; Campbell et al., 2011; Tadjbakhsh, 2011; Richmond and Mitchell, 2012). In these approaches, 'liberal' regimes of international peacebuilding, seen as relying on top-down frameworks of markets, liberal democracy, and the rule of law, were viewed as problematic in societies designated as 'non-liberal'.

However, these critical approaches, while useful in drawing attention to the impasse of international peacebuilding, were unable to provide a programme of policymaking that went beyond the impasse that they established themselves in opposition to. Either liberal framings of rights and law were seen as too abstract and distant from the 'realities' of 'every-day life', often with unintended and problematic consequences, or there was the perceived danger of cultural relativism, undermining democracy and human rights, where law was seen as problematically adapting to 'local' sociocultural differences.

This chapter analyses how resilience approaches, informed by philoso-phical pragmatism, began to enable both critics and policymakers to over-come the international peacebuilding impasse through focusing on the transformative power of local practices and understandings. Resilience was often defined 'as the capacity to positively or successfully adapt to external problems or threats' (Chandler, 2012, p. 217), but as Philippe Bourbeau noted in his cross-disciplinary survey, a broader definition could under-stand 'resilience as the process of patterned adjustments adopted by a society or an individual in the face of endogenous or exogenous shocks' (Bourbeau, 2013, p. 10). The key point highlighted here is that resilience increasingly focused on working with and upon the capacities, capabilities, processes, and practices already 'to hand' rather than the external provi-sion of policies or programmes.

Resilience-informed policy thinking built upon critiques of the formal and abstract nature of liberal modernist understandings of universal con-stitutional and legal rights frameworks but sought to avoid the peace-building-as-statebuiding policy impasse of essentialising sociocultural difference (considered in Chapters 5 and 6). These approaches neither advocated for the export of liberal institutions nor worked on transform-ing the societal level with the goal of enabling these institutions to take root. Resilience approaches evaded the problematic of liberal goals and universal framings, targeting communities to enhance their existing local capacities. These approaches took a much 'flatter' and more agent-centred approach than that of the peacebuilding-as-statebuilding paradigm, which understood problems in terms of discursive, cognitive, and ideational frameworks, seen to constitute the 'gap' between liberal universalist ideals and the problematic realities on the ground. Resilience approaches did not start from the problematic of socio-cultural difference but from a different set of problems that no longer involved a focus on a 'hermeneutics of suspicion' (Ricoeur, 1970, p. 27): problematising the understanding or rationality of those seen to be in need of intervention.

These 'resilience' framings suggested that, in a complex and flatter world, liberal forms of institutional and legal understanding were themselves problematic: that formal frameworks of law could no longer be understood to work to shape or direct social processes in a top-down or hierarchical manner. From this starting point, 'everyday life' was neither conceived of as a problem nor romanticised as 'resisting' (as considered in the previous chapter) but seen as providing a problem-solving resource of practices to be drawn upon. This shift evaded the problems of the external imposition of abstract, 'unreal', liberal universalist frameworks, but also evaded cultural relativism, because there was no external yardstick or comparison at play in such understandings and thereby no articulation of an external subject position of a superior approach or rationality.

While international peacebuilding approaches, with clear goals and sets of technical expertise, involved the assumption of a universalist subject position – described by Ole Jacob Sending as an external 'Archimedean' position (2009) – resilience approaches moved away from this external subject position. In focusing on how everyday practices could provide the resources to address the problems faced, problems and solutions were no longer debated in the formal framings of the export of liberal institutions, laws and rights; instead resilience approaches were based on how practices worked in a particular context. The growing attention to concrete practices rather than to explaining the 'gap' between theory and the world through the attention to discursive structures was reflected in the growing attention to practice theory and actor-network approaches, (see, for example, Kratochwil and Friedrichs, 2009; Neumann, 2002; Bueger, 2012; Kessler and Guillaume, 2012).

This approach, which could best be grasped in the conceptual paradigm of philosophical pragmatism, started neither from universalist nor cultural relativist assumptions with regard to formal institutional frameworks but with the effects of their application in particular circumstances (see Dewey, 1954).

The core aspect was the empiricist attitude of concern with practical consequences rather than abstract concepts and beliefs. Philosophical pragmatism sought to overcome the divide between Cartesian understandings of objective truth and sceptical perspectives, that truth was always relative or subjective, through the emphasis on practical consequences (see, for example, Dewey, 2008). It was this framing which was at the heart of resilience approaches which went beyond universalist/cultural relativist understandings of international peacebuilding as a 'liberal' paradigm (see further, Chandler, 2014).

It is the connection between resilience and philosophical pragmatism, which is important to draw out here. International peacebuilding frameworks, with their binary focus on the universalist understandings of international interveners and pluralist constructions of the non-liberal barriers to these understandings at the local level, forced a discussion of policy accountability on to the agenda, allocating agency and responsibility to either internationals or locals. Pragmatic approaches of resilience sought to overcome this problematic and hierarchical binary by removing the 'external' nature of international policy actors, as the focus upon the practices of the 'everyday' was understood to generate the policy goals of intervention through community development itself. As Moe and Simojoki noted, 'the forms of peace evolving through such pragmatic engagement would be qualitatively different from prevailing notions of liberal peace... building on local practices may involve increasing rather than reducing plurality and diversity... rather than striving for known endpoints' (2013, p. 411).

This chapter takes as an example of this shift, the policy discussion on the limits of international peacebuilding intervention with regard to security and the 'war on drugs' in the Americas. This discussion was cohered through the publication of a high-profile report from the General Secretariat of the Organisation of American States, suggesting that international peacebuilding interventions had failed in this area (OAS, 2013a). The 'war on drugs' had been framed in the terminology of international peacebuilding for fragile and conflict-prone states in the region (see, for example, Morton, 2011; Cammack et al., 2006; Miraglia et al., 2012; Tokatlián, 2011; Sogge, 2009) and therefore was a good example of how peacebuilding interventions were refocused in the early 2010s. International, essentially US-led, approaches to the problem had focused primarily on drug production and distribution in Latin American states and the prominence of international criminal organisations and networks operating with relative impunity where many states had fragile frameworks of law and rights enforcement.

Heuristically, it is possible to draw out three different approaches to the problem. Firstly, what might be called a 'top-down' universalist peacebuilding approach, where resources were put into strengthening state capacity: training police and security forces, improving the operation and independence of the judiciary, increasing state level coordination and information sharing and developing the strength of legal regimes in terms of democracy and human rights. Richmond described this 'liberal peace' approach as 'a model through which Western-led agency, epistemology and institutions, have attempted to unite the world order under a hegemonic system that replicates liberal institutions, norms, and political, social and economic systems' (2011a, p. 1).

The second, the more pluralist and culturally sensitive 'bottom-up' peacebuilding-as-statebuilding approach, more typical of the 2000s, started with the perceived failures of exporting institutional frameworks and focused instead on societal capacity-building, working in the impasse described in the previous part of this book. This approach paid much more attention to deeper sociocultural values and understandings, suggesting that success at the state-level was dependent upon 'local' understandings – that norms and values change was the key to peace and the institutionalisation of a 'rule of law' regime (see, for example, Fukuyama, 1995; Risse et al., 1999; Cortell and Davis, 2000; Chandler, 2013).

The third approach – the 'resilience' approach – did not start from the position of an external liberal subject equipped with superior interventionist knowledge or instrumental goals. Resilience approaches sought to work through understanding the concrete context in which social practices and everyday 'tactics' produced problematic consequences: in this case, the conflicts and instability caused by the criminal production, trafficking and consumption of drugs. Through a process-based or relational understanding of the construction of a concrete problem (or set of problems), everyday contexts and practices were seen to provide the key to mitigating both the causes and consequences. For example the security questions posed by 'the drug problem' in the Americas:

> Resilience is the story of a profound change in perspective about where the solution to the hemispheric drug problem can be found. Rather than focusing primarily on suppressing drug production and trafficking, or changing the legal or regulatory regime, national and local leaders recognize that

the best approach is to focus on people rather than drugs and to rebuild and strengthen communities from the grassroots level up. Like a healthy body, a healthy community fights off an 'epidemic', whether it is an epidemic of violence or of drug dependence, through its own capacity to respond effectively – its own resilience. (OAS, 2013b, p. 55)

The shift from understanding local sociocultural values – as the problem or barrier to be overcome – to resilience approaches, which understood local practices, in the context of the production of a concrete problem and its solution, was crucial. Here, local responses and practices were seen as key to positive transformation once the relational context, through which the problem was understood to be generated, could be understood and addressed.

The following section draws out how the impasse of international peacebuilding-as-statebuilding was initially reproduced through the extension of international peacebuilding interventions in the societal sphere – where cultural sensitivities led either to increasingly problematic universalist attempts to remake cultural norms or to the perceived problem of a cultural relativist adaption to the status quo. Then the example of the Organisation of American States initiative to rethink the 'war on drugs' will be used to demonstrate how a discussion about how to export institutional frameworks and the 'rule of law' pragmatically shifted to one about how to deal with a set of varied problems, once they were re-presented as contextually embedded social practices.

The Limits of Culture

Whereas earlier international peacebuilding approaches to institutional frameworks of governance assumed a more universalist approach, in peacebuilding-as-statebuilding understandings, the efficacy or capacity of state institutions and the 'rule of law' was increasingly understood to be dependent upon their sociocultural foundations (see, for example, North, 1990; Mahoney and Thelen, 2010; Peters, 2005; Scott, 2008). This perspective was probably most famously articulated by Friedrich von Hayek, in his view that modern liberal institutions could not be exported or created by edicts or plans but had to emerge organically from society (von Hayek, 1960, p. 22; see also; Tamanaha, 2004; Cesarini and Hite, 2004). In this organic or culturalist perspective, the constitutional history of Great Britain was often highlighted to argue that even without a written (codified) constitution, the rule of law had more de facto purchase than in the former colonies where the rule of law needed to be produced through de jure democratic constitutions. This gap, between de facto legal standing and a purely de jure one, began to enter the sphere of international legal and political understandings of sovereignty with the end of the Cold War (see Jackson, 1990).

For peacebuilding-as-statebuilding approaches, law could not provide its own legitimacy – its own basis, limits, or constraints – anymore than democratic theory could explain the constitution of the demos. In this context, research projects and, in fact, even entire research institutes worked on the basis of the need to investigate 'law as culture' (see Gephart, 2010). The universal, 'natural' or 'Cartesian' assumptions of the liberal rationalist autonomous subject were subject to devastating critique from these sociologically informed and pragmatic positions. But while operating to highlight the limits of universalist peacebuilding constructions of the rule of law there appeared to be little that could be done to overcome these limits. The sphere of sociocultural understandings appeared to pose a formidable policy challenge. Often, in peacebuilding discourse, this contrast, between the 'reality' of the everyday and the formal framework of law, was understood in terms of two – opposing – spatially constructed rationalities: that of the 'international' and the 'local' (as considered in the previous chapter).

This clash, between the formal and the real, was captured in critical conceptual approaches that focused on the hybrid outcomes of international interventions that attempted to transform societies through top-down mechanisms such as legal and constitutional reforms (see, for example, Roberts, 2008; Richmond, 2009; Mac Ginty, 2011; Richmond and Mitchell, 2012). In the framings of hybridity approaches: 'the "laws" of the society can easily overrule the laws of the state' (Zimmermann, 2007, p. 29). As Zimmermann argued: 'Socially speaking, the former can be far more institutionalized than the latter, which means that the state law can easily be undermined by the lack of connection between its formal precepts and observed behavior' (2007, p. 29).

These 'hybrid', sociological approaches understood 'local', national, or community cultures and values as a socially constructed barrier to the export or development of constitutional frameworks and the rule of law (see, Chandler, 2013). The discursive framework in which these approaches developed was that of analysing and explaining the limits of external interventions based on universal understandings. Universalist framings of law were held to fail where societies were understood to be 'non-liberal' and therefore not ready for, or incapable of, organising on the basis of law standing above social and economic conflicts. These barriers to the 'rule of law' were often understood to have deep cultural roots in the colonial era or in the parallel power structures that emerged during internal conflicts, and seen to be similarly deep-rooted. It is these deep societal roots that were held to explain the limits of international peacebuilding.

The limits of peacebuilding-as-statebuilding framings, which sought to promote liberal institutional outcomes, through interventions at the deeper, sociocultural level, were clearly highlighted in 'culture of lawfulness' policy interventions that attempted to transform culture to enable the rule of law. These programmes had been particularly prevalent in the peacebuilding frameworks of the 'war on drugs' in Latin America. Heavily funded by the US Government and the World Bank, initiatives led by the US-based NGO the National Strategy Information Centre (NISC) placed the culture of lawfulness at the centre of the US's global security strategy of peacebuilding. According to US Under Secretary of State for Global Affairs, Paula Dobriansky: 'Government efforts to enforce the law are insufficient in and of themselves to establish the rule of law in a country. This is a result of the fact that lawlessness and corruption often stem from social norms and historic practices' (Dobriansky, 2004). For Dobriansky, historic path dependencies and sociocultural norms meant that the rule of law could not operate universally. She argued therefore that sociocultural interventions were necessary to educate and win over the 'hearts and minds' of recalcitrant subjects (Dobriansky, 2004).

A typical example was that of the National Strategy Information Center 'culture of lawfulness' three-year project in the city of Pereira, Columbia, funded from 2008 to 2010. The project's starting presupposition was that the local culture was a central barrier to the rule of law: 'Prior to this project, rule of law principles had few public advocates and were not well understood by the people of Pereira. Apathy and fatalism were the norm for large segments of the population, and many engaged in or tolerated illicit behaviour' (NSIC, 2011, p. ii). The project started with local knowledge and understandings, developing 'a Pereiran rule of law narrative, locally driven and cognizant of Pereira's unique history, customs and culture' and with the desire of government and civil society leaders to tackle the barriers of the local culture (NSIC, 2011, p. ii). With the zeal of nineteenth-century missionaries, the NSIC attempted to align USAID and local funding, using local knowledge and access to society – at the level of

government leaders, civil society organisations, faith groups, local businesses, the media, and schools – to initiate awareness of the rule of law,
educate and inform, and begin to change ingrained patterns of behaviour.

Local culture was to be engaged with on the basis that the locals needed
to adapt to and learn about universal liberal understandings of the 'rule of
law':

> ...training judges and prosecutors, rewriting laws, and building investigative
> facilities for police are not sufficient. To be effective, these efforts need to be
> accompanied by the development of societal support for rule of law princi-
> ples. This entails educating citizens about the importance of the rule of law,
> how it enhances their quality of life, and the role they can play in making it a
> reality. When education and culture supportive of lawfulness are combined
> with enhanced law enforcement and institutional reforms, justice and order
> can be strengthened and crime and corruption reduced – even within one
> generation. However, reform efforts that do not address the culture at large,
> neglect a cost efficient, effective, and long-lasting way to deepen democracy.
> (NISC, 2011, p. 1)

It was understood that if the barrier of local culture could be successfully
overcome, liberal institutions and frameworks could take root 'even
within one generation', while reforms that worked at the state and
institutional level would be doomed to failure, just remaining at the
superficial level of the formal framework and not touching the local
reality. To this end, local leaders were encouraged to buy into the
programme, and an all-out 'counter-insurgency' campaign was launched
to win over the 'hearts and minds' of the community: 'A comprehensive
citywide CoL [culture of lawfulness] campaign...touched Pereirans at
nearly every point of contact – at school, at work, in transit (buses, taxis,
billboards), through television/radio/print, at community events and in
houses of worship' (NISC, 2011, p. iii).

The NISC evaluated their own project positively, arguing that over the
three year period it had a substantial impact on the community 'measured
through the degree of the institutionalization of CoL in long-term community processes, activities and planning as well as significant shifts seen
during the program in popular knowledge and attitudes – a foundation of
behavioral change' (NISC, 2011, p. iii). It is important to note that these
institutionalist framings operated at the level of intersubjective understandings – the empowerment that they offered to the 'local' level was

that of individuals having a different understanding of the importance of the rule of law and their role as active citizens. These cognitive changes then were to lead to changes in behaviour, enabling liberal transformation, facilitating the rule of law (NISC, 2011, p. 1).

Although there was the language of local knowledge and resources, needs and interests and the empowerment of local people, it was clear that the agenda was very much one in which enlightened Western interveners, equipped with the external subject position of liberal universalist understandings, attempted to transform the barrier of local cultural-social frameworks. Because intervention was consciously aimed at transforming the minds and understanding of local people – and thereby necessarily setting up a hierarchy of understanding – the gap between the external perspective and the 'local' arena became clearer the more the international 'empowerment' agenda extended into the society (see also Pupavac, 2005).

This became clear in projects such as the comprehensive 'multi-sectoral' campaign, considered here. In fact, reading their report it becomes clear how patronising and demeaning this work was for those they sought to 'empower'. Examples of good work highlighted in the report included a 60-hour Culture of Lawfulness course to be taught in schools (NISC, 2011, p. 2), encouraging the media to incorporate culture of lawfulness themes into documentaries, soap operas, game and talk shows (ibid, p. 9), therapeutic workshops for citizens to 'give voice to the obstacles and frustrations they faced along their "journey" to a culture of lawfulness' (ibid, p. 11), an annual 'Most Legal and Most Safe Neighborhood' competition (ibid), culture of lawfulness supported hip hop and rap festivals – including 'The Culture of Lawfulness is an Awesome Challenge' rap contest (ibid, pp. 12; 27), public education billboards with personal testimonies concluding with the phrase: 'and YOU, what are YOU going to do for lawfulness?' (ibid, p. 13), mime and theatre to discourage speeding and jay walking (ibid, p. 14), pledges for lawfulness by the town mayor in front of primary school children (ibid, p. 16), local Chamber of Commerce prize 'Culture of Lawfulness is my Business' (ibid, p. 18), and a Culture of Lawfulness 'paint fest' (ibid, p. 24). Local pastors and lay preachers were even given manuals on how to introduce rule of law themes into their services (ibid, p. 26). Of course, the paradox was that the more multi-sectoral and comprehensive the culture of lawfulness intervention was, the more artificial and patronising it became; while any single activity on its own seemed clearly unable to tackle the task at hand, 'to transform an entire culture' (ibid, p. 20).

These approaches were limited by the insitutionalist peacebuilding-as-statebuilding framings that they explicitly drew upon (and explicitly defended). Here 'the rule of law' was consciously articulated as an external rationality, as somehow the preserve of the West (where, as noted above, it was often held that there was no cultural or societal mismatch), meaning that any attempt to 'artificially' construct rule of law regimes, even though 'culture of lawfulness' attempts to 'transform entire cultures', hardly appeared feasible. Even the best and most determined attempts to engage with the 'local', in order to transform cultural values, fell prey to the problems of 'artificiality' (which had already beset international attempts to export the 'rule of law' through state and institutional level legal and constitutional reforms). Furthermore, no matter how culturally sensitive these interventions were, they still – in fact, inevitably – produced hierarchical understandings, which problematised (even pathologised) local understandings and values, and came across as patronising and neocolonial.

There were clear limits to attempts to overcome the impasse of international peacebuilding approaches on the basis of interventions to transform 'local' sociocultural understandings. Local sociocultural understandings and values were usually grounded upon contextual realities, such as structural and socioeconomic frameworks of inequality and exclusion, and thereby were not necessarily amenable to interventions at the level of formal understanding (see further, Acharya, 2000; Belloni, 2008; Paffenholz, 2009). However, the alternative approach to these barriers – of adapting liberal understandings of legal and constitutional practices to local sociocultural contexts – appeared to be equally problematic in terms of leaving international organisations vulnerable to accusations of providing support to 'illiberal' actors or undermining human rights norms (Moe and Simiojoki, 2013, p. 400). The impasse of international peacebuilding was fully highlighted in attempts to defend international intervention, but which denied that local culture would necessarily be seen in these liberal, 'problematic' ways by external interveners.

For more critical or radical peacebuilding theorists, intervention needed to be done in more self-reflexive ways, which similarly sought to problematise Western understandings of liberal universality. These critical approaches were often drawn towards pluralist anthropological frameworks in order to develop an ethical methodology of intervention, which could break free of the hierarchical understandings explicit in liberal universalism. Here, the plural and 'hybrid' outcomes of international intervention were seen as positive and to be encouraged. In fact, the experience of intervention, it was alleged, could be a mutual learning exchange between intervener and those intervened upon, as fixed cultural understandings on both sides could be challenged through 'unscripted conversations' and 'the spontaneity of unpredictable encounters' (see, for example, Duffield, 2007, pp. 233–4; Richmond, 2009; also Jabri, 2007, p. 177).

The obvious problem with the 'unscripted conversations' approach was the question: 'Why then intervene in the first place?' The answer was that intervention was essentially a mechanism of intersubjective enlargement of reflexivity, enabling an emancipation of both the peacebuilding intervener and those intervened upon, through the opening up of possibilities for both to free themselves from the sociocultural constraints of their own societies and to share a pluralised ethos of peace which, through pluralising, went beyond both liberal universalism and non-liberalism. As Morgan Brigg and Kate Muller argued:

> Conflict resolution analysts and practitioners might facilitate this process [of increasing exchange and understanding across difference] – something which has already begun – by openly examining and discussing their own cultural values within their practice. This can generate possibilities for more dynamic conflict resolution processes by extending the practice, also already underway, of opening to and learning from local and Indigenous capacities, including different ways of knowing, approaching and managing conflict. (Brigg and Muller, 2009, p. 135)

For Richmond, this plural and emancipatory peace, based on mutual learning and exchange, was thereby 'post-liberal' (Richmond, 2009). Here, cultural understandings were also seen as malleable and open to intersubjective transformation, enabling 'post-liberal' peacebuilding approaches to overcome the problems of conflict, crime, and reconstruction but without privileging universalist understandings – although these views could be critiqued as no more than the anthropological ethics of cosmopolitan liberalism (see Shannon, 1995) this is not the focus here.

The impasse of international peacebuilding-as-statebuilding was merely brought into full focus in these critical approaches, which found it impossible to escape the focus on sociocultural norms and values. The ethics of radical 'post-liberal' peacebuilding were those of cultural pluralism and the 'respect and the recognition of difference' beyond the divide of 'liberal and non-liberal contexts' (Richmond, 2009, p. 566). However, it was clear that the problematic was one that still shared much with the liberal universalist vision, merely questioning its ability to fully accept the existence of plurality (see also Sabaratnam, 2013). As Richmond argued: 'Behind all of this is the lurking question of whether liberal paradigms are able to engage with, and represent equitably non-liberal others – those for which it infers a lesser status' (2009, p. 570).

For Richmond, the need to overcome the universalism of international peacebuilding approaches shaped the understanding of the problem as one of pluralisation, that 'requires a privileging of non-liberal voices' and the 'ongoing development of local-liberal hybrid forms of peace' (2009, p. 578). However, as Audra Mitchell, among others, highlighted, this framing problematically focused on fixed or essentialised sociocultural understandings, counter-positioning an external 'liberal' internationalist subject to a 'non-liberal' local one (Mitchell, 2011). Mitchell pointed further beyond 'liberal' peacebuilding framings, in articulating practices as the key to understanding outcomes of intervention rather than focusing on the binary and hybrid perspectives of liberal/non-liberal and international/local. The focus on effects rather than on cultural difference was key to the discursive moves of resilience approaches, which took policy debates beyond the 'liberal' peacebuilding paradigm and its impasse of engineering liberal goals without developing hierarchical and divisive forms of regulation.

The starting point for resilience was a reinterpretation of the liberal discursive construction of 'culture' itself as a fixed or settled spatial community of intersubjective, constructed meanings, which external interveners were somehow external to. As Ann Swindler noted 'a culture is not a unified system that pushes action in a consistent direction... it is more like a "tool kit" or repertoire' (1986, p. 277; see also Sewell, 1999). The peacebuilding-as-statebuilding approach could thereby be understood to operate merely through inversing hierarchical liberal understandings of universal reason (see Scott, 2003). The epistemological privileging of 'local' knowledge then became the basis of value pluralism, but always from the standpoint of the problems of liberal democracy and universalist approaches to public institutions and the rule of law (see, for example, Brigg, 2010; Mac Ginty, 2008). As long as the discourse remained on the level of shared rationalities of spatially differentiated inter-subjective collectivities, both academic and policy discussion stayed on the terrain of liberal universalism and value relativism, based upon the judgement of the intervener, self-understood as external to the problematic (Richmond, 2009).

It was only in the sphere of practices and strategies in relation to concrete problems that there could be a shift away from spatial constructions to social practices. The 'local' or the 'everyday' then became the focal point, not on the basis of the epistemological differences of liberal reason but on the ontological basis of the practical production of the world. This was where practice-based understandings became particularly useful. Annemarie Mol's work, for example, on medical intervention in the treatment of diabetes provided a methodological template by drawing out how seemingly universal or objective medical understandings, in fact, were produced through diverse assemblages of social practices. Thus understandings and meanings needed to be grasped in their concrete context as 'a part of ongoing practices: practices of care as well as practices to do with work, school, family, friends, holidays and everything else that might be important in a person's life' (see Mol, 2008, p. 53).

THE RISE OF RESILIENCE

While the international peacebuilding problematic deployed external standards of judgement and downplayed the critical and agential capacity of actors, philosophical pragmatism argued that the world was made 'from below' (Boltanski, 2011, p. 44), through the practices of the 'everyday', and that the only purpose of external intervention could be to facilitate and respond reflexively to these practices rather than seek to remake or constrain them through either liberal universalist or peace-building-as-statebuilding approaches. The importance of understanding society 'from the bottom-up' rather than 'from the top-down' was well articulated by a number of authors with a growing impact on debates on international policymaking. Perhaps the classic text in this regard was Michel de Certeau's *The Practice of Everyday Life* (1998). In his analysis of the practices of the 'everyday', de Certeau shared much with the actor-network theory of Bruno Latour and the work of the French pragmatist theorist, Luc Boltanski (Latour, 2004a, 2005; Boltanski, 2011). Just as Latour argued that 'we have never been modern' – in his devastating critique of the artificial division between science and culture (Latour, 1993) – so de Certeau hinted at the ever-present reality of the practices of local and 'everyday' agency outside the reach of liberal representational theory (see also Thrift, 2008). Rather than seeing the 'everyday' as only operating on the margins, or merely as a barrier or limit, 'altering or defeating' the instruments of power, de

Certeau argued that it was the external grand narratives and strategies of power which should be seen as marginal, artificial, phenomenological constructs (1998, p. 41).

What was vital about the pragmatist framework was not so much the fact that policy attention was drawn to the everyday but its methodological centrality. Authors such as James C. Scott had focused on everyday life as the sphere of resistance (see the previous chapter), but the transformative capacities of the 'everyday' remained marginal, erupting on the surface only on rare occasions (see, for example, Scott, 1990; also a similar framing in Rancière, 1999). Similarly, Henri Lefebvre's understanding of the 'everyday' could be seen as one that was under the surface of modernity rather than constituting its appearances (see, Lefebvre, 1987). What differentiated the pragmatist philosophy of authors such as de Certeau, Boltanski, and Latour was their critique of the structural discursive understandings, which marginalised the concrete and specific practices of the everyday. As Boltanski argued, the resources of the local provided the empirical material for a 'sociology of critique', which gave agency to previously marginalised subjects, seen as constrained by discursive structures of power in the 'critical sociology' of authors such as Althusser, Foucault, and Bourdieu (Boltanski, 2011; Latour, 2004b; de Certeau, 1998, pp. 45–60; also Celikates, 2006).

For Boltanski, pragmatic sociology, with its rigorous empiricism could offer 'better descriptions of the activity of actors in particular situations' (2011, p. 23). Rather than starting from the external subject position of critical sociological theory, pragmatic sociology 'refocused the sociologist's attention on actors en situation, as the main agencies of performance of the social' (ibid, p. 24). As Boltanski argued, the key intent was to go beyond both the universalist and culturalist frameworks:

> The universalist framework is explicitly rejected, because the polities are treated as historical constructs. As to the culturalist framework, it is displaced from culture in the sense of anthropology towards the political... The social actors whose disputes are observed by the sociologist are realistic. They do not demand the impossible. Their sense of reality is sustained by the way they grasp their social environment. (Boltanski, 2011, p. 31)

Informed by philosophical pragmatism, resilience approaches did not start from liberal universalist assumptions of the rational autonomous subject and thus were no longer concerned with explaining the limits of liberal universalism, or attempting to work on culture to overcome the 'gap' between liberal assumptions and 'everyday' reality. Even in Western societies it was argued that everyday realities trumped any attempts to use the law for purposes of societal regulation: 'Under late modern conditions, where law's normativity can no longer find a durable foothold in fleeting social structures, legal measures aimed at generating new patterns of behaviour or social change grow evermore ineffective' (Banakar, 2013, p. 21).

It is important to note that, in these approaches, the complexity and fluidity of social practices was highlighted and the spatial dispersal of 'communities' with net-worked connections, which lacked a strong sense of shared intersubjective values. Law failed to connect with society but not on the basis of the structured or cohered 'gap' between culture(s) and law. In fact, it was possible to argue that the attempts to renegotiate liberal frameworks of representation, on the basis of cultural differences and multi-culturalism, could retrospectively be seen as precursors to the discussion of governing complexity in terms of resilience (see further, Walzer, 1983; Kymlicka, 1995; Tully, 1995; Gutman, 1994). Resilience approaches started from the assumption that there could be no 'organic', 'cultural', or intersubjective construction of community, which gave legal frameworks a purchase on social complexity. Instead, their concern was with how societal regulation could operate on the basis of fluidity and complexity. As the Stockholm Resilience Centre argued:

> Law is traditionally characterised by 'thou shalts' rather than opening doors for new approaches. As a reaction to this, the concept of reflexive law has emerged. Reflexive law is less rule-bound and recognises that as long as certain basic procedures and organisational norms are respected, participants can arrive at positive outcomes and correct their projects along the way, basically learning by doing. In response to growing complexity, detailed rules are replaced by procedures for regulated entities to follow. Reflexive law is a social innovation which seeks to promote multi-level governance and preserve diversity and experimentation at local level. (SRC, 2014, p. 14)

Law and society were not to be treated separately, not because there was a clash between liberal universalism and cultural relativism but because universal frameworks of law were understood to be the barrier to governing complexity rather than a solution. These approaches shared the focus on the local societal milieu of international peacebuilding debates, but in these framings the milieu was seen as providing the sphere in which transformative agency was generated through practice. In effect, resilience approaches reposed the problem not in terms of a 'gap' between law and society (or the binaries of abstract and concrete or 'local' and 'international') but in pragmatic terms of specific problems or consequences, which could no longer be meaningfully addressed through the mechanisms of law (or external subject positions) as a guide to practice.

It was the internal processes of practical relations and outcomes that needed to be understood and worked upon, not the external mechanisms and frameworks which needed to be refined. As Manuel DeLanda noted, the key to non-linear understandings of complexity was that the internal organisation of an entity was more important that the external or extrinsic factors, which 'are efficient solely to the extent to which they take a grip on the proper nature and inner processes of things'. One and the same external set of policies or causal actions 'may produce very different effects' (2006, p. 20). This pragmatic approach evaded the problems of 'liberal' discourses of peacebuilding, neither imposing a universal framework over sociocultural difference, nor recognising or privileging 'local' choices as emancipatory. The problem was the contextual assemblage within which practices took place. The 'local', or the 'everyday' was understood neither as a product of social and economic structures or fixed ideological and cultural values nor as a barrier or limit but rather as a set of fluid microprocesses of practices in a constant interaction driven by the agency of ordinary people in concrete circumstances.

In this way, 'everyday' life operated across or outside of the structural spatial orderings of critical sociological theory and the homogenising assumptions of top-down understandings of science, law, and politics. For the advocates of resilience approaches, it was the 'tactics' of the everyday which constituted the world and its problems, not the universalist 'strategies' of liberal regimes of power shaped by an external viewpoint somehow 'outside' the problematic. As Foucault indicated, this shift away from the sovereign and disciplinary power of law, focused on the real lives or the 'everyday' of individuals and communities 'and their environment, the milieu in which they live … to the extent that it is not a natural environment, that it has been created by the population and therefore has effects on that population' (Foucault, 2003, p. 245). It was this 'milieu' of societal practices which thereby 'appeared as a field of intervention' rather than the formal sphere of law (Foucault, 2007, pp. 20–1). In this framework, governance operated through societal processes rather than over or against them.

THE DRUG PROBLEM IN THE AMERICAS

A good example of the resilience approach to law and institutional frameworks was that of the discussion with regard to international peacebuilding and the 'war on drugs', which had been reposed not as a question of law enforcement but in terms of 'the drug problem in the Americas' (OAS, 2013a). What made the OAS report particularly interesting was that it was produced in two parts: the Analytical Report based on a series of case studies, which analysed the problem; and a Scenarios Report based on a hypothetical analysis of four possible futures. It is the Scenarios Report, which will be focused upon here. The four possible future scenarios were categorised as 'Together', 'Pathways', 'Resilience' and 'Disruption'. These different scenarios could be heuristically categorised, respectively, as: international peacebuilding-as-statebuilding; peacebuilding as a turn to 'the local' to align law and sociocultural norms; resilience-based approaches concerned with the problem in terms of the contextual framing of local practices; and accepting the perceived status quo, which would lead to diverse responses, including compromising with criminal networks where the costs of controlling them was considered too high.

The international peacebuilding approach to the insecurities caused by the drug problem was just one of the options in the OAS report. The universalist peacebuilding approach focused on state-level institutions, arguing that the drug problem 'is part of a larger insecurity problem, with weak state institutions unable to control organized crime and the violence and corruption it generates' (OAS, 2013b, p. 23). The response was then that of strengthening the capacity of judicial and public institutions, improving their professional status and bringing in new techniques, benchmarks, and success indicators. Collectively, states in the region would then be able to launch a sustained campaign against transnational criminal organisations. In this scenario, liberal institutional changes were seen to be effective: reducing the power of criminal organisations and trafficking gangs through increasing the strength and effectiveness of democratic and legal institutions. This liberal good governance framing was also understood to strengthen economies in these states and to transform local values and understandings, lessening support for organised criminal groups and enabling liberal institutional frameworks, based on human rights and transparent procedures, to extend even in outlying areas where drugs were grown and produced (OAS, 2013b, p. 30).

The report argued that there was also plenty of evidence against such approaches, which were the sine qua non of international peacebuilding programmes in the 1990s and 2000s. The complexity of drug production, trade, and consumption in the Americas and the different contexts, which state institutions were faced with, could also be argued to undermine such universalist understandings of 'good government'. For many of the states concerned, the focus on law enforcement and drug prohibition 'produces more damage that the drugs themselves' (OAS, 2013b, p. 41). It was understood that peacebuilding enforcement efforts not only failed to sufficiently reduce the supply and the demand for drugs but that they also had the unintended consequence of providing illegal criminal gangs with huge profit margins, while risking the security of their citizens and the integrity of their democracies (ibid, p. 42).

The second approach of cultural pluralism sought to move beyond the 'liberal' peacebuilding paradigm in a turn to the 'local'. It argued that there was no such thing as a universal solution to the security problem, particularly at the level of formal framings of law, good government, and institutional capacity. While drugs might be a problem, using the law to prohibit drug production, transportation, and use was also a problem where the sociocultural context militated against its effective operation, or produced even more problematic unintended consequences in the increase of police and paramilitary power. It argued that the impasse of peacebuilding-as-statebuilding policies was that the unintended consequences of their adoption appeared to be just as problematic as the problems they were intended to resolve. The 'impasse' or 'contradictions' of international peacebuilding approaches, based on universalist assumptions, were by this stage much more commonly accepted (see, for example, Paris and Sisk, 2009a).

Pluralist approaches attempted to escape this impasse through either working to adapt local cultures to the rule of law or (using the same ontological framing, but privileging 'local' rather than 'international' voices) adapting law to the social context. The pluralist approach as portrayed in the OAS report appeared to adopt the latter perspective, advocated both by the radical critics of liberal peacebuilding and the pragmatic advocates of scaling back intervention (see Merilee Grindle's conception of 'good enough governance', Grindle, 2004, 2007). This was outlined in the 'Pathways' scenario, which rearticulated the drug problem in less universalist terms (OAS, 2013b, p. 43). The reason for a pluralist approach, it was argued, was that the drug problem and the use of law enforcement to address it could not be properly grasped outside of the specific cultural-socio-political context:

> ...the international drug control framework may operate well enough for some countries but generates serious problems for others. For example, harms and costs related to drug consumption in the region (loss of productivity, dependency, treatment costs, stress on families) and those related to drug control enforcement are unevenly distributed and do not affect every country in the hemisphere in the same way or to the same extent. Political leaders in some Central and South American countries where there is drug crop cultivation believe that problems of drug-related violence, high homicide rates, insecurity, overcrowded prisons, and human rights violations are made worse or are even largely caused by efforts to prevent the illicit production and trafficking of drugs. (OAS, 2013b, p. 45)

This argument to a certain extent reflected the discussion in the United States where the war on drugs was seen to be a war on the poor and marginalised (both inside and outside America) and it was argued that the balance needed to be refocused in a more 'emancipatory' way to concerns of human rights, health provision, and the development and protection of cultural and indigenous rights (OAS, 2013b, p. 47).

The cultural pluralist understanding focused much less on the institutional frameworks and more on the specific cultural context in which the law operated, and in this way sought to mitigate the unintended consequences of universalist approaches. The location of the solution was shifted downwards to experiment with alternative legal and regulatory frameworks. The most consensual regulatory shift in this regard was experimentation with the decriminalisation of softer drugs such as cannabis and focusing more resources on major criminal networks than on small-scale production and consumption. In this way, resources could be better distributed, lifting the burden on police, prisons, and courts as well as reducing the drug market and enabling drugs, which were decriminalised, to be better regulated.

Of course, it could be noted that, in this framing, law was being adapted to the sociocultural reality rather than making a 'culture of lawfulness' attempt to adapt sociocultural reality to the law. However, the problems of privileging local culture and values and of adapting law to the reality of the 'local' – the paradox discussed above – became clear. In relation to the discussion in the US, regarding the decriminalisation of cannabis, the contradictions were highlighted by critics, such as *The Wire* creator David Simon, who argued that such changes would be just as 'artificial', merely benefitting privileged 'middle-class white kids' while intensifying the criminalisation of poor African-Americans in crack-infested communities (Vulliamy and Ray, 2013). There were clear limits to the capacity of adapting law to local reality, as removing the universal 'detachment' of law from reality left the law open to accusations of arbitrariness and cultural relativism. If law really was 'culture' then these accusations were hard to avoid.

The third, 'Resilience', approach was notable in that the focus was no longer upon law and its enforcement nor upon how law may be pluralised but instead was placed upon states' 'improved social capital to build community-based approaches, in which the underlying emphasis shifts from treating drug use and related violence as primarily a legal or security matter to responding to the drug problem by strengthening community resilience' (OAS, 2013b, p. 20). The resilience approach located the security problem as an outcome of complex societal practices not as something which could be dealt with as a discrete problem to be tackled by law. Rather, 'the drug problem is a manifestation and magnifier of underlying social and economic dysfunctions that lead to violence and addiction' (ibid, p. 23).

It should be clear that not only was the drug problem not a discrete problem to be solved in isolation, resilience approaches, of necessity, constructed the drug problem as a matter of community practices and amenable to community solutions. In resilience approaches, communities imbricated within the production and trade of illegal drugs were less likely to be seen as criminal objects of the law and more likely to be understood as in need of facilitating intervention to enable them to be the leading agents of transformation. The individuals most likely to be involved in the production, trafficking and consumption of drugs, and the communities in which they lived, would be subject to enabling interventions designed to use cultural, communal, and informal networks to produce less problematic practices.

Rather than intervene coercively to enforce the law or adapt law to the differentiated level of the 'local', resilience approaches sought to use the 'really existing' power of the local community as a transformative mechanism. As Moe and Simiojoki noted, key to interventions based on pragmatic rather than international peacebuilding understandings was the mobilising and organising of 'existing capacities' (2013, p. 407). It was this element of internalisation of the problem (rather than the 'internationalisation' of the problem) and focus on local transformative agency that distinguished resilience approaches from those of the external subject positions of international peacebuilding, both the liberal top-down approaches – which saw individuals as objects of law and subject to social engineering – and those of a turn to the 'local', which understood local cultural-socio-political milieus as barriers to universal frameworks of law and thereby sought to adapt the law to the circumstances.

As the OAS scenarios report suggested, the resilience approach worked directly with – and not over or against – individuals and communities caught up in the drugs problem (OAS, 2013b, p. 58). Rather than a cultural pluralist or a peacebuilding-as-statebuilding approach, which both emphasised the hold of the past, in terms of path dependencies and deep cultural values, resilience approaches argued that everyday settings could be enabling and transformative. As well as focusing on the 'roots' of the problem in terms of those directly involved in the practices of producing, trafficking, and consuming drugs, there was also a great deal of attention to the community networks and relationships seen to provide the context for practices (OAS, 2013b, p. 58).

The emphasis, as stated, moved away from drugs per se to a focus on resilient people and communities. As the OAS report stated, in this framing: 'citizens gradually become aware that they are fundamental part of the solution and not just victims of the problem' (OAS, 2013b, p. 61). With this shift, the focus was no longer on the problem of community understandings and values – the problem was not understood to be 'in the heads' of local people, but in the context shaping the outcomes of their practices. Law was no longer the key framework for measuring success in dealing with the 'drug problem', instead the metrics concerned everyday practices from parenting to employment training: 'The paradigm change of focussing on building resilient societies forces people and governments to look inward for solutions and to acknowledge the need for social reforms' (OAS, 2013b, p. 62).

CONCLUSION

The shift away from liberal peacebuilding formulations, towards the pragmatic philosophy of resilience, moved beyond the 'abstractions' of formal frameworks to focus on the 'reality' of the everyday. However, there seemed to be little evidence to suggest that reframing international intervention without the baggage of international peacebuilding understandings would lead to the improved outcomes through 'practical learning', which pragmatist thought promised. Jettisoning 'liberal' concerns with the formal constitution of a political community did little to enable the broader structural and socioeconomic context of decision-making to come under consideration while the shift of interventionist policymaking from the public sphere of constitutionalism and law did little to clarify accountability for policymaking. At least international peacebuilding-as-statebuilding frameworks forced a discussion of power and policy accountability on to the agenda and thereby a discussion of the allocation of agency and responsibility to either internationals or locals.

Pragmatic approaches of resilience removed this possibility of external accountability, as the focus upon the practices of the 'everyday' allowed the insinuation of international intervention into mechanisms of community development in informal, and much less accountable, ways. In removing the external subject position of international interveners, the international peacebuilding impasse, which reproduced hierarchical and binary understandings – continually reproducing the divide between international interveners and the communities in which they acted – appeared to be overcome. However, the cost of this removal was the internalisation of both the policy problem and its solution in the closed system of the differentiated local production of differentiated local worlds. Resilience removed the external intervener from external intervention and with this made local capacities, practices, and understandings the means and the ends of intervention. Rather than enlarging our understanding of problems and their solutions, the removal of the 'big picture', universalist metanarratives, and critical sociological understandings constructed a new and potentially more problematic paradigm. The end of 'liberal' universalist approaches to peacebuilding may well be welcomed by analysts and commentators but the rise of the pragmatic philosophy of resilience should not necessarily be seen as a step forward, as considered further in the concluding chapter.

PART V

Conclusion

CHAPTER 9

The End of the Liberal Episteme

INTRODUCTION

This concluding chapter summarises the transformation in the conceptual understanding of international peacebuilding over the last two decades; analysed through the framework of 'The Twenty Years' Crisis'. It suggests that the conceptual shifts within and beyond the impasse of the 2000s can be usefully interrogated through their imbrication within broader epistemological shifts highlighting the limits of causal knowledge claims. These are heuristically framed in this chapter in terms of the shift from peacebuilding interventions within the problematic of causation to those concerned with the pragmatic management of effects. In this shift, the means and mechanisms of international peacebuilding have been transformed, no longer focused on the universal application of Western causal knowledge through policy interventions but rather on the effects of specific and unique local and organic processes at work in societies themselves. The focus on effects takes the conceptualization of international peacebuilding out of the traditional terminological lexicon of politics and international relations theory and instead recasts problems in increasingly organic ways, suggesting that artificial or hubristic attempts at socio-political intervention should be excluded or minimized.

This chapter conceptualizes the fundamental shift in the understanding of international peacebuilding as one from the universalist liberal perspectives of the 1990s, through the institutionalist impasse of peacebuilding-as-statebuilding in the 2000s and the problems of the 'local turn', towards

© The Author(s) 2017
D. Chandler, *Peacebuilding*, Rethinking Peace and Conflict Studies,
DOI 10.1007/978-3-319-50322-6_9

the dominance of the pragmatic perspective by the mid-2010s. In the pragmatic perspective, to all intents and purposes, peacebuilding no longer exists as a separate policy area. This shift reflects both the declining relevance of traditional disciplinary understandings of liberal modernist political categories and an increasing scepticism towards Western, liberal or modernist forms of knowledge. Both of these are considered here. The conclusion of this book is thus that the decline of both modernist political framings and broader modernist understandings of causality have been central to the erasure of the particular space and goals of international peacebuilding.

Over the last two decades, debates over international peacebuilding saw a shift from political concerns of sovereign rights under international law to concerns of knowledge claims of cause and effect, highlighted through the problematization of peacebuilding policy interventions' unintended consequences. This can be illustrated through contrasting the difference between the confidence – today, critics would, of course, say 'hubris' (Mayall and Soares de Oliveira, 2011) – of 1990s' understandings of the transformative possibilities held out by the promise of international peacebuilding with the much more pessimistic approaches prevalent in 2017.

In the late 1990s, leading advocates understood international peacebuilding intervention as a clear exercise of Western power in terms of a 'solutionist' approach to problems that would otherwise have increasingly problematic knock-on effects in a global and interconnected world (see, for example, Blair, 1999). Twenty years later, analysts are much more likely to highlight that the complexity of global interactions and processes, in fact, mitigate against ambitious schemas for intervention – aspiring to address problems at the level either of universalizable or generalizable solutions, exported from the West ('top-down' interventions), or through ambitious projects of social and political engineering (attempting to transform society through institutionalist approaches of peacebuilding-as-statebuilding) (see, for example, Ramalingam et al., 2008; Ramalingam, 2013).

When peacebuilding is condemned for being 'liberal' in 2017, this is much more likely to be a pragmatist critique of the epistemological or cause-and-effect assumptions involved in external claims of peacebuilding effectiveness, rather than a statement concerning any understanding of the rights of sovereignty, self-government or political equality. 'Liberal' thus equates to the modernist episteme rather than to political or philosophical questions of sovereignty and individual rights. Today, it is increasingly argued that causal relations cannot be grasped in the frameworks which constituted international peacebuilding intervention in terms of either 'top-down' liberal universalism or 'bottom-up' institutional capacity-building understandings of the mechanisms of socio-political transformation. In a more complex world, the lines of debate and discussion have shifted away from a political critique of peacebuilding, grounded in political theory and claims of rights to self government vis-à-vis external hegemony, to an epistemic critique of linear or reductionist assumptions of policy efficacy. Peacebuilding has thus been discredited not on traditional 'political' grounds but on the 'pragmatist' basis of a growing awareness that any forms of external peacebuilding intervention or social engineering will have unintended side effects.

It is in the attempt to minimize these unintended consequences that the focus of policy-makers has shifted to the pragmatic governance of effects (focusing on the fluid and specific context of engagements) rather than seeking to address ostensible universalist or structural cause-and-effect understandings of 'root causes'. For example, rather than seeking to solve conflict or to end it (resulting in possibly problematic unintended consequences) international peacebuilding intervention is increasingly articulated as 'managing' conflict, developing societal strategies to cope better and thereby limit its effects (BSOS, 2011). Focusing on managing effects rather than engaging with causative chains makes the forms and practices of peacebuilding intervention quite different.

The shift beyond between conceptual discussions of rights and sovereignty and towards epistemic questions of knowledge is undertaken here through developing Giorgio Agamben's heuristic framing of a shift from a concern with causation to that of effects, which he rightly understood to be a depoliticizing move (Agamben, 2014). Debates about addressing causation involved socio-political analysis and policy choices, putting decision-making and the question of sovereign power and political accountability at the forefront. Causal relations assume power operates 'from the top down' with policy outcomes understood to be direct products of conscious choices, powers and capacities. Agamben argued that whilst the governing of causes was the essence of politics, the pragmatic governance of effects reversed the political process:

> We should not neglect the philosophical implications of this reversal. It means an epoch-making transformation in the very idea of government, which overturns the traditional hierarchical relation between causes and effects. Since governing the causes is difficult and expensive, it is more safe and useful to try to govern the effects. (Agamben, 2014)

The governance of effects can therefore be seen as a pragmatic retreat from the commitments of the international peacebuilding approaches of the 1990s and 2000s, in terms of both resources and policy goals. However, the shift from causation to effects involved a shifting conceptualization of peacebuilding itself; it is this conceptual connection that is the central concern of this concluding chapter.

Peacebuilding policy intervention conceptualized as the governance of effects relocates the subject position of the peacebuilder in relation to both the problem under consideration, which is no longer amenable to external policy solutions, and the society or community being peacebuilt, which is no longer constructed as lacking knowledge or resources, but as being the key agency of peacebuilding transformation. Transformation comes not through external cause-and-effect policy interventions but through the facilitation or empowerment of local agential capacities. The regulation of effects thus shifts the focus away from the formal public, legal and political sphere to the more organic and generative sphere of everyday life (as considered in the previous chapter). The management of effects involves on-going facilitative engagement in social processes and evades the question of government as political decision-making (see further, Chandler, 2014).

THE CONCEPTUALIZATION OF PEACEBUILDING AS POLITICS

In the policy debates of the 1990s, international peacebuilding intervention was often conceived in political terms as an exception to the norm of international politics, which was legally based on a sovereign order. Peacebuilding interventions were posed as necessary in the case of crises that threatened the peace and security of international society and the UN Security Council incrementally relaxed its restrictions, making peacebuilding interventions increasingly feasible (see IICK, 2000; ICISS, 2001a; Chesterman, 2002a). The legal and political exception to accepted international norms assumed the problem-solving capabilities of external international actors and led to the undermining of sovereign rights. As we have seen, this political extension of direct international accountability for peacebuilding in states seen as prone to conflict marked the start of peacebuilding's 'Twenty Years' Crisis' in 1997. The ceding of sovereign power to international peacebuilding institutions was legitimized through the hierarchical assumption of the superior knowledge and resources of the peacebuilding interveners. Thus discourses of international intervention necessarily assumed that knowledge and power operated in, what are increasingly seen today to be, linear and reductive ways.

This chapter thereby concludes the book with an analysis of how the crisis of peacebuilding was brought to a close, highlighting the importance to policy-makers and peacebuilding critics of the shift from debates within a political framework of rights and responsibility to those around knowledge and the problems of the liberal or modernist episteme. The 'liberal' peacebuilding problematic was one of linear causal understandings and asymmetrical and hierarchical discourses of problem-solving intervention (based on the superior knowledge and resources of peacebuilding actors and international agencies). The pragmatist problematic that has displaced it instead emphasises the problems of linear and reductive understandings of intervention and the unintended consequences of such mechanistic approaches to peacebuilding transformation.

The shifting understanding challenged disciplinary conceptions of peacebuilding as universalising liberal institutions of governance (Chandler, 2010) and concepts of peacebuilding-as-statebuilding as progress towards these liberal institutional frameworks through developing more organicist understandings of emerging order, immune to traditional mechanisms of intervention. The shift to conceptualizations of peacebuilding as the governance of effects thus removed policy approaches to peace from the paradigmatic normative power and knowledge assumptions at the heart of the disciplines of politics and international relations.

International Relations theory had traditionally been concerned with the questions of power and international order: how power-politics and conflict could be tamed by international institutions and norms. In the traditional concerns of the discipline, the institution of sovereignty was seen to be key and intervention was therefore problematized (and contained) as destabilizing international order and potentially leading to the internationalization of conflict (see, for example, Schmitt, 2003; Bull, 1995). For this reason, advocates of peacebuilding intervention were keen to either keep intervention indirect or to legitimize intervention on the basis of redefining sovereignty to enable peacebuilding intervention without destabilizing international legal norms (see, for example, Krasner, 1999). As Cynthia Weber (1995, p. 11) noted, it was not possible to speak of peacebuilding intervention without speaking of sovereignty: without sovereignty there could be no framework of understanding, enabling judgements to be made as to 'who would be the target of intervention and what would be violated or transgressed'.

Without a co-constitutive relationship with state sovereignty it was not possible to conceptualize peacebuilding in the political terminology of intervention. Critical constructivist theorist Helle Malmvig succinctly argued:

> Whether any given event constitutes an intervention or a non-intervention, is hence dependent on what meaning sovereignty is attributed in advance. In order for something to be portrayed as an intervention, there must always already be an idea of what falls and what does not fall within the sovereign sphere of the state. (Malmvig, 2006, p. 16)

Malmvig argued that the relationship worked both ways as the concept of state sovereignty was also dependent on intervention. In discourses of peacebuilding intervention, at stake was the boundary line to be drawn between the inside and the outside of states: what counted as a national and as an international concern. Constructivists thereby argued that the content of state sovereignty was not given in advance – prior to intervention – but was constituted in the process of intervention itself (Malmvig, 2006, p. 17).

Constructivist approaches were undoubtedly insightful in understanding sovereignty and intervention as mutually constitutive concepts (see further, Biersteker and Weber, 1996) and in providing useful conceptual tools for the analysis of how the concepts of sovereignty and intervention had been discursively deployed in the field of international politics. However, these approaches were unable to grasp the transformation and then the severing of the ties between sovereignty and intervention during the heated debates of the 1990s and early 2000s. Today, it is clear that the intervention/sovereignty binary no longer operates as a paradigm or 'research assemblage', able to stabilize the meaning of peacebuilding in terms of a political intervention (see further, Law, 2004).

In analysing the radical shifts in the formal disciplinary understanding of the concept of peacebuilding, from the 1990s to the 2010s, three frameworks or models can be illustrated heuristically. These frameworks can be demarcated both in their conceptualization of the formal political categories of sovereignty and peacebuilding intervention and in their approach to causal knowledge claims. It is these discursive linkages that enabled evolving forms of peacebuilding that tended to no longer engage at the level of formal political authority and thus no longer required legitimization on the basis of hierarchical claims of power or knowledge superiority.

SOLUTIONISM: THE ROOTS OF THE CRISIS OF PEACEBUILDING

The view of peacebuilding intervention and sovereignty as conceptually opposites was predominant in the 1990s. In this period, there were heated debates about the clash of rights of intervention and rights of sovereignty, demonstrating the hold of the traditional international relations and international law perspectives of the co-constitution of these two concepts. Even the *Responsibility to Protect* report of 2001 sought to maintain this conceptual binary: arguing, in the constructivist vein, that sovereignty was conditional on the state's will and ability to maintain human rights and that therefore the increasing permissibility of peacebuilding intervention to ensure security meant the definition of sovereignty was changing to make this a condition of sovereignty (ICISS, 2001a). Sovereignty and intervention were still co-constitutive opposites, affirmed by the fact that states were understood to lose their sovereignty if they failed to uphold the security and human rights of their citizens.

The 'solutionist' cause-and-effect model was the archetypal model of peacebuilding intervention in the policy debates in the late 1990s and early 2000s. The necessity of peacebuilding arose directly as a legal, political and ethical concern in the context of the aftermath of humanitarian intervention and regime change under the auspices of the War on Terror. Peacebuilding thus initially emerged as a distinct set of transformative policy goals on the basis of state failure and perceived break down of the domestic security order. In this framing, the policy response tended to be one of centralized direction, under United Nations or United States and NATO command, based upon military power or bureaucratic organization, which often assumed that policy-interveners operated in a vacuum, where social and political norms had broken down, and little attention needed to be given to the particular policy context.

This hierarchical model was articulated in universalist terms. Intervening states and international institutions were understood to have the power, resources and objective scientific knowledge necessary to solve the problems of conflict and to be able to build the framework for future peace and stability. This framework of intervention reached its apogee in international peacebuilding in the Balkans, with long-term protectorates established over Bosnia and Kosovo, and was reflected in the RAND Corporation's reduction of such interventions to simple cost and policy formulas that could be universally applied (Dobbins et al., 2007). Debates informing peacebuilding in the mid- and late-1990s assumed that Western states had the knowledge and power to act and therefore focused on the question of the political will of Western states (see, for example, Held, 1995; Wheeler, 2000). Of particular concern was the fear that the United States might pursue national interests rather than global moral and ethical concerns (Kaldor, 2007, p. 150). In this framework, problems were seen in terms of a universalist and linear understanding.

For 'solutionists', peacebuilding interventions, even including regime change and post-conflict management, could be successful on the basis that a specific set of policy solutions could solve a specific set of policy problems. This set up a universalist understanding of good policy-making – the idea that certain solutions were timeless and could be exported or imposed – like the rule of law, democracy and markets. This policy framework now stands condemned for being highly mechanistic. The problems of post-conflict or conflict-prone states were seen in simple terms of the need to restore the equilibrium of the status quo – which was understood as being disrupted by new forces or events. Illustrated, for example, in the popular 'New Wars' thesis, which argued that stability was disrupted by exploitative elites seeking to destabilize society in order to cling to resources and power (Kaldor, 1999) or that the lack of human rights could be resolved through constitutional reforms (Brandt et al., 2011).

The assumption was that society was fundamentally healthy and that the problematic individuals or groups could be removed or replaced through external peacebuilding intervention that would enable the equilibrium to be restored. This was a mechanistic view of how societies operated – as if they were machines and a single part had broken down and needed to be fixed. There was no holistic engagement with society as a collective set of processes, interactions and inter-relations. The assumption was that external peacebuilding interveners could come up with a 'quick fix' – perhaps maintaining troop levels to quell conflict while legal experts wrote constitutions – followed by an exit strategy.

The universalist framework legitimizing policy intervention thereby established a hierarchical and paternalist framework of understanding. Western liberal democratic states were understood to have the knowledge and power necessary to solve the problems that other post-conflict or 'failing' and conflict-prone states were alleged to lack. It was therefore little surprise that these interventions challenged sovereign rights to self-government, which had long been upheld after decolonization in the 1950s and 1960s. Many commentators therefore raised problems with the idealization of liberal Western societies and the holding up of abstract and unrealistic goals that tended to exaggerate the incapacity or lack of legitimacy of non-Western regimes (see, for example Heathershaw and Lambach, 2008; Lemay-Hébert, 2009). Beneath the universalist peacebuilding claims of promoting the interest of human rights, human security or human development, critical 'political' theorists also suggested new forms of international domination were emerging, institutionalizing market inequalities or restoring traditional hierarchies of power reminiscent of the colonial era (see, for example, Chandler, 1999, 2006a; Bain, 2003; Bickerton, 2007; Hehir and Robinson, 2007; Douzinas, 2007; Duffield, 2007; Pugh et al., 2008; Dillon and Reid, 2009; Barnett, 2010).

The critiques of international peacebuilding up to the 2000s are thereby categorised in this book (see Chapter 2) as being couched in the traditional terminology of modern 'political' radicalism. In other words they were concerned with power inequalities and the open nature of international hierarchy expressed in the new peacebuilding mandates. Both the goals of peacebuilding were seen to be political, focused on the institutional structures of the states and societies concerned, and the critical focus upon these practices was political, flagging up the dangers of formalising unequal relations and establishing new forms of international hegemony. In seeking to deconstruct or to delegitimise the policies and practices of peacebuilding, critics flagged up the ideological nature of the claims to be bringing democracy and rights through new forms of direct and indirect protectorates and problematized the counter-productive effects of interfering in domestic political processes. Retrospectively, as we have seen, the birth of peacebuilding and the hierarchical assumptions informing it have been recast not as a problem of politics, rights and equality but as a problem of knowledge and of understanding, or even (as seen in Chapter 1) as a problem of international actors 'caring too much'.

ENDOGENOUS CAUSALITY: PROLONGING THE IMPASSE OF PEACEBUILDING

The 'solutionist' perspective, with its clear hierarchies of power and knowledge, began to be transformed with less linear and universal and more plural and endogenous views of causation. This shift began to be articulated – though the discourse of peacebuilding-as-statebulding – in ways that understood sovereignty and intervention to be compatible, becoming increasingly predominant in the 2000s. This second model increasingly took local context much more into account, understanding problems as results of complex processes of social and historical path dependencies that needed to be carefully intervened in and adjusted. Thus the relation between external intervening actors (as agents or causes of policy changes) and the subsequent policy outcomes became understood to be much more socially, politically and historically mediated and contingent. This model was exemplified by the work of Roland Paris on the need for 'Institutionalization before Liberalization', in which it was argued that external interventions needed to work 'bottom-up' on the social and historical preconditions for peacebuilding rather than 'top-down' with the wholesale export of Western models and assumptions (Paris, 2004, p. 179).

This position gained further traction as international peacebuilding interventions led international interveners to expand the remits of their policy interventions well beyond the initial problem-solving policy interventions with their short time-spans and exit strategies. The response to the shock terrorist attacks of 9/11 appeared to intensify the trend towards extended international policy interventionism. The 2002 US National Security Strategy expanded and securitized the interventionist remit, arguing that: 'America is now threatened less by conquering states than we are by failing ones' (NSS, 2002, p. 1). The recognition that we lived in a globalized and inter-connected world seemed to bind the needs of national security with those of human rights, democracy and development, creating a powerful interventionist consensus around peacebuilding-as-statebuilding (see Mazarr, 2014).

Peacebuilding-as-statebuilding shifted from addressing causes in universal and linear ways and towards a focus on endogenous processes and institutionalist framings, eventually laying the basis for a transition to the governance of effects. Rather than going for quick problem-solving fixes, policy advocates increasingly argued that policy needed to be concerned more holistically with social processes and analysis of state-society relations in order to overcome the 'sovereignty gap' (Ghani et al., 2005; Ghani and Lockhart, 2008). However, this perspective still reproduced the impasse of peacebuilding, maintaining the legacies of universalist cause-and-effect understandings in that it aimed at establishing viable market-based democracies and still presupposed that external policy-interveners had the necessary superior knowledge and resources to shape policy outcomes (see, for example, Bliesemann de Guevara, 2012; Kühn, 2011; Tadjbakhsh, 2011).

Thus, while international peacebuilders rapidly moved away from their views that liberal institutions themselves were adequate and worked instead to build the basis for sustainable institutions through focusing on social and ideational change, the extension of international mandates was framed in liberal terms. Liberal goals were to be achieved through highly non-liberal means of social engineering and withholding democratic freedoms of self-government. Peacebuilding was at an impasse and there appeared to be little way out of the crisis as the more international peace-builders tried to engage with the 'local' the more they reproduced the hierarchical binaries problematizing society further (see discussions in Chapters 7 and 8).

However, the attention to the 'local' and to the differentiated processes and path-dependencies and societal rigidities gradually enabled peace-building discourses to shift from the accountability of external actors for their interventionist policy-making to seeing agency as located at the local level itself. Once this shift was naturalised or reified as a problem of knowledge and the need to pay attention to context, a way out of the impasse appeared: international peacebuilding aspirations could be put aside, not on the basis of recognising equal rights to sovereignty and political equality but, on the contrary, through seeing liberal goals as hubristic and problematic in themselves.

GOVERNING EFFECTS: BEYOND THE IMPASSE

The end of peacebuilding, shifting beyond the impasse of peacebuilding intervention, came via the acceptance, increasingly prevalent today, that governing effects should be done without a concern for causation. This 'post-peacebuilding' paradigm no longer worked on the cuts and binaries of problem-solving intervention and evaded any discussion of the political or legal relationship between intervention and sovereignty. International 'peacebuilders' thus increasingly claim not to be taking over decision-making processes, to be setting external goals, or to be measuring progress using external yardsticks.

Rather than the external provision of policy solutions or the use of 'conditionality' to guide states in specific directions, international actors are more likely to understand peacebuilding in terms of enabling organic systems and existing knowledges, practices and capacities. This model puts to the fore more pragmatist forms of policy intervention designed to enhance autonomous processes rather than undermine or socially engi-neer them (see, for example, Drabek and McEntire, 2003; Kaufmann, 2013). These forms of intervention cannot be grasped within the paradigm of political and legal claims for political authority central to the discipline of International Relations.

The shift from intervention at the level of causation to intervention at the level of effects was predominantly discussed in relation to the need to take into account the 'law of unintended consequences'. The problem of 'unintended consequences' became a policy trope regularly used as a shorthand expression for the profound shift in the understanding of peacebuilding intervention, addressed in this book. This could be seen as a generalized extension of Ulrich Beck's view of 'risk society', with the determinate causal role of 'side effects', or Bruno Latour's similar analysis of today's world as modernity 'plus all its externalities' (see further, Beck, 1992; Latour, 2003). By the mid-2010s it seemed that there was no way to consider peacebuilding in terms of intended outcomes without considering the possibility that the unintended outcomes would outweigh these.

The transformation in peacebuilding from being a central policy concern to being no longer on the policy agenda was so rapid that it was little surprise that it caught peacebuilding scholarship unawares. While, in 2002, the US State Department was focusing on extensive peacebuilding operations to address the crucial question of state failure, already, by 2012, just a decade later, after admitting defeat in Iraq and Afghanistan, the US Defense Strategic Guidance policy was illustrative of a different set of assumptions: that US forces would pursue their objectives through 'innovative, low-cost, and small-footprint approaches' rather than the conduct of 'large-scale, prolonged stability operations' (DSG, 2012, pp. 3; 6).

In 2013, for example, discussion over potential coercive intervention in Syria was dominated by fears that the unintended outcomes would outweigh the good intentions of external actors (Ackerman, 2013). General Martin Dempsey, chairman of the US Joint Chiefs of Staff, warned that policy caution was necessary as: 'We must anticipate and be prepared for the unintended consequences of our action' (Ackerman, 2013; see also Phillips, 2013). As Michael Mazarr argued in the influential US foreign policy journal *Foreign Affairs*, in 2014, securing US goals of peace, democracy and development in failing and conflict-ridden states could not, in fact, be done by instrumental cause-and-effect external peacebuilding interventions: 'It is an organic, grass-roots process that must respect the unique social, cultural, economic, political, and religious contexts of each country... and cannot be imposed' (Mazarr, 2014).

For Mazarr, policy would now follow a more 'resilient mindset, one that treats perturbations as inevitable rather than calamitous and resists the urge to overreact', understanding that peacebuilding intervention must work with rather than against local institutions and 'proceed more organically and authentically' (Mazarr, 2014). This shift was also reflected by high-level policy experts in the US State Department; according to Charles T. Call, senior adviser at the Bureau of Conflict and Stabilization Operations, US approaches increasingly sought not to impose unrealistic external goals but instead to facilitate local transformative agency through engaging with local 'organic processes and plussing them up' (personal communication).

Peacebuilding, today, thus no longer exists as a distinct policy sphere as the goals and approaches have been increasingly discredited and seen as being problematically based upon the grand narratives of liberal internationalism, which informed and drove the debates on international peacebuilding intervention in the late 1990s, when issues of intervention and non-intervention in Africa and the Balkans were at the centre of international political contestation. International peacebuilding intervention was not successfully opposed on the grounds of political or legal principles, but on the basis of the universalist and hierarchical knowledge assumptions which informed peacebuilding interventions and produced the hubristic and reductionist promises of transformative outcomes (see, for example, Owen, 2012; Stewart and Knaus, 2012; Mayall and De Oliviera, 2011; Mazarr, 2014).

'ORGANIC' VERSUS 'POLITICAL' UNDERSTANDINGS OF PEACEBUILDING

The critique of cause-and-effect understandings of peacebuilding could draw on similar pragmatist critiques of modern medical interventions based upon antibiotics and other artificial chemical and technical remedies (see, for example, Thacker and Artlett, 2012; Krans, 2014; O'Neal et al., 2014, pp. 877–78). The reductionist understanding of intervention in the biomedical sciences has often been problematized for its lack of attention to unintended consequences, which could easily mean that the cure was worse for individual and societal healthcare than the initial affliction. These critiques thus operated as a readily available template for the rapid development of a critical conceptualization of peacebuilding intervention in the discipline of International Relations – one that bore little relation to traditional concerns of international stability, international law, sovereign rights of independence or to post-colonial sensibilities.

These critiques of linear and reductionist cause-and-effect approaches tended to focus upon the value of organic, natural, or endogenous powers of resistance and resilience which were understood to be unintentionally undermined through the mechanistic assumptions of modern Western science (see, for example, Capra, 1983, pp. 118–65). In the parallel arguments in discourses of intervention and peacebuilding, the organic processes of endogenous development have been prioritized over universalizing, mechanistic or reductionist approaches to policy intervention that sought to introduce policy solutions from the outside. For example, while markets, development, democracy, security and the rule of law might be good when they developed organically, it was often argued that when they were extracted from their context and applied in a 'pure' form they were dangerous as they lacked the other ingredients connected to institutions and culture.

The basis for this perspective was first developed in relation to the impasse of peacebuilding intervention in the Balkans in the late-1990s and early-2000s, when interventionist policy-making began to shift attention to the endogenous or internal capacities and capabilities of the local society rather than seeking externally managed 'military solutions, quick fixes [and] easy, early exits', associated with simple cause-and-effect understandings (Bildt, 2003). However, the critique of cause-and-effect assumptions, which focused on the knowledge and expertise of external policy-interveners, rapidly extended to include 'bottom-up' attempts at socio-political engineering, associated with institutionalist peacebuilding-as-statebuilding goals of promoting markets, democracy and the rule of law.

The governance of effects, increasingly taken up by international peacebuilders, thereby insists that problems cannot be dealt with merely at the level of causation, by identifying and categorizing a problem as if it could be understood in the reductionist terms of cause and effect. Peacebuilding based on the governance of effects therefore had no need for ready-made international policy solutions that could simply be applied or implemented, and therefore implied little possibility of learning generic lessons from intervention that could be applied to all other cases of conflict or of underdevelopment on the basis that if the symptoms appeared similar the cause must be the same. Crucially, this framing removed peacebuilding from the context of policy-making and the political sphere of democratic debate and decision-making.

The focus therefore shifted away from international peacebuilding policies (supply-driven policy-making) and towards engagement with the internal capacities and capabilities that were already held to exist. In other words, there was a shift from the agency, knowledge and practices of peacebuilding interveners to that of the society, which was the object of policy concerns. As the 2013 updated UK Department for International Development's *Growth and Resilience Operational Plan* stated: 'We will produce less "supply-driven" development of product, guidelines and policy papers, and foster peer-to-peer, horizontal learning and knowledge exchange, exploiting new technologies such as wiki/huddles to promote the widest interaction between stakeholders' (DfID, 2013, p. 8).

'Supply-driven' policies – the stuff of politics and of democratic decision-making – are understood to operate in an artificial or non-organic way, and to lack an authentic connection to the effects, which need to be addressed. The imposition of (accountable) external institutional and policy frameworks has become increasingly seen as artificial and as having counterproductive or unintended outcomes. Pragmatist, effects-based approaches thereby seek to move away from the impasse of 'liberal' peacebuilding interventions – wishing to export constitutional frameworks, to train and equip military and police forces, to impose external conditionalities on the running of state budgets, to export managerial frameworks for civil servants and political representatives or to impose regulations to ensure administrative transparency and codes of conduct – which were at the heart of international policy prescriptions in the late 1990s and early 2000s (World Bank, 2007; Eurodad, 2006; ActionAid, 2006).

It is argued that the 'supply-driven' approach of external experts exporting or developing liberal institutions did not grasp the complex processes generative of instability or insecurity. Instead, the cause-and-effect model of peacebuilding intervention is seen to create problematic 'hybrid' political systems and fragile states with little connection to their societies (Roberts, 2008; Mac Ginty, 2010; Richmond and Mitchell, 2012; Millar, 2014). The imposition of institutional frameworks, which have little connection to society, is understood as failing, not only in not addressing causal processes but in making matters worse through undermining local capacities to manage the effects of problems; shifting problems elsewhere and leaving states and societies even more fragile or vulnerable to conflict.

This approach is alleged to fail to hear the 'message' of problematic manifestations or to enable societies' own organic and homeostatic processes to generate corrective mechanisms. Triggering external peacebuilding interventions is said to shortcut the ability of societies to reflect upon and take responsibility for their own affairs and is increasingly seen as a counter-productive 'over-reaction' by external powers (see further, Desch, 2008; Maor, 2012). There is an increasingly prevalent view that, contrary to earlier assumptions, peacebuilding solutions can only be developed through practice by actors on the ground.

As noted above, following Agamben, the pragmatic conceptualization of peacebuilding interventions in terms of the governance of effects evades the traditional disciplinary understanding of intervention as an exercise of external political power and authority. It does this through denying intervention as an act of external decision-making and policy direction as understood in the political paradigm of liberal modernist discourse. This can be illustrated through highlighting some examples of policy shifts in key areas of international peacebuilding concern: security, the rule of law, democracy and human rights.

Peacebuilding interventions are increasingly shifting in relation to the understanding of conflict. There is much less talk of conflict prevention or conflict resolution and more of conflict management. As the UK government argued, in a 2011 combined DfID, Foreign and Commonwealth Office and Ministry of Defence document, conflict per se is not now considered to be the problem: 'Conflict is a normal part of human interaction, the natural result when individuals and groups have incompatible needs, interests or beliefs' (BSOS, 2011, p. 5). The problem which needs to be tackled is the state or society's ability to manage conflict: 'In stable, resilient societies conflict is managed through numerous formal and informal institutions' (BSOS, 2011, p. 5).

Conflict management, as the UK government policy indicates, is increasingly understood as an organic set of societal processes and practices, which international peacebuilding intervention can influence but cannot import solutions from outside or impose them. This understanding very much follows the approach long advocated by influential peace theorist Jean Paul Lederach (1997, p. 94), who argued that: 'The greatest resource for sustaining peace in the long term is always rooted in the local people and their culture'. For Lederach, managing conflict meant moving away from cause-and-effect forms of instrumental external intervention which saw people as 'recipients' of policy, and instead seeing people as 'resources', integral to peace processes, therefore it was essential that:

> ...we in the international community adopt a new mind-set – that we move beyond a simple prescription of answers and modalities for dealing with

> conflict that come from outside the setting and focus at least as much attention on discovering and empowering the resources, modalities, and mechanisms for building peace that exist within the context. (Lederach, 1997, p. 95)

One of the central shifts in understanding conflict as something that needs to be 'coped with' and 'managed' rather than something that can be 'solved' or 'prevented' is the view that state-level interventions are of limited use. Peace treaties can be signed by state parties but unless peace is seen as an ongoing and transformative inclusive societal process these agreements will be merely superficial and non-sustainable (Lederach, 1997, p. 135).

Just as peace and security are less understood as able to be secured through cause-and-effect forms of intervention, reliant on policy interveners imposing solutions in mechanical and reductive ways, there has also been a shift in understanding the counterproductive effects of attempts to export the rule of law (as considered in the previous chapter; see also Cesarini and Hite, 2004; Zimmermann, 2007). The pragmatist approach is driven by a realization of the gap between the formal sphere of law and constitutionalism and the social 'reality' of informal power relations and informal rules. This perspective has also been endorsed by Douglass North (1990, p. 140), the policy guru of new institutionalist economics, who has highlighted the difficulties of understanding how exported institutions will interact with 'culturally derived norms of behaviour'. The social reality of countries undergoing post-conflict 'transition' is thereby not grasped merely by an analysis of laws and statutes. In fact, there increasingly appears to be an unbridgeable gap between the artificial constructions of legal and constitutional frameworks and the realities of everyday life, revealed in dealings between individual members of the public and state authorities.

As emphasized above, the pragmatist approach does not seek to assert sovereign power or Western hierarchies of power and knowledge; in fact, the governance of effects operates as both an epistemological and ontological challenge to the cause-and-effect understandings of intervention, dominant until the last decade. These points are highlighted, for example, in Bruno Latour's (2013, p. 343) critical engagement with modernist modes of understanding: arguing that Western societies have forgotten the lengthy processes which enabled them to build liberal institutions dependent on the lengthy process of the establishment of a political culture, which has to be steadily maintained, renewed and extended and cannot be exported or imposed (see also Collier, 2010).

This shift away from formal universalist understandings of democracy and human rights is increasingly evidenced in the shifting understanding of human rights-based approaches to empowerment. Understanding empowerment in instrumental cause-and-effect terms based upon the external provision of legal and political mechanisms for claims is increasingly seen to be ineffective. Rights-based NGOs now seek not to empower people to access formal institutional mechanisms but to enable them to empower themselves. The pragmatist approach places the emphasis on the agency and self-empowerment of local actors, not on the introduction of formal frameworks of law, supported by international human rights norms (Moe and Simojoki, 2013, p. 404).

The approach of 'finding organic processes and plussing them up' (as articulated by the US State Department policy advisor, cited earlier) is not limited to government policy interventions but has been increasingly taken up as a generic approach to overcome the limits of cause-and-effect understandings. A study of Finnish development NGOs highlighted that rather than instrumentally selecting groups of civil society elites, new forms of intervention appear as anti-intervention, denying any external role in this process and stressing that there is no process of external management or selection as policy interveners work with whatever groups or associations already exist and 'have just come together...it is not our NGO that brought them together but we just found them that way' (Kontinen, 2014).

A similar study, in south-eastern Senegal, noted that policy interveners were concerned to avoid both the 'moral imperialism' of imposing Western human rights norms, but also to avoid a moral relativism which merely accepts local traditional practices (Gillespie and Melching, 2010, p. 481). The solution forwarded was that of being non-prescriptive and avoiding and 'unlearning' views of Western teachers as 'authorities' and students as passive recipients (ibid, p. 481). Peacebuilding intervention was articulated as the facilitation of local people's attempts to uncover traditional practices and in 'awakening' and 'engaging' their already existing capacities: 'By detecting their own inherent skills, they can more easily transfer them to personal and community problem solving' (ibid, p. 490). These processes could perhaps be encouraged or assisted by external policy interveners but they cannot be transplanted from one society to another, and even less can they be imposed by policy actors.

CONCLUSION

The pragmatic shift in understanding peacebuilding intervention from addressing causes to the governance of effects, focusing on the problem society's own capacities and needs and internal and organic processes, has been paralleled by a growing scepticism of attempts to export or impose Western models. The pragmatic governance of effects thereby evades the political problematic of sovereign power and is often understood as non-interventionist because of its organicist conceptualization. Any international interventions of this sort can no longer be construed as 'peacebuilding' as there would be no separate or discrete realm of policy in this area. They also would not require any specialist 'peacebuilding' knowledge and, in fact, tend to problematize any such knowledge claims, instead requiring therapeutic capacities and sensitivities, more attuned to open and unscripted forms of engagement, mutual processes of learning and unpredictable and spontaneous forms of knowledge exchange (see, for example, Duffield, 2007, pp. 233–34; Jabri, 2007, p. 177; Brigg and Muller, 2009, p. 130).

In the illustrative examples of the governance of effects given above, it is clear that problems are no longer conceived as amenable to political solutions in terms of instrumental governing interventions on the basis of cause-and-effect understandings. Those subject to new pragmatic forms of 'post-peacebuilding' goals of empowerment and capacity-building are not understood as citizens of states – capable of negotiating, debating, deciding and implementing policy agendas – but instead are caught up in never-ending processes of governing effects at the local or community level. Politics disappears from the equation and with it the clash of the co-constitutive concepts of sovereignty and intervention and the legitimating claims of power and knowledge through which these peacebuilding claims were contested.

The end of peacebuilding as an evolving set of problem-solving prescriptions should not necessarily be seen as cause for celebration. As this concluding chapter has outlined, peacebuilding projects have not been shelved because of a progressive political challenge reasserting the rights of sovereignty and self-government, democracy and political equality. The counter-productive effects of international peacebuilding have not been seen as caused by the non-liberal, hierarchical, moralising, patronising, elitist and often racist assumptions behind the peacebuilding impulse of Western problem-solving. Quite the opposite, new discourses of ontological difference, plural ways of being, non-linear forms of causality, complexity, self-organising systems, resilience, pragmatism and liberal hubris have fed into a new consensus that it was the West's transformative aspirations that were the problem rather than its hegemonic theories and practices. Peacebuilding may be over but the problems of conflict and fragility affecting much of the population of the world remain and the international order is no less hierarchical for the fact that international institutions and Western governments are under no pressure to promise a more peaceful and secure world.

REFERENCES

Abrahamsen, R (2000) *Disciplining Democracy: Development Discourse and Good Governance in Africa.* London: Zed Books.

Acharya, A (2000) 'How Ideas Spread: Whose Norms Matter? Norm Localization and Institutional Change in Asian Regionalism', *International Organization 2*, no. 1: 65–87.

Ackerman, S (2013) 'US Military Intervention in Syria would Create "Unintended Consequences"', *Guardian*, 22 July.

ActionAid (2006) *What Progress? A Shadow Review of World Bank Conditionality.* Johannesburg: ActionAid.

AFP (1999) 'Allies Told Peace Dividend is Over, More Defense Spending Needed', Agence-France Presse, 2 December.

Agamben, G (2014) 'For a Theory of Destituent Power', *Chronos* 10.

Agger, I and Mimica, J (1996) *Psycho-social Assistance to Victims of War: An Evaluation.* Brussels: European Community Humanitarian Office.

al-Khafaji, I (2003) 'I did not want to be a Collaborator', *Guardian*, 28 July.

Althusser, A (2008) 'Ideology and Ideological State Appraratuses', in *On Ideology.* London: Verso, 1–60.

Amnesty (1996) *Bosnia: The International Community's Responsibility to Ensure Human Rights.* New York: Amnesty International Report.

Anon (1996) 'Human Rights in Peace Negotiations', *Human Rights Quarterly* 18: 249–58.

Archibugi, D, Held, D and Kohler, M (eds) (1998) *Re-imagining Political Community: Studies in Cosmopolitan Democracy.* London: Polity Press.

Arendt, H (1979) *The Origins of Totalitarianism* (new edition). New York: Harvest.

© The Author(s) 2017
D. Chandler, *Peacebuilding,* Rethinking Peace and Conflict Studies,
DOI 10.1007/978-3-319-50322-6

Ashdown, P (2003a) 'Broken Communities, Shattered Lives: Winning the Savage War of Peace', Speech to the International Rescue Committee, London, 19 June.

Ashdown, P (2003b) 'What Baghdad can learn from Bosnia', *Guardian*, 22 April.

Bain, W (2003) *Between Anarchy and Society: Trusteeship and the Obligations of Power*. Oxford: Oxford University Press.

Balkanologie (1999) Special issue, 'South-Eastern Europe: History, Concepts, Boundaries', *Balkanologie* 3, no. 2: 47–127.

Banakar, R (2013) 'Law and Regulation in Late Modernity', in R Banakar and M Travers (eds) *Law and Social Theory*. Oxford: Hart Publishing.

Barbara, J (2008) 'Rethinking Neo-liberal State Building: Building Post-Conflict Development States', *Development in Practice* 18, no. 3: 307–18.

Barnett, M (2006) 'Building a Republican Peace: Stabilizing States after War', *International Security* 30, no. 4: 87–112.

Barnett, M (2010) *The International Humanitarian Order*. Abingdon: Routledge.

Barnett, M and Zürcher, C (2009) 'The Peacebuilder's Contract: How External Statebuilding Reinforces Weak Statehood', in R Paris and TD Sisk (eds) *The Dilemmas of Statebuilding: Confronting the Contradictions of Postwar Peace Operations*. London: Routledge, 23–52.

Beck, U (1992) *Risk Society: Towards a New Modernity*. London: Sage.

Begby, E and Burgess, B (2009) 'Human Security and Liberal Peace', *Public Reason* 1, no. 1: 91–104.

Bellamy, A (2008) 'The "Next Stage" in Peace Operations Theory', in A Bellamy and P Williams (eds) *Peace Operations and Global Order*. London: Routledge, 17–38.

Belloni, R (2008) 'Civil Society in War-to-Democracy Transitions', in AK Jarstad and TD Sisk (eds) *From War to Democracy: Dilemmas of Peacebuilding*. Cambridge: Cambridge University Press, 182–210.

Bennett, J (2010) *Vibrant Matter: A Political Ecology of Things*. London: Duke University Press.

Bertsch, GK (1973) 'The Revival of Nationalisms', *Problems of Communism* 22, no. 6: 1–15.

Bickerton, CJ (2007) 'State-building: Exporting State Failure', in Bickerton, P Cunliffe and A Gourevitch (eds) *Politics without Sovereignty*. London: University College Press, 93–111.

Bieber, F (2001) 'Croat Self-Government in Bosnia – A Challenge for Dayton'. *European Centre for Minority Issues (ECMI) Brief*, no. 5, May.

Biersteker, TJ and Weber, C (1996) *State Sovereignty as Social Construct*. Cambridge: Cambridge University Press.

Bildt, C (1996a) 'The Important Lessons of Bosnia', *Financial Times*, 3 April.

Bildt, C (1996b) 'Response to Henry Kissinger's Article in the *Washington Post* of 8 Sept. entitled, "In the Eye of a Hurricane", OHR Article by the High Representative', 14 September, Sarajevo: OHR.

Bildt, C (1998) *Peace Journey: The Struggle for Peace in Bosnia.* London: Weidenfeld & Nicolson.

Bildt, C (2003) 'Europe's Future in the Mirror of the Balkans', *OpenDemocracy*, 3 April.

Bisenić, D (2002) 'Interview: Wolfgang Petritsch, the High Representative in Bosnia-Herzegovina: "New Solutions are not emergency measures for Balkans"', *Danas*, 10 April.

Blair, T (1999) 'Doctrine of the International Community.' 24 April.

Bliesemann De Guevara, B (ed.) (2012) *Statebuilding and State-Formation: The Political Sociology of Intervention.* London: Routledge.

Boltanski, L (2011) *On Critique: A Sociology of Emancipation.* Cambridge: Polity.

Bone, J (2003) 'Dashing Diplomat Favoured by Bush', *The Times*, 20 August.

Bougarel, X (1996) 'Bosnia and Herzegovina - State and Communitarianism', in DA Dyker and I Vejvoda (eds) *Yugoslavia and After: A Study in Fragmentation, Despair and Rebirth.* London: Longman, 87–115.

Bourbeau, P (2013) 'Resiliencism: Premises and Promises in Securitisation Research', *Resilience: International Policies, Practices and Discourses* 1, no. 1: 3–17.

Boyd, CG (1998) 'Making Bosnia Work', *Foreign Affairs* 77, no. 1: 42–55.

Brandt, M, Cottrell, J, Ghai, Y and Regan, A (2011) *Constitution-making and Reform: Options for the Process.* Geneva: Interpeace.

Brigg, M (2010) 'Culture: Challenges and Possibilities', in Richmond ed., *Palgrave Advances in Peacebuilding: Critical developments and Approaches.* Basingstoke: Palgrave, 329–46.

Brigg, M and Muller, K (2009) 'Conceptualising Culture in Conflict Resolution', *Journal of Intercultural Studies* 30, no. 2: 120–21.

Brown, C (1995) *Serpents in the Sand: Essays on the Non-Linear Nature of Politics and Human Destiny.* Ann Arbor: University of Michigan Press.

BSOS (2011) *Building Stability Overseas Strategy.* London: Department for International Development, Foreign and Commonwealth Office and Ministry of Defence.

Bueger, C (2012) 'From Epistemology to Practice: A Sociology of Science for International Relations', *Journal of International Relations & Development* 15, no. 1: 97–109.

Bull, H (1995) *The Anarchical Society: A Study of Order in World Politics* (2nd edition). Basingstoke: Palgrave.

Burg, SL (1997) 'Bosnia Herzegovina: A Case of Failed Democratization', in K Dawisha and B Parrot (eds) *Politics, Power, and the Struggle for Democracy in South-East Europe.* Cambridge: Cambridge University Press, 122–45.

Cammack, P (2004) 'What the World Bank Means by Poverty Reduction and Why It Matters', *New Political Economy* 9, no. 2: 189–211.

Cammack, P (2006) 'Global Governance, State Agency and Competitiveness: The Political Economy of the Commission for Africa', *British Journal of Politics and International Relations* 8, no. 3: 331–50.

Cammack, D, McLeod, D, Menocal, AR and Christiansen, K (2006) *Donors and the 'Fragile States' Agenda: A Survey of Current Thinking and Practice*. London: Overseas Development Institute.

Campbell, D (1998) *National Deconstruction: Violence, Identity and Justice in Bosnia*. Minneapolis: University of Minnesota Press.

Campbell, S, Chandler, D and Sabaratnam, M (eds) (2011) *A Liberal Peace? The Problems and Practices of Peacebuilding*. London: Zed Books.

Capra, F (1983) *The Turning Point: Science, Society and the Rising Culture*. London: Flamingo.

Carr, EH (2001) *The Twenty Years' Crisis 1919–1939: An Introduction to the Study of International Relations*. Basingstoke: Palgrave.

elador, GC (2002) 'International Civilian Police Missions in War-Torn Societies – From Theory to Practice in Bosnia and Kosovo', Paper presented at the Fifth International Seminar 'Democracy and Human Rights in Multiethnic Societies, Institute for Strengthening Democracy in Bosnia, Konjić, 8–12 July.

Celikates, R (2006) 'From Critical Social Theory to a Social Theory of Critique: On the Critique of Ideology after the Pragmatic Turn', *Constellations* 13, no. 1: 21–40.

Cesarini, P and Hite, K (2004) 'Introducing the Concept of Authoritarian Legacies', in K Hite and P Cesarini (eds) *Authoritarian Legacies and Democracy in Latin America and Southern Europe*. Notre Dame: University of Notre Dame Press, 1–10.

CfA (2005) Commission for Africa, *Our Common Interest*, 11 March. London: Commission for Africa.

Chandler, D (1999) *Bosnia: Faking Democracy after Dayton*. London: Pluto Press.

Chandler, D (2000) 'International Justice', *New Left Review* 2, no. 6: 55–66.

Chandler, D (2002a) *From Kosovo to Kabul: Human Rights and International Intervention*. London: Pluto Press.

Chandler, D (2002b) 'Anti-Corruption Strategies and Democratization in Bosnia-Herzegovina', *Democratization* 9, no. 2: 101–20.

Chandler, D (ed.) (2005a) *Peace without Politics? Ten Years of International State-Building in Bosnia*. London: Routledge.

Chandler, D (2005b) 'From Dayton to Europe', *International Peacekeeping* 12, no. 3: 336–49.

Chandler, D (2006a) *Empire in Denial: The Politics of State-Building*. London: Pluto Press.

Chandler, D (2006b) 'Back to the Future? The Limits of Neo-Wilsonian Ideals of Exporting Democracy', *Review of International Studies* 32, no. 3: 475–94.

Chandler, D (2006c) 'The Bureaucratic Gaze of International Human Rights Law', in S Meckled-Garcia and B Cali (eds) *The Legalization of Human Rights: Multidisciplinary Perspectives.* London: Routledge, 117–33.

Chandler, D (2010) *International Statebuilding: The Rise of Post-Liberal Governance.* London: Routledge.

Chandler, D (2012) 'Resilience and Human Security: The Post-Interventionist Paradigm', *Security Dialogue* 43, no. 3: 213–29.

Chandler, D (2013) 'Promoting Democratic Norms? Social Constructivism and the "Subjective" Limits to Liberalism', *Democratization* 20, no. 2: 215–39.

Chandler, D (2014) 'Democracy Unbound? Non-Linear Politics and the Politicisation of Everyday Life', *European Journal of Social Theory* 17, no. 1: 42–59.

Chesterman, S (2002a) *Just War or Just Peace? Humanitarian Intervention and International Law.* Oxford: Oxford University Press.

Chesterman, S (2002b) 'Walking Softly in Afghanistan: The Future of UN State-Building', *Survival* 44, no. 3: 37–46.

Chesterman, S, Ignatieff, M and Thakur, R (2005) *Making States Work: State Failure and the Crisis of Governance.* New York: UN University Press.

Chomsky, N (2000) 'The Kosovo Peace Accord', in T Ali (ed.) *Masters of the Universe: NATO's Balkan Crusade.* London: Verso, 387–96.

Chopra, J (2003) 'Building State Failure in East Timor', in J Milliken (ed.) *State Failure, Collapse and Reconstruction.* Oxford: Blackwell, 223–43.

Clover, C (2003) 'Row Mars First Meeting of Iraq Interim Council', *Financial Times*, 14 July.

Cohen, JL and Arato, A (1992) *Civil Society and Political Theory.* Cambridge, MA: MIT Press.

Coleman, PT, et al. (2011) 'Navigating the Landscape of Conflict: Applications of Dynamic Systems Theory to Addressing Protracted Conflict', in R Körppen and HJ Giessmann (eds) *The Non-Linearity of Peace Processes: Theory and Practice of Systemic Conflict Transformation.* Opladen: Barbara Budrich Verlag, 39–56.

Collier, P (2010) *War, Guns and Votes: Democracy in Dangerous Places.* London: Vintage.

Connolly, W (2011) *A World of Becoming.* London: Duke University Press.

Cooper, R (2003) *The Breaking of Nations: Order and Chaos in the Twenty-first Century.* London: Atlantic Books.

Cordell, K (ed.) (1998) *Ethnicity and Democratisation in the New Europe.* London: Routledge.

Cortell, AP and Davis, JW (2000) 'Understanding the Domestic Impact of International Norms: A Research Agenda', *International Studies Review* 2, no. 1: 65–87.

Cox, M (2001) 'Introduction', in EH Carr (ed.) *The Twenty Year's Crisis 1919–1939: An Introduction to the Study of International Relations*. Basingstoke: Palgrave.

Cox, RW (1981) 'Social Forces, States and World Orders', *Millennium: Journal of International Studies* 10, no. 2: 126–55.

CPA (2003a) Coalition Provisional Authority, Order No.1, 'De-Baathification of Iraqi Society', 15 May.

CPA (2003b) Coalition Provisional Authority, Order No.2, 'Dissolution of Entities', 23 May.

CPA (2003c) Coalition Provisional Authority, Regulation No.6, 'Governing Council of Iraq', 13 July.

Cramer, C (2006) *Why Civil War is Not a Stupid Thing: Accounting for Violence in Developing Countries*. London: Hurst & Co.

Crawford, G (2006) 'The World Bank and Good Governance: Rethinking the State or Consolidating Neo-Liberalism?', in A Paloni and M Zanardi (eds) *The IMF, the World Bank and Policy Reform*. London: Routledge, 115–41.

Dahrendorf, R (1990) *Reflections on the Revolution in Europe: In a Letter Intended to Have Been Sent to a Gentleman in Warsaw, 1990*. London: Chatto & Windus.

D'Amato, A (1994) 'Peace Vs. Accountability in Bosnia', *American Journal of International Law* 88, no. 3: 500–06.

DD (1997) Dialogue Development, *Survey of Bosnian Civil Society Organizations: Mapping, Characteristics, and Strategy*. Copenhagen: Dialogue Development.

Deacon, B and Stubbs, P (1998) 'International Actors and Social Policy Development in Bosnia-Herzegovina: Globalism and the "New Feudalism"', *Journal of European Social Policy* 8, no. 2: 99–115.

Dean, M (2010) *Governmentality: Power and Rule in Modern Society* (2nd edition). London: Sage.

de Certeau, M (1998) *The Practice of Everyday Life*. Berkeley, CA: University of California Press.

De Coning, C (2016) 'From peacebuilding to sustaining peace: Implications of complexity for resilience and sustainability', *Resilience: International Policies, Practices and Discourses* 4, no. 3: 166–81.

DeLanda, M (2006) *A New Philosophy of Society: Assemblage Theory and Social Complexity*. London: Continuum.

Denitch, B (1996) *Ethnic Nationalism: The Tragic Death of Yugoslavia* (revised edition). London: University of Minnesota Press.

Desch, MC (2008) 'America's Liberal Illiberalism: The Ideological Origins of Overreaction in US Foreign Policy', *International Security* 32, no. 3: 7–43.

Dewey, J (1954) *The Public and its Problems*. Athens: Swallow Press.

Dewey, J (2008) *The Later Works, 1925–1953, Volume 4: The Quest for Certainty*. Carbondale: Southern Illinois University Press.

DfID (2013) Department for International Development, *Operational Plan 2011–2015 DFID Growth and Resilience Department*. London: DfID.

Diamond, L (1994) 'Rethinking Civil Society: Toward Democratic Consolidation', *Journal of Democracy* 5, no. 3: 4–17.

Dicey, AV (1959) *Introduction to the Study of the Law of the Constitution*. London: Macmillan.

Dillon, M and Reid, J (2009) *The Liberal Way of War: Killing to Make Life Live*. London: Routledge.

Dobbins, J, Jones, SG, Crane, K and DeGrasse, BC (2007) *The Beginners' Guide to Nation-Building*. Santa Monica, CA: RAND Corporation.

Dobriansky, PJ (2004) 'Promoting a Culture of Lawfulness', Remarks at Georgetown University, Washington, DC, 13 September.

Douzinas, C (2007) *Human Rights and Empire: The Political Philosophy of Cosmopolitanism*. Abingdon: Routledge-Cavendish.

Doyle, M and Sambanis, N (2006) *Making War and Building Peace: United Nations Peace Operations*. Princeton, NJ: Princeton University Press.

DPI (2002) Democratization Policy Institute, *An Agenda for Bosnia's Next High Representative*, 1 May.

Drabek, TE and McEntire, DA (2003) 'Emergent Phenomena and the Sociology of Disaster: Lessons, Trends and Opportunities from the Research Literature', *Disaster, Prevention and Management* 12, no. 2: 97–112.

DSG (2012) Defense Strategic Guidance, *Sustaining US Global Leadership: Priorities for 21st Century Defense*. Washington, DC: White House.

Duffield, M (2001) *Global Governance and the New Wars: The Merging of Development and Security*. London: Zed Books.

Duffield, M (2007) *Development, Security and Unending War: Governing the World of Peoples*. Cambridge: Polity.

du Pont, Y (1999) 'Levelling the Political Playing Field: Democratization through Supporting a Pluralistic and Moderate Party System in Bosnia and Herzegovina', *OSCE Yearbook 1999*. Hamburg: IFSH (Institute for Peace Research and Security Policy), University of Hamburg, 301–14.

Easterly, W (2006) *The White Man's Burden: Why the West's Efforts to Aid the Rest Have Done so Much Ill and so Little Good*. Oxford: Oxford University Press.

EC (2001) 'The Stabilisation and Association Process and CARDS Assistance 2000 to 2006', European Commission paper for the Second Regional Conference for South East Europe.

Eschler, C and Maiguashca, B (eds) (2005) *Critical Theories, International Relations and 'the Anti-Globalisation Movement': The Politics of Global Resistance*. London: Routledge.

ESI (2002a) European Stability Initiative, 'Imposing Constitutional Reform? The Case for Ownership: A Discussion Paper', *ESI Bosnia Report*, no. 13, 20 March. Berlin/Sarajevo: ESI.

ESI (2002b) European Stability Initiative, *From Dayton to Europe: Land, Development and the Future of Democratic Planning* (draft version for circulation to OHR only), 12 December. Berlin/Sarajevo: ESI.

ESI (2005) European Stability Initiative, *The Helsinki Moment: European Member State Building in the Balkans*, 1 February. Berlin: ESI.

Etzione, A (2016) Back to Nation Building? *Huffington Post*, 30 March 2016. http://www.huffingtonpost.com/amitai-etzioni/back-to-nation-building_b_9576390.html.

EU (2001) 'Review of the Stabilisation and Association Process', European Union General Affairs Council Report.

EU (2005) European Partnership for Bosnia and Herzegovina, Medium Term Priorities Realisation Programme. Available at: http://www.dei.gov.ba/en/pdf/Complet_EP_PSP.pdf.

Eurodad (2006) *World Bank and IMF Conditionality: A Development Injustice.* Brussels: European Network on Debt and Development.

Evans, G and Sahnoun, M (2002) 'The Responsibility to Protect', *Foreign Affairs* 81, no. 6: 1–8.

EWI/ESI (2001) EastWest Institute and European Stability Initiative, *Democracy, Security and the Future of the Stability Pact for South Eastern Europe: A Framework for Debate*, April. Brussels: ESI.

Falk, RA (1999) 'Kosovo, World Order, And The Future of International Law', *American Journal of International Law* 93: 847–57.

Fearon, JD and Laitin, DD (2004) 'Neo- trusteeship and the Problem of Weak States', *International Security* 28, no. 4: 5–43.

Feldman, N (2004) *What We Owe Iraq: War and the Ethics of Nation Building.* Princeton, NJ: Princeton University Press.

Ferdinand, P (1997) 'Nationalism, Community and Democratic Transition in Czechoslovakia and Yugoslavia', in D Potter et al. (eds) *Democratization.* Cambridge: Open University, 466–89.

Fine, KS (1996) 'Fragile Stability and Change: Understanding Conflict during the Transitions in East Central Europe', in A Chayes and AH Chayes (eds) *Preventing Conflict in the Post-Communist World.* Washington, DC: Brookings Institution, 541–81.

Foucault, M (1981) *The History of Sexuality. Volume 1: An Introduction.* London: Penguin.

Foucault, M (2003) *Society must be Defended: Lectures at the Collège de France 1975–76.* London: Allen Lane/Penguin.

Foucault, M (2007) *Security, Territory, Population: Lectures at the Collège de France 1977–1978.* Basingstoke: Palgrave.

Foucault, M (2008) *The Birth of Biopolitics: Lectures at the Collège de France 1978–1979.* Basingstoke: Palgrave-MacMillan.

Foucault, M (2010) *The Government of the Self and Others: Lectures at the Collège de France 1982–1983.* Basingstoke: Palgrave.

Fukuyama, F (1995) 'The Primacy of Culture', *Journal of Democracy* 6, no. 1: 7–14.

Fukuyama, F (2004) *State-Building: Governance and World Order in the Twenty-First Century.* London: Profile Books.

Gallagher, T (1995) 'Democratization in the Balkans: Challenges and Prospects', *Democratization* 2, no. 3: 337–61.

Gallagher, T (1997) 'A Culture of Fatalism Towards the Balkans: Long-Term Western Attitudes and Approaches', paper presented at the British International Studies Association, 22nd Annual Conference, Leeds, 15–17 December.

Garton Ash, T (1999) 'The Legacy of Appeasement', *Independent*, 31 March.

Gellner, E (1994) *Conditions of Liberty: Civil Society and its Rivals.* London: Hamish Hamilton.

Gephart, W (2010) *Law as Culture: For a Study of Law in the Process of Globalization from the Perspective of the Humanities.* Frankfurt am Main: Vittorio Klostermann.

GFA (1995) *General Framework Agreement for Bosnia-Herzegovina.*

Ghani, A and Lockhart, C (2008) *Fixing Failed States: A Framework for Rebuilding a Fractured World.* Oxford: Oxford University Press.

Ghani, A, Lockhart, C and Carnahan, M (2005) 'Closing the Sovereignty Gap: An Approach to State-Building', *Overseas Development Institute Working Paper*, no. 253, September.

Giessman, HJ (2011) 'Foreword', in R Körppen and HJ Giessmann (eds) *The Non-Linearity of Peace Processes: Theory and Practice of Systemic Conflict Transformation.* Opladen: Barbara Budrich Verlag, 7–9.

Gillespie, D and Melching, M (2010) 'The Transformative Power of Democracy and Human Rights in Nonformal Education: The Case of Tostan', *Adult Education Quarterly* 60, no. 5: 477–98.

Goldhagen, DJ (1999) 'German Lessons', *The Guardian*, 29 April.

Gow, J (1998) 'A Region of Eternal Conflict? The Balkans – Semantics and Security', in W Park and GW Rees (eds) *Rethinking Security in Post-Cold War Europe.* London: Longman.

Gray, J (2000) 'Crushing Hatreds', *The Guardian*, 28 March.

Grindle, MS (2004) 'Good Enough Governance: Poverty Reduction and Reform in Developing Countries', *Governance: An International Journal of Policy, Administration and Institutions* 17, no. 4: 525–48.

Grindle, MS (2007) 'Good Enough Governance Revisited', *Development Policy Review* 25, no. 5: 553–74.

Guardian (2003) 'Remember Afghanistan?', editorial, *Guardian*, 19 August.

Gunther, R et al. (1996) 'Debate: Democratic Consolidation: O'Donnell's "Illusions": A Rejoinder', *Journal of Democracy* 7, no. 4: 151–59.

Gutman, A (ed.) (1994) *Multiculturalism: Examining the Politics of Recognition*. Princeton, NJ: Princeton University Press.

Hameiri, S (2010) *Regulating Statehood: State Building and the Transformation of the Global Order*. Basingstoke: Palgrave Macmillan.

Hardt, M and Negri, A (2005) *Multitude: War and Democracy in the Age of Empire*. London: Penguin.

Harrison, G (2001) 'Post-Conditionality Politics and Administrative Reform: Reflections on the Cases of Uganda and Tanzania', *Development and Change* 32, no. 4: 634–65.

Harrison, G (2004) *The World Bank and Africa: The Construction of Governance State*. London: Routledge.

Hatzopoulos, P (2005) 'Non-Nationalist Ideologies in the Balkans: The Interwar Years', unpublished thesis, London School of Economics.

Hay, C (2007) *Why We Hate Politics*. Cambridge: Polity.

Heartfield, J (1996) 'Rights and the Legal Subject', unpublished Freedom and Law discussion paper.

Heartfield, J (2002) *The Death of the Subject Explained*. Sheffield: Sheffield Hallam University.

Heath, RE (1981) 'Education', in S Fischer-Galati (ed.) *Eastern Europe in the 1980s*. London: Croom Helm, 225–55.

Heathershaw, J and Lambach, D (2008) 'Introduction: Post-Conflict Spaces and Approaches to Statebuilding', *Journal of Intervention and Statebuilding* 2, no. 3: 269–89.

Hehir, A (2008) *Humanitarian Intervention after Kosovo: Iraq, Darfur and the Record of Global Civil Society*. Basingstoke: MacMillan.

Hehir, A and Robinson, N (eds) (2007) *State-Building: Theory and Practice*. Abingdon: Routledge.

Heimerl, D (2002) 'The Return of the Refugees: Fiction and Reality', paper presented at Fifth International Seminar, 'Democracy And Human Rights In Multiethnic Societies', Institute For Strengthening Democracy in Bosnia, Konjić, 8–12 July.

Held, D (1995) *Democracy and the Global Order: From the Modern State to Cosmopolitan Governance*. Cambridge: Polity.

Helman, GB and Ratner, SR (1993) 'Saving Failed States', *Foreign Policy*, no. 89: 3–21.

Herbst, J (2004) 'Let Them Fail: State Failure in Theory and Practice: Implications for Policy', in RI Rotberg (ed.) *When States Fail: Causes and Consequences*. Princeton: Princeton University Press.

Hollander, JA and Einwohner, RL (2004) 'Conceptualizing Resistance', *Sociological Forum* 19, no. 4: 533–54.

Holsti, K (1996) *The State, War, and the State of War*. Cambridge: Cambridge University Press.

Huntington, S (1968) *Political Order in Changing Societies*. New Haven: Yale University Press.

Hutton, W (2003) 'Alone the US will fall', *Observer*, 24 August.

ICB (1996) *Unfinished Peace: Report of the International Commission on the Balkans*. Washington, DC: Carnegie Endowment for International Peace/ Aspen Institute Berlin.

ICB (2005) International Commission on the Balkans, *The Balkans in Europe's Future*.

ICG (1996) 'Aid and Accountability: Dayton Implementation', *ICG Bosnia Report* No. 17. Sarajevo: International Crisis Group.

ICG (1997) International Crisis Group Report, *Going Nowhere Fast: Refugees and Internally Displaced Persons in Bosnia and Herzegovina*. Sarajevo: International Crisis Group.

ICG (2001) International Crisis Group, 'Turning Strife to Advantage: A Blueprint to Integrate the Croats in Bosnia and Herzegovina', *ICG Balkans Report*, no. 106, 20 March. Sarajevo/Brussels: ICG.

ICG (2002a) 'The Continuing Challenge of Refugee Return in Bosnia and Herzegovina', *ICG Balkans Report*, no. 137, 13 November. Sarajevo/ Brussels: ICG.

ICG (2002b) International Crisis Group, 'Policing the Police in Bosnia: A Further Reform Agenda', *ICG Balkans Report*, no. 130, 10 May. Sarajevo/Brussels: ICG.

ICISS (2001a) International Commission on Intervention and State Sovereignty, *Responsibility to Protect*. Ottawa: International Development Research Centre.

ICISS (2001b) International Commission on Intervention and State Sovereignty, *The Responsibility to Protect: Research, Bibliography, Background*. Ottawa: International Development Research Centre.

Ignatieff, M (2000) 'A Bungling UN Undermines Itself', *New York Times*, 15 May.

Ignatieff, M (2003) *Empire Lite: Nation-Building in Bosnia, Kosovo and Afghanistan*. London: Vintage.

Ignatieff, M (2005) 'Human Rights, Power and the State', in S Chesterman, M Ignatieff and R Thakur (eds) *Making States Work: State Failure and the Crisis of Governance*. New York: UN University Press, 59–75.

IICK (2000) Independent International Commission on Kosovo, *The Kosovo Report*. Oxford: Oxford University Press.

IMF (2005) International Monetary Fund, *World Economic Outlook, September 2005: Building Institutions*. Washington, DC: IMF.

Jabri, V (2007) *War and the Transformation of Global Politics*. Basingstoke: MacMillan.

Jackson, R (1990) *Quasi-states: Sovereignty, International Relations and the Third World*. Cambridge: Cambridge University Press.

Jacoby, T (2007) 'Hegemony, Modernisation and Post-War Reconstruction', *Global Society* 21, no. 4: 521–37.

Jahn, B (2007a) 'The Tragedy of Liberal Diplomacy: Part One', *Journal of Intervention and Statebuilding* 1, no. 1: 87–106.

Jahn, B (2007b) 'The Tragedy of Liberal Diplomacy: Part Two', *Journal of Intervention and Statebuilding* 1, no. 2: 211–29.

Jervis, R (1998) *System Effects: Complexity in Political and Social Life*. Princeton, NJ: Princeton University Press.

Joseph, J (2012) *The Social in the Global: Social Theory, Governmentality and Global Politics*. Cambridge: Cambridge University Press.

Kahler, M (2009) 'Statebuilding after Afghanistan and Iraq', in R Paris and TD Sisk (eds) *The Dilemmas of Statebuilding: Confronting the Contradictions of Postwar Peace Operations*. London: Routledge, 287–303.

Kaldor, M (1999) *New and Old Wars: Organized Violence in a Global Era*. Oxford: Polity Press.

Kaldor, M (2007) *Human Security: Reflections on Globalization and Intervention*. Cambridge: Polity.

Kaldor, M and Selchow, S (2012) *The 'Bubbling Up' of Subterranean Politics in Europe*. London: Civil Society and Human Security Research Unit, London School of Economics and Political Science.

Kaplan, M (1997) 'Was Democracy Just a Moment?', *Atlantic Monthly*, December.

Kasapovic, M (1997) '1996 Parliamentary Elections in Bosnia and Herzegovina', *Electoral Studies* 16, no. 1: 117–21.

Kaufmann, M (2013) 'Emergent Self-Organisation in Emergencies: Resilience Rationales in Interconnected Societies', *Resilience: International Policies, Practices and Discourses* 1, no. 1: 53–68.

Keane, J (1988) *Democracy and Civil Society*. London: Verso.

Keck, ME and Sikkink, K (1998) *Activists beyond Borders: Advocacy Networks in International Politics*. Ithaca, NY: Cornell University Press.

Kelly, M (1998) 'Step by Step, Preventing the Destruction of Bosnia', *International Herald Tribune*, 22 January.

Kemp, I and Van Meurs, W (2003) 'Europe Beyond EU Enlargement', in W van Meurs (ed.) *Prospects and Risks Beyond EU Enlargement: Southeastern Europe: Weak States and Strong International Support*. Opladen: Leske & Budrich.

Keohane, RO (2002) 'Ironies of Sovereignty: The EU and the US', *Journal of Common Market Studies* 40, no. 4: 743–65.

Keohane, RO (2003) 'Political Authority after Intervention: Gradations in Sovereignty', in JL Holzgrefe and RO Keohane (eds) *Humanitarian Intervention: Ethical, Legal and Political Dilemmas*. Cambridge: Cambridge University Press.

Kessler, O and Guillaume, X (2012) 'Everyday Practices of International Relations: People in Organizations', *Journal of International Relations & Development* 15, no. 1: 110–20.

King's College (2003) *A Review of Peace Operations: A Case for Change*. London: King's College and International Policy Institute.

Klein, JP (2002) 'UN Security Council Briefing', 19 June. New York: United Nations.

Klein, N (2005) 'Baghdad Year Zero', in Klein et al. (eds) *No War: America's Real Business in Iraq*. London: Gibson Square Books.

Kontinen, T (2014) 'Rights-based Approach in Practice? Dilemmas of Empowerment in a Development NGO', paper presented at After Human Rights workshop, University of Helsinki, March 13–14.

Körppen, D and Ropers, N (2011) 'Introduction: Addressing the Complex Dynamics of Conflict Transformation', in R Körppen and HJ Giessmann (eds) *The Non-Linearity of Peace Processes: Theory and Practice of Systemic Conflict Transformation*. Opladen: Barbara Budrich Verlag, 11–20.

Krans, B (2014) '5 Frightening Consequences of Overusing Antibiotics', *Healthline-News*, 11 March.

Krasner, S (1999) *Sovereignty: Organized Hypocrisy*. Princeton: Princeton University Press.

Krasner, S (2004) 'Sharing Sovereignty: New Institutions for Collapsing and Failing States', *International Security* 29, no. 2: 5–43.

Krasner, S (2005) 'The Case for Shared Sovereignty', *Journal of Democracy* 16, no. 1: 69–83.

Krastev, I (2004) *Shifting Obsessions: Three Essays on the Politics of Anticorruption*. Budapest: CEU Press.

Kratochwil, F and Friedrichs, J (2009) 'On Acting and Knowing: How Pragmatism Can Advance International Relations Research and Methodology', *International Organization* 63, no. 3: 701–31.

Kühn, F (2011) 'Less is More: International Intervention and the Limits of External Stabilization', *Canadian Foreign Policy Journal* 17, no. 1: 62–74.

Kymlicka, W (1995) *Multi-cultural Citizenship*. New York: Oxford University Press.

Lake, D (2016) *The Statebuilder's Dilemma: On the Limits of Foreign Intervention*. Ithaca: Cornell University Press.

Latour, B (1993) *We Have Never Been Modern*. Cambridge, MA: Harvard University Press.

Latour, B (2003) 'Is Re-modernization Occurring—And If So, How to Prove It? A Commentary on Ulrich Beck', *Theory, Culture & Society* 20, no. 2: 35–48.

Latour, B (2004a) *Politics of Nature: How to Bring the Sciences into Democracy*. London: Harvard University Press.

Latour, B (2004b) 'Why has Critique run out of Steam?', *Critical Inquiry* 30: 225–48.

Latour, B (2005) *Reassembling the Social: An Introduction to Actor-Network Theory*. Oxford: Oxford University Press.

Latour, B (2013) *An Inquiry into Modes of Existence: An Anthropology of the Moderns*. Cambridge, MA: Harvard University Press.

Law, J (2004) *After Method: Mess in Social Science*. Abingdon: Routledge.

Lederach, JP (1997) *Building Peace: Sustainable Reconciliation in Divided Societies*. Washington, DC: United States Institute of Peace.

Lefebvre, H (1987) 'The Everyday and Everydayness', *Yale French Studies* 73: 7–11.

Lemay-Hébert, N (2009) 'Statebuilding without Nation-Building? Legitimacy, State Failure and the Limits of the Institutionalist Approach', *Journal of Intervention and Statebuilding* 3, no. 1: 21–45.

Leonard, M (2005) *Why Europe Will Run the 21st Century*. London: Fourth Estate.

Lewis, N (1997) 'Human Rights and Democracy in an Unfree World', paper presented to the 38th Annual Convention of the International Studies Association, Toronto, 18–23 March.

Leys, C (1996) *The Rise and Fall of Development Theory*. Oxford: Indiana University Press.

Linklater, A (1998) *The Transformation of Political Community*. Cambridge: Polity.

Littman, M (1999) *Kosovo: Law and Diplomacy*. London: Centre for Policy Studies.

Lloyd, J (1999) 'Prepare for a Brave New World', *New Statesman*, 19 April.

Lynch, C (2016) 'How to Crowdsource the Syrian Cease-Fire', *Foreign Policy*, 23 March.

Mac Ginty, R (2008) 'Indigenous Peace-Making versus the Liberal Peace', *Cooperation and Conflict* 43, no. 2: 139–63.

Mac Ginty, R (2010) 'Hybrid Peace: The Interaction between Top-Down and Bottom-Up Peace', *Security Dialogue* 41, no. 4: 391–412.

Mac Ginty, R (2011) *International Peacebuilding and Local Resistance: Hybrid Forms of Peace*. Basingstoke: Palgrave Macmillan.

Maclean, SM, Black, DR and Shaw, TM (eds) (2006) *A Decade of Human Security: Global Governance and New Multilateralisms*. Aldershot: Ashgate.

Mahoney, J and Thelen, K (eds) (2010) *Explaining Institutional Change: Ambiguity, Agency, and Power*. Cambridge: Cambridge University Press.

Malmvig, H (2006) *State Sovereignty and Intervention: A Discourse Analysis of Interventionary and Non-Interventionary Practices in Kosovo and Algeria*. London: Routledge.

Malone, DM (2005) 'Foreword', in S Chesterman, M Ignatieff and R Thakur (eds) *Making States Work: State Failure and the Crisis of Governance*. New York: UN University.

Mani, R (2002) *Beyond Retribution: Seeking Justice in the Shadows of War*. Cambridge: Polity.

Maor, M (2012) 'Policy Overreaction', *Working paper*, Hebrew University of Jerusalem.

Mayall, J and De Oliviera, RS (eds) (2011) *The New Protectorates: International Tutelage and the Making of Liberal States*. London: Hurst & Co.

Mazarr, MJ (2014) 'The Rise and Fall of the Failed-State Paradigm: Requiem for a Decade of Distraction', *Foreign Affairs* 93, no.1: 113–21.

McFarlane, B (1988) *Yugoslavia: Politics, Economics and Society*. London: Pinter.

Millar, G (2014) 'Disaggregating Hybridity: Why Hybrid Institutions do not Produce Predictable Experiences of Peace', *Journal of Peace Research* 51, no. 4: 501–14.

Miller, P and Rose, N (2008) *Governing the Present: Administering Economic, Social and Personal Life*. Cambridge: Polity.

Mills, K (1997) 'Reconstructing Sovereignty: A Human Rights Perspective', *Netherlands Quarterly of Human Rights* 15, no. 3: 267–90.

Mimica, J (1995) 'Ethnically Mixed Marriages from the Perspective of the Universal Declaration of Human Rights', in I Agger (ed.) *Mixed Marriages: Voices from a Psycho-Social Workshop held in Zagreb, Croatia*. Brussels: European Community Humanitarian Office.

Miraglia, P, Ochoa, R and Briscoe, I (2012) 'Transnational Organised Crime and Fragile States', *OECD Development Cooperation Working Paper*, no. 3.

Mitchell, A (2011) 'Quality/Control: International Peace Interventions and "The Everyday"', *Review of International Studies* 37, no. 4: 1623–45.

Moe, LW and Simojoki, MV (2013) 'Custom, Contestation and Cooperation: Peace and Justice in Somaliland', *Conflict, Security & Development* 13, no. 4: 393–416.

Mol, A (2008) *The Logic of Care: Health and the Problem of Patient Choice*. London: Routledge.

Morgenthau, H (1970) *Truth and Power: Essays of a Decade, 1960–1970*. New York: Praeger.

Morton, AD (2011) 'Failed-State Status and the War on Drugs in Mexico', *Global Dialogue* 13, no. 1.

Neier, A (1996) 'The New Double Standard', *Foreign Policy*, no. 105: 91–101.

Neumann, IB (2002) 'Returning Practice to the Linguistic Turn: The Case of Diplomacy', *Millennium: Journal of International Studies* 31, no. 3: 627–51.

Newman, E, Paris, R and Richmond, OP (eds) (2009) *New Perspectives on Liberal Peacebuilding*. New York: United Nations University.

NISC (2011) National Strategy Information Centre, *Fostering a Culture of Lawfulness: Multi-Sector Success in Pereira, Columbia 2008–2010.* Washington, DC: NISC.

North, DC (1981) *Structure and Change in Economic History.* New York: Norton.

North, DC (1990) *Institutions, Institutional Change and Economic Performance.* Cambridge: Cambridge University Press.

North, DC and Thomas, RP (1973) *The Rise of the Western World: A New Economic History.* Cambridge: Cambridge University Press.

NSS (2002) *The National Security Strategy of the United States of America.* Washington, DC: The White House.

OAS (2013a) Organization of African States, *The Drug Problem in the Americas.* Washington, DC: OAS.

OAS (2013b) Organization of African States, *Scenarios for the Drug Problem in the Americas 2013–2025.* Washington, DC: OAS.

O'Connor, M (1998) 'West sees Payoff from Backing Flexible Leaders in Bosnia', *New York Times,* 24 January.

O'Donnell, G (1996) 'Illusions about Consolidation', *Journal of Democracy 7,* no. 2: 34–51.

OECD (2005) *OECD Principles for Good International Engagement in Fragile States.* OECD.

OHR (1996a) Office of the High Representative Bulletin, 8, 23 June. Sarajevo: OHR.

OHR (1997a) Office of the High Representative Bulletin, 40, 13 March. Sarajevo: OHR.

OHR (1997b) Office of the High Representative Bulletin, 49, 28 May. Sarajevo: OHR.

OHR (1997c) Office of the High Representative Bulletin, 50, 4 June. Sarajevo: OHR.

OHR (1997d) Office of the High Representative Bulletin, 61, 1 October. Sarajevo: OHR.

OHR (1997e) SRT Banja Luka News Summary, 10 December. Sarajevo: OHR.

OHR (1998) 'Decision suspending decision-making on claims to apartments in the Federation for which a permanent occupancy right was issued after 30 April 1991, and imposing a moratorium on sale of apartments to persons who acquired their occupancy right after 30 April', 5 November. Sarajevo: OHR.

OHR (1999) 'Decision cancelling all permanent occupancy rights issued in the RS during and after the war in BIH and converting them into temporary occupancy rights', 14 April. Sarajevo: OHR.

OHR (2000) 'Decision on re-allocation of socially owned land, superseding the 26 May 1999 and 30 December 1999 Decisions', 27 April. Sarajevo: OHR.

OHR (2001a) 'Decision establishing interim procedures to protect vital interests of Constituent Peoples and Others, including freedom from Discrimination', 11 January. Sarajevo: OHR.

OHR (2001b) 'Amending the Law on Sale of Apartments with Occupancy Rights', Office of the High Representative, 17 July. Sarajevo: OHR.

OHR (2002a) 'Agreement on the Implementation of the Constituent Peoples' Decision of the Constitutional Court of Bosnia and Herzegovina', 27 March. Sarajevo: OHR.

OHR (2002b) 'Press Conference of the High Representative, Wolfgang Petritsch, on the Completion of the Constitutional Reform Process in Bosnia and Herzegovina's Entities', 19 April. Sarajevo: OHR.

OHR (2002c) 'A New Strategic Direction: Proposed Ways Ahead For Property Law Implementation in a Time of Decreasing International Community Resources, Property Law Implementation Plan', 12 September. Sarajevo: OHR.

OHR (2002d) 'Report to the European Parliament by the OHR and EU Special Representative for Bosnia, July–December 2002', 23 December. Sarajevo: OHR.

O'Malley, P (2004) *Risk, Uncertainty and Government*. London: Routledge.

O'Neal, H, Thomas, CB and Karam, G (2014) 'Principles Governing Antimicrobial Therapy in the Intensive Care Unit', in JE Parrillo and RP Dellinger (eds) *Critical Care Medicine: Principles of Diagnosis and Management in the Adult*. Philadelphia, PA: Elsevier, 870–85.

OSCE (1997a) OSCE Democratization Branch, Monthly Report, 1, February. Sarajevo: OSCE.

OSCE (1997b) OSCE Democratization Branch, Monthly Report, 2, March. Sarajevo: OSCE.

OSCE (1997c) OSCE Democratization Branch, Monthly Report, 3, April. Sarajevo: OSCE.

OSCE (1997d) OSCE Democratization Branch, 'Regional Centre Tuzla Priority and Strategy Paper: Summary, Planned Activities, Head Office Suggestions', unpublished paper.

OSCE (1997e) OSCE Democratization Branch, 'Regional Centre Sokolac priority and strategy paper: summary, planned activities, Head Office suggestions', unpublished paper.

OSCE (1997f) OSCE Democratization Branch, Regional Centre Mostar priority and strategy paper: summary, planned activities, Head Office suggestions (first draft), unpublished paper.

OSCE (1997g) OSCE Democratization Branch, Democratization Programme: Strategies and Activities for 1997. Sarajevo: OSCE.

OSCE (1997h) Rule of Law Analysis Report, February. Sarajevo: OSCE Democratization Branch.

OSCE (1997i) Rule of Law Analysis Report, March. Sarajevo: OSCE Democratization Branch.

OSCE (1997j) Democratization Branch, untitled information document, 26 February. Sarajevo: OSCE Democratization Branch.

OSCE (1997k) OSCE Democratization Branch, Semi-Annual Report. Sarajevo: OSCE Democratization Branch.

Owen, D (2012) *The Hubris Syndrome: Bush, Blair and the Intoxication of Power* (revised edition). York: Methuen.

Owens, P (2012) 'Human Security and the Rise of the Social', *Review of International Studies* 38, no. 3: 547–67.

Paffenholz, T (2009) *Civil Society and Peacebuilding: A Critical Assessment.* Boulder, CO: Lynne Rienner.

Paffenholz, T (2012) 'Conflict Transformation Theory: A Reality Check', paper presented at the International Studies Association annual convention, San Diego, California, USA, 1–4 April.

Paris, R (2002) 'International Peacebuilding and the "Mission Civilisatrice"', *Review of International Studies* 28, no. 4: 637–56.

Paris, R (2004) *At War's End: Building Peace after Civil Conflict.* Cambridge: Cambridge University Press.

Paris, R and Sisk, TD (eds) (2009a) *The Dilemmas of Statebuilding: Confronting the Contradictions of Postwar Peace Operations.* London: Routledge.

Paris, R and Sisk, TD (2009b) 'Introduction: Understanding the Contradiction of Postwar Statebuilding', in Paris and Sisk (eds) *The Dilemmas of Statebuilding: Confronting the Contradictions of Postwar Peace Operations.* London: Routledge, 1–20.

Paris, R and Sisk, TD (2009c) 'Conclusion: Confronting the Contradiction', in R Paris and TD Sisk (eds) *The Dilemmas of Statebuilding: Confronting the Contradictions of Postwar Peace Operations.* London: Routledge, 304–15.

Pender, J (2001) 'From "Structural Adjustment" to "Comprehensive Development Framework": Conditionality Transformed?', *Third World Quarterly* 22, no. 3: 397–411.

Peters, GB (2005) *Institutional Theory in Political Science: The 'New Institutionalism'.* London: Continuum.

Phillips, DL (2013) 'Unintended Consequences of Striking Syria', *World Post*, 11 September.

PIC (1996) Peace Implementation Council, 'PIC Chairman's Conclusions of the Peace Implementation Council', Florence, 13–14 June 1996. Sarajevo: OHR.

PIC (1997a) 'Peace Implementation Council Communique: Political Declaration from Ministerial Meeting of the Steering Board of the Peace Implementation Council, Sintra, 30 May'. Sarajevo: OHR.

PIC (1997b) 'Peace Implementation Council Bonn Conclusions: Bosnia and Herzegovina 1998: Self-Sustaining Structures', Bonn, 10 December. Sarajevo: OHR.

PIC (1998) 'Peace Implementation Council Declaration of the Ministerial Meeting of the Steering Board of the Peace Implementation Council', Luxembourg, 9 June. Sarajevo: OHR.

Pieterse, JN (1997) 'Sociology of Humanitarian Intervention: Bosnia, Rwanda and Somalia Compared', *International Political Science Review* 18, no. 1: 71–93.

Poels, J (1998) 'Bosnia and Herzegovina: A new "neutral" flag', *Flagmaster* 98: 9–12.

Popolo, D (2011) *A New Science of International Relations: Modernity, Complexity and the Kosovo Conflict.* Farnham: Ashgate.

Pugh, M (2005) 'The Political Economy of Peacebuilding: A Critical Theory Perspective', *International Journal of Peace Studies* 10, no. 2: 23–42.

Pugh, M and Cooper, N (2004) *War Economies in a Regional Context: Challenges of Transformation.* Boulder, CO: Lynne Rienner.

Pugh, M, Cooper, N and Turner, M (eds) (2008) *Whose Peace? Critical Perspectives on the Political Economy of Peacebuilding.* Basingstoke: MacMillan.

Pugliese, D (2016) 'Traditional peace-keeping not enough to maintain a Syrian deal: UN report looks to satellites, crowdsourcing', *National Post,* 9 February.

Pupavac, V (2005) 'Human Security and the Rise of Global Therapeutic Governance', *Conflict, Security and Development* 5, no. 2: 161–81.

Radin, CA (2000) 'UN's Peacekeeping a Failure, Report Says', *Boston Globe,* 24 August.

Ramalingam, B (2013) *Aid on the Edge of Chaos: Rethinking International Cooperation in a Complex World.* Oxford: Oxford University Press.

Ramalingam, B, Jones, H, Reba, T and Young, J (2008) 'Exploring the Science of Complexity: Ideas and Implications for Development and Humanitarian Efforts', *ODI Working Paper,* no. 285. London: Overseas Development Institute.

Ramsbotham, O and Woodhouse, T (1996) *Humanitarian Intervention in Contemporary Conflict: A Reconceptualization.* Cambridge: Polity Press.

Rancière, J (1999) *Disagreement: Politics and Philosophy.* Minneapolis: University of Minnesota Press.

Rau, Z (ed.) (1991) *The Reemergence of Civil Society in Eastern Europe and the Soviet Union.* Oxford: Westview Press.

RFE/RL (2000) 'Confronting Evil', *RFE/RL Balkan Report* 4, no. 52, 14 July.

Richards, D (ed.) (2000) *Political Complexity: Non-Linear Models of Politics.* Ann Arbor: University of Michigan Press.

Richmond, OP (2005) *The Transformation of Peace.* Basingstoke: MacMillan.

Richmond, OP (2008a) *Peace in International Relations.* London: Routledge.

Richmond, OP (2008b) 'Reclaiming Peace in International Relations', *Millennium: Journal of International Studies* 36, no. 3: 439–70.

Richmond, OP (2009) 'A Post-Liberal Peace: Eirenism and the Everyday', *Review of International Studies* 35, no. 3: 557–80.

Richmond, OP (2010) 'Resistance and the Post-Liberal Peace', *Millennium: Journal of International Studies* 38, no. 3: 665–92.

Richmond, OP (2011a) *A Post-Liberal Peace*. London: Routledge.

Richmond, OP (2011b) 'Critical Agency, Resistance and a Post-Colonial Civil Society', *Cooperation and Conflict* 46, no. 4: 419–40.

Richmond, OP and Kappler, S (2011) 'Peacebuilding and Culture in Bosnia and Herzegovina: Resistance or Emancipation?', *Security Dialogue* 42, no. 3: 261–78.

Richmond, OP and MacGinty, R (2007) Special Issue, 'The Liberal Peace and Post-War Reconstruction', *Global Society* 21, no. 4: 491–610.

Richmond, OP and Mitchell, A (2012) *Hybrid Forms of Peace: From Everyday Agency to Post-Liberalism*. Basingstoke: Palgrave Macmillan.

Ricoeur, P (1970) *Freud and Philosophy: An Essay on Interpretation*. New Haven: Yale University Press.

Risse, T, Ropp, SC and Sikkink, K (eds) (1999) *The Power of Human Rights: International Norms and Domestic Change*. Cambridge: Cambridge University Press.

Roberts, D (2008) 'Hybrid Polities and Indigenous Pluralities: Advanced Lessons in Statebuilding from Cambodia', *Journal of Intervention and Statebuilding* 2, no. 1: 63–86.

Roberts, D (2009) 'The Superficiality of Statebuilding in Cambodia; Patronage and Clientelism as Enduring Forms of Politics', in R Paris and TD Sisk (eds) *The Dilemmas of Statebuilding: Confronting the Contradictions of Postwar Peace Operations*. London: Routledge, 149–69.

Robertson, G (1999) *Crimes Against Humanity: The Struggle for Global Justice*. London: Allen Lane/Penguin Press.

Rose, N (1989) *Governing the Soul: Shaping of the Private Self*. London: Free Association.

Rose, N (1999) *Powers of Freedom: Reframing Political Thought*. Cambridge: Cambridge University Press.

Rosenau, JN and Czempiel, E (eds) (1992) *Governance Without Government: Order and Change in World Politics*. Cambridge: Cambridge University Press.

Rosenberg, J (1994) *The Empire of Civil Society: A Critique of the Realist Theory of International Relations*. London: Verso.

Rotberg, RI (2004) 'The Failure and Collapse of Nation-States: Breakdown, Prevention and Repair', in RI Rotberg (ed.) *When States Fail: Causes and Consequences*. Princeton: Princeton University Press.

Sabaratnam, M (2013) 'Avatars of Eurocentrism in the Critique of the Liberal Peace', *Security Dialogue* 44, no. 3: 259–78.

Sachs, J (2005) *The End of Poverty: How We Can Make It Happen In Our Lifetime.* London: Penguin.

Schmitt, C (2003) *The Nomos of the Earth: In the International Law of the Jus Publicum Europaeum.* New York: Telos Press.

Schmitter, PC and Karl, TL (1991) 'What Democracy is . . . and is Not', *Journal of Democracy* 2, no. 3: 4–17.

Scott, D (2003) 'Culture in Political Theory', *Political Theory* 31, no. 1: 92–115.

Scott, JC (1990) *Domination and the Arts of Resistance: Hidden Transcripts.* New Haven, CT: Yale University Press.

Scott, RW (2008) *Institutions and Organizations: Ideas and Interests.* London: Sage.

Seligman, AB (1992) *The Idea of Civil Society.* New York: Free Press.

Semenova, E (2012) 'Representative Elites in Central and Eastern Europe: Recruitment and Development, 1990 to 2010', paper presented at the international conference 'Domestic Elites and Public Opinion: The Neglected Dimension of Externally Induced Democratization', University of Konstanz, 5–7 September.

Sen, A (1999) *Development as Freedom.* Oxford: Oxford University Press.

Sending, OJ (2009) 'Why Peacebuilders Fail to Secure Ownership and be Sensitive to Context', *NUPI Working Paper*, no. 755. Oslo: Norwegian Institute of International Affairs.

Seroka, J (1988) 'The Interdependence of Institutional Revitalization and Intra-Party Reform in Yugoslavia', *Soviet Studies* 40, no. 1: 84–99.

Seroka, J (1989) 'Economic Stabilization and Communal Politics in Yugoslavia', *Journal of Communist Studies* 5, no. 2: 125–47.

Sewell, WH Jr (1999) 'The Concept(s) of Culture', in V Bonnell and L Hunt (eds) *Beyond the Cultural Turn: New Directions in the Study of Society and Culture.* California: University of California Press, 35–61.

Shannon, C (1995) 'A World Made Safe for Differences: Ruth Benedict's "Chrysanthemum and the Sword"', *American Quarterly* 47, no. 4: 659–80.

Shaw, M (1999) 'War and Globality: The Role and Character of War in the Global Transition', in Ho-won Jeong (ed.) *The New Agenda for Peace Research.* London: Ashgate, 61–80.

Simma, B (1999) 'NATO, the UN and the Use of Force: Legal Aspects', *European Journal of International Law* 10: 1–22.

Smillie, I (1996) *Service Delivery or Civil Society? Non-Governmental Organizations in Bosnia and Herzegovina.* Canada: CARE.

Smith, JR (2000) 'Kosovo Still Seethes as UN Official Nears Exit', *Washington Post*, 18 December.

Smith, JR (2003) 'Now for Nation Change. Law and Order: The Military doesn't want to Touch it. Who Will?', *Washington Post*, 13 April.

Snyder, J (2000) *From Voting to Violence: Democratization and Nationalist Conflict.* New York: W. W. Norton.

Sogge, D (2009) *Repairing the Weakest Links: A New Agenda for Fragile States.* Madrid: FRIDE.

Sokolović, D (2003) 'Bosnia-Herzegovina Country Report', in Wim van Meurs (ed.) *South Eastern Europe: Weak States and Strong International Support, Prospects and Risks Beyond EU Enlargement, Vol. 2.* Opladen: Leske and Budrich/Bertelsmann Foundation.

Solana, J (2009) 'Five Lessons in Global Diplomacy', *Financial Times*, 21 January.

Sorenson, JS (1997) 'Pluralism or Fragmentation?', *War Report*, May.

SRC (2014) Stockholm Resilience Centre, *What is Resilience: An Introduction to Social-Ecological Research.* Stockholm: SRC.

Steele, J (2003a) 'De Mello Knew Sovereignty, not Security, was the Issue', *Guardian*, 21 August.

Steele, J (2003b) 'US Decree Strips Thousands of their Jobs', *Guardian*, 30 August.

Stewart, R and Knaus, G (2012) *Can Intervention Work?* London: W. W. Norton & Co.

Stiglmayer, A (2002) 'Constitutional Reform in Bosnia: RS is Becoming Multi-ethnic', *Jutarnje Novine*, 15 April.

Straw, J (2002) 'Order out of Chaos: The Challenge of Failed States', in M Leonard (ed.) *Reordering the World.* London: Foreign Policy Centre.

Swindler, A (1986) 'Culture in Action: Symbols and Strategies', *American Sociological Review* 51, no. 2: 273–86.

Szasz, P (1996) 'Current Developments: The Protection of Human Rights through the Dayton/Paris Peace Agreement on Bosnia', *American Journal of International Law* 90: 301–15.

Sztompka, P (1996) 'Looking Back: The Year 1989 as a Cultural and Civilizational Break', *Communist and Post-Communist Studies* 29, no. 2: 115–29.

Tadjbakhsh, S (ed.) (2011) *Rethinking the Liberal Peace: External Models and Local Alternatives.* London: Routledge.

Tadjbakhsh, S and Chenoy, AM (2007) *Human Security: Concepts and Implications.* London: Routledge.

Tamanaha, BZ (2004) *On the Rule of Law: History, Politics, Theory.* Cambridge: Cambridge University Press.

Thacker, JD and Artlett, CM (2012) 'The Law of Unintended Consequences and Antibiotics', *Open Journal of Immunology* 2, no. 2: 59–64.

Thrift, N (2008) *Non-Representational Theory: Space, Politics, Affect.* Abingdon: Routledge.

Tilly, C (1985) 'War Making and State Making as Organized Crime', in PB Evans, D Rueschemeyer and T Skocpol (eds) *Bringing the State Back In.* Cambridge: Cambridge University Press.

Tokatlián, JG (2011) *Organised Crime, Illicit Drugs and State Vulnerability.* Oslo: Norwegian Peacebuilding Centre.

Tully, J (1995) *Strange Multiplicity: Constitutionalism in an Age of Diversity.* Cambridge: Cambridge University Press.

UKFAC (2000) United Kingdom House of Commons Foreign Affairs Committee, *Fourth Report, Session 1999–2000*, 23 May.

UKJCC (2000) United Kingdom House of Commons Joint Consultative Committee, 'United Nations Reform: Peace and Security', September.

UKPMSU (2005) UK Prime Minister's Strategy Unit Report. *Investing in Prevention - An International Strategy to Manage Risks of Instability and Improve Crisis Response*, February.

UKSCD (1998) United Kingdom House of Commons Select Committee on Defence. Eighth Report Session 1997–1998, 10 September.

Ulbrich, J (2000) 'In Europe, "Neutrality" is a Concept Whose Time has Passed', *Associated Press*, 29 August.

United Nations (1945) *The Charter of the United Nations.* New York: United Nations.

United Nations (1992) *An Agenda for Peace, Preventive Diplomacy, Peacemaking and Peace-keeping: Report of the Secretary-General pursuant to the statement adopted by the Summit Meeting of the Security Council on 31 January 1992.* New York: United Nations.

United Nations (1994) Secretary-General's Report, *Agenda for Development.* New York: United Nations.

United Nations (1995a) *Supplement to an Agenda for Peace: Position Paper of the Secretary-General on the Occasion of the Fiftieth Anniversary of the United Nations.* New York: United Nations.

United Nations (1995b) Secretary-General Report, *Support by the UN System of the Efforts of Governments to Promote and Consolidate New or Restored Democracies.* New York: United Nations.

United Nations (1996) Secretary-General Report, *Agenda for Democratization.* New York: United Nations.

United Nations (2000a) *Millennium Report of the Secretary-General, "We the Peoples": The Role of the United Nations in the 21st Century.* New York: United Nations.

United Nations (2000b) *Brahimi Report, Report of the Panel on United Nations Peace Operations, United Nations General Assembly Security Council*, 21 August. New York: United Nations.

United Nations (2005) *World Summit Outcome*, United Nations General Assembly, September. New York: United Nations.

United Nations (2015a) *Uniting our Strengths for Peace: Politics, Partnership and People, Report of the high-level independent panel on United Nations peace operations.* New York: United Nations.

United Nations (2015b) *The Challenge of Sustaining Peace, Report of the Advisory Group of Experts for the 2015 Review of the United Nations Peacebuilding Architecture.* New York: United Nations.

UNMP (2005) UN Millennium Project, *Investing in Development: A Practical Plan to Achieve the Millennium Development Goals.* New York: United Nations.

USDoS (1996) 'Statement by Secretary of State Warren Christopher on the Bosnian Elections', released by the Office of the Spokesman, 18 September. Washington: US Department of State.

USDoS (1997) Bosnia and Herzegovina Country Report on Human Rights Practices for 1996, released by the Bureau of Democracy, Human Rights, and Labour. Washington: US Department of State.

USDoS (1998) Bosnia and Herzegovina Country Report on Human Rights Practices for 1997, released by the Bureau of Democracy, Human Rights, and Labour US Department of State. Washington: US Department of State.

USIP (2003) United States Institute of Peace, Establishing the Rule of Law in Iraq, *Special Report* 104, April.

von Hayek, F (1960) *The Constitution of Liberty.* London: Routledge.

Vulliamy, E and Ray, S (2013) 'David Simon, creator of The Wire, says new US drug laws help only "white, middle-class kids"', *Observer*, 25 May.

Walker, RBJ (1992) *Inside/Outside: International Relations as Political Theory.* Cambridge: Cambridge University Press.

Walker, J and Cooper, M (2011) 'Genealogies of Resilience: From Systems Ecology to the Political Economy of Crisis Adaptation', *Security Dialogue* 42, no. 2: 143–60.

Walzer, M (1983) *Spheres of Justice.* New York: Basic Books.

Washington Post (1997) 'Clearing the Bosnian Air', editorial, *Washington Post*, 6 October.

Washington Post (2002) 'After the War', editorial, *Washington Post*, 24 November.

Weber, C (1995) *Simulating Sovereignty: Intervention, the State and Symbolic Exchange.* Cambridge: Cambridge University Press.

Weiss, TG (1999) 'Principles, Politics and Humanitarian Action', *Ethics and International Affairs* 13: 1–22.

Westendorp, C (1997) 'Interview', *Slobodna Bosna*, 30 November.

Wheeler, NJ (1997) 'Agency, Humanitarianism and Intervention', *International Political Science Review* 18, no. 1: 9–26.

Wheeler, NJ (2000) *Saving Strangers: Humanitarian Intervention in International Society.* Oxford: Oxford University Press.

Wight, M (1979) *Power Politics.* Harmondsworth: Penguin.

Williams, R (2000) 'Democracy, Development and Anti-Corruption Strategies: Learning from the Australian Experience', in A Doig and R Theobald (eds) *Corruption and Democratisation.* London: Frank Cass, 135–48.

Woodger, W (1997) 'The Letter of Democracy and the Spirit of Censorship: The West Runs the Media in Bosnia', unpublished paper.

Woodward, SL (1995) *Balkan Tragedy: Chaos and Dissolution After the Cold War.* Washington, DC: Brookings Institution.

Woodward, SL (1996) 'Implementing Peace in Bosnia and Herzegovina: A Post-Dayton Primer and Memorandum of Warning', *Brookings Discussion Papers*. Washington, DC: Brookings Institution.

Woodward, SL (2007) 'Do the Root Causes of Civil War Matter? On Using Knowledge to Improve Peacebuilding Interventions', *Journal of Intervention and Statebuilding* 1, no. 2: 143–70.

World Bank (1989) *Sub-Saharan Africa: From Crisis to Sustainable Growth: A Long-Term Perspective Study*. Washington, D.C.: World Bank.

World Bank (1992) *Governance and Development*. Washington, DC: World Bank.

World Bank (1997) *The State in a Changing World: World Development Report, 1997*. New York: Oxford University Press.

World Bank (1998) *Assessing Aid: What Works, What Doesn't, and Why. A World Bank Policy Research Report*. New York: Oxford University Press.

World Bank (2002) *World Development Report 2002: Building Institutions for Markets*. Washington, DC: Oxford University Press.

World Bank (2007) *Conditionality in Development Policy Lending*. Washington, DC: World Bank.

Yannis, A (2002) 'The Concept of Suspended Sovereignty in International Law and its Implications in International Politics', *European Journal of International Law* 13, no. 5: 1037–52.

Young, H (1999) 'The Free World Does Need a Leader, but Clinton is Not It', *The Guardian*, 11 May.

Zakharia, F (2003) *The Future of Freedom; Illiberal Democracy at Home and Abroad*. New York: W. W. Norton.

Zartman, IW (2005) 'Early and "Early Late" Prevention', in S Chesterman, M Ignatieff and R Thakur (eds) *Making States Work: State Failure and the Crisis of Governance*. New York: UN University.

Zaum, D (2007) *The Sovereignty Paradox: The Norms and Politics of International Statebuilding*. Oxford: Oxford University Press.

Zimmermann, A (2007) 'The Rule of Law as a Culture of Legality: Legal and Extra-legal Elements for the Realisation of the Rule of Law in Society', *Elaw-Murdoch University Electronic Journal of Law* 14, no. 1: 10–31.

Zürcher, C (2012) 'Costly Democracy: Peacebuilding and Democratic Transition', paper presented at the international conference 'Domestic Elites and Public Opinion: The Neglected Dimension of Externally Induced Democratization', University of Konstanz, 5–7 September.

Zürcher, C, Manning, C, Evenson, K, Hayman, R, Riese, S and Roehner, N (2013) *Costly Democracy: Peacebuilding and Democratization after War*. Palo Alto, CA: Stanford University Press.

INDEX

© The Author(s) 2017
D. Chandler, *Peacebuilding*, Rethinking Peace and Conflict Studies,
DOI 10.1007/978-3-319-50322-6

Printed by Printforce, the Netherlands